The Cuban Policy of the United States: A Brief History

AMERICA AND THE WORLD

A series of books on the History of United States Foreign Policy

EDITOR: *Robert A. Divine*

The Cuban Policy of the United States: A Brief History

LESTER D. LANGLEY

The Cuban Policy of the United States:

A Brief History

LESTER D. LANGLEY

Central Washington State College

John Wiley and Sons, Inc., New York · London · Sydney

Library of Congress Catalog Card Number: 68–19335

GB 471 51713X

PRINTED IN THE UNITED STATES OF AMERICA

For

Charles L. Stansifer

Teacher, Scholar, and Friend

Foreword

From the days when Spanish authority in the Caribbean centered in Havana to the grim two weeks in October 1962 when John F. Kennedy challenged the Soviet missile sites, Cuba has played a major role in American foreign policy. Americans have long coveted Cuba, envisioning it variously as a ripe apple bound to fall into their outstretched arms, a fertile tropical land offering room for the expansion of the slave-plantation society of the Old South, a vast sugar bowl with unlimited opportunity for investment and profit, and even as a strategic island pointed like a pistol at the heart of America. The United States fought a war to free Cuba from Spain and time after time American citizens joined with exiles in mounting filibustering expeditions designed to liberate the island. Yet in the second half of the twentieth century, Cuba finally succeeded in liberating itself from the cloying embrace of the United States and stands today proudly and defiantly as the sole Communist nation in the Western Hemisphere.

Professor Langley captures the sense of frustration and the contradictions that run through this experience by focusing on the interplay between self-interest and idealism that has characterized American policy toward Cuba. He demonstrates that, from the very outset, United States policy toward Cuba was separate and distinct from the nation's Latin American policy. In the 1820's, when the United States favored independence for the other nations of the hemisphere, American diplomats denied their own revolutionary heritage by upholding continued Spanish sovereignty in Cuba. As the nineteenth century advanced, Americans gradually came to support Cuban independence in the belief that the introduction of democracy and free enterprise would automatically enable the Cuban people to achieve political stability and economic prosperity. The decision to fight Spain in 1898, as Professor Langley interprets it, was a natural outgrowth of this Jacksonian ideology, and the resulting American economic domination of the island was the consequence of the same naive belief in the American mission. By showing us how the United States treated Cuba differently than the other Latin American countries, Professor Langley enables us to understand why Cuba became the most vulnerable area for Soviet penetration of the hemisphere in the Cold War. Castro emerged to torment Eisenhower and Kennedy, but the policies of John Quincy Adams, Franklin Pierce, William McKinley, and Franklin D. Roosevelt created the hatreds, jealousies, and resentments that led to the Cuban rejection of the United States.

This book is the first in a new series of volumes tracing the history of American foreign policy toward those nations with which the United States has had significant relations over a long period of time. By stressing the continuity of diplomatic themes through the decades, each author will seek to identify the distinctive character of America's international relationships. It is hoped that this country-by-country approach will not only enable readers to understand more deeply the diplomatic history of their nation but make them aware that past events and patterns of behavior exert a continuous influence on American foreign policy.

ROBERT A. DIVINE

Preface

Since the founding of the nation, Cuba has occupied a position of preeminence in the Latin American policy of the United States. The writings of Thomas Jefferson, John Adams, James Monroe, Henry Clay, John C. Calhoun, and John Quincy Adams contain numerous references to the strategic and economic importance of Cuba to the United States. The generations of the 1850's and 1870's watched as Cuban (and American) filibusters and revolutionaries employed bases in the United States in their efforts to overthrow Spanish colonialism. The generation of 1898 fought for Cuban independence and attempted to implant Anglo-Saxon political and economic institutions in the Cuban republic. Since 1934, when the protectorate ended, the American imprint on the island has appeared economically in the form of private investment and politically in the acceptance of the Batista dictatorship. The Castro revolution, especially the incorporation of Cuba into the Soviet bloc, has brought nationalization of American industries and a rupture in diplomatic relations. But the United States cannot escape the legacy of history. The Bay of Pigs invasion and the "Missile Crisis" dramatically illustrated the continued strategic and political significance of an island lying only a hundred miles from American soil.

The most crucial episodes in Cuban-American relations, such as the Spanish-American War (what Cuban historians call the Cuban-Spanish-American War) or the Castro revolution, have spawned hundreds of books and articles. Another important epoch, the Ten Years' War (1868-1878), unfortunately has received less attention from scholars, perhaps because it is less attractive as a subject than Gilded Age politics. Yet, there exists no adequate one-volume historical summary of the Cuban policy of the United States. The present work strives to survey the major events in Cuban-American relations — the era of the Monroe Doctrine, the annexationist movement of the 1850's, the Ten Years' War, the Spanish-American War, the protectorate period, and the years of Batista and Castro — with the aim of presenting these occurrences in historical perspective. Hopefully, this book will fill a scholarly void and give the student and citizen a definition of the Cuban policy of the United States.

I thank these individuals and organizations for aid in the preparation of this work: the Organized Research Fund of Texas A&M University, which supplied necessary financial assistance; Marjorie Moeller, Janet Spadora, and Mrs. Joseph M. Nance, Cushing Memorial Library, who procured nineteenth century Spanish works on Cuba; Dr. Joseph Milton Nance, Head, Department of History and Government, Texas A&M University, who gratefully assisted with the original research request; Dr. Frank Hubert, Dean, College of Liberal Arts, Texas A&M University, who facilitated completion of the typing; Professors Irving Linger and Lee Martin, who presented the original proposal to the Research Council; and Mrs. Pam Rowe, who typed the entire manuscript. In Washington I was aided by the Hon. Olin E. Teague (Democrat, Texas), whose office assisted in the search for adequate housing in 1966.

All diplomatists owe a special debt to the able assistants in the National Archives, Library of Congress Reading Room, and Library of Congress Manuscripts Division. My views on the late nineteenth century changed considerably under the scholarly guidance of George L. Anderson, Department of History, University of Kansas. Finally, I extend my sincere thanks and appreciation to Professor Robert Divine, Department of History, University of Texas, who read the entire manuscript and made several perceptive comments.

The statements, judgments, and opinions expressed in this work are mine. I accept full responsibility for any errors of fact or interpretation.

May 1967 LESTER D. LANGLEY

Contents

MAPS

(Maps by John V. Morris)

The Cuban Policy of the United States:
A Brief History

CHAPTER I

The Formation of a Cuban Policy

SPANISH CUBA WAS BORN IN VIOLENCE. For years before the island became a domain of Spain, it had served as a refuge for runaway slaves from Santo Domingo, where a vicious plantation system had reduced the Indian inhabitants to slavery. The subjugation of Cuba, which began in 1509, was undertaken in part to close this escape route. By 1513 the Spanish conquerors dominated the island's periphery. Hounded into the interior, the Indian population fought valiantly but was systematically annihilated by a superior military machine. Unlike later mainland conquests, which were struggles between two civilizations, as in Mexico, or two races, as in Chile, Cuba's defeat turned into a carnage. Much of the brutality escaped official censure, for attention concentrated on the Mexican mainland, where rumor said that an empire filled with riches was ripe for the taking. The island of Cuba became a stopping place on the way to the more lucrative fields of *Tierra Firme.*[1]

In the evolution of Spanish colonial policy, Cuba became a bulwark against foreign encroachment in the trade of the Indies. Its geographic position called for the construction of forts for the protection of galleons laden with gold and silver. Neither France nor England paid attention to Spanish assertions that the Indies constituted a "closed" empire. Both considered the Caribbean as "open" waters: Spanish shipping was fair game. Many of the diminutive islands of the Lesser Antilles had been avoided by

[1] Vidal Morales y Morales, *Inciadores y primeros mártires de la revolución cubana* (Habana, 1963), I, 13–14; Irene Wright, *The Early History of Cuba, 1492–1584* (New York, 1916), 23–38.

the Spanish conquerors, who feared the cannibalistic Carib Indians. These islands now became bases for French and, later, English buccaneers, who roamed the Caribbean with the tacit approval of their respective governments. A blow struck at Spain's Caribbean possessions had repercussions in Europe. Frantically, the Spanish sought to strengthen Cuban defenses. Havana's first fort resulted from fear of France, and Punta and Morro Castles, which later gained fame as island landmarks, were erected for protection against English raiders. From a strategic viewpoint, the development of a viable and stable Cuban economy was secondary. Cuba's growth as a bastion against Spain's continental enemies was symbolic of the island's worth.[2]

What was doubly tragic, as far as the inhabitants of the island were concerned, was that Spain often abandoned the populace residing in the smaller towns or remote districts to self-defense. The taking of a galleon on the high seas or the shelling of a fort was a serious threat to the empire, but the sacking of a coastal town was viewed by the officialdom in Madrid as an unfortunate occurrence. This helps to explain why so many of the English and French buccaneers attacked isolated towns with impunity and little fear of capture. Elizabethan sea dogs received their apprenticeship in Caribbean escapades. The future successes of the English navy could be measured by the derring-do of the buccaneers on the Spanish Main. Sir Francis Drake, perhaps the most famous of this band, so terrified inhabitants of the Spanish colonies that the mention of his presence near a city was sufficient to send the citizenry scurrying into the interior to escape the wrath of the terrible "Draques." Drake sailed along Cuba's coast in 1586, when Spain and England were headed for a European confrontation, and appeared off Havana, where the *cabildó* (town council) anxiously awaited his next move. This time he sailed away. But the repetition of such daring maneuvers soon convinced Madrid that the Indies required increased protection. More attention was now given to the firepower of major forts and the number of coast guard

[2] Irene Wright, ed., *Spanish Documents Concerning English Voyages to the Caribbean, 1527–1568* (London, 1929), 10; Wright, *Early History of Cuba*, 224.

ships. The Cuban population was expected to organize its own militias for defense.[3]

The relative neglect of the island, compared with intensive development for the mainland colonies, provoked a series of minor revolts in the seventeenth and eighteenth centuries. In 1692 Don Francisco Manuel de Roca and 300 armed men seized the Spanish governor, threatened the authorities, but capitulated in the face of vigorous counterrevolution. A short time later, minor protests broke out in Santiago and Camagüey. Neither impaired the grip of Spanish authority. More serious was the so-called tobacco revolt of 1721 and 1723 against the hated tobacco monopoly. A restrictive colonial policy purposely created commercial monopolies for *Peninsulares* (those born in Spain) and denied *Creole* (those of Spanish blood born in the New World) planters an opportunity to exploit the more lucrative benefits of free trade. For the remainder of the eighteenth century, except for a brief respite during the French and Indian War, the island's entrepreneurs endured onerous official restrictions on trade. Communications were poor or almost nonexistent between the interior towns. The smaller coastal cities were nearly as isolated, for the Spanish merchants' ships made visits only at six-month intervals.[4]

Ironically, it was in the agony of defeat and occupation that many Cubans found commercial freedom. In 1762 a British naval force under the command of Sir George Pocock laid siege to Havana. The effects were devastating: one-third of the Spanish ships destroyed, a booty of 750,000 pounds (most of which was divided up by the officers), and widespread suffering from disease and starvation. For ten months, England was master of Havana, richest port of the Spanish Main. Free trade, or the nearest thing to free trade ever known in Havana, fattened the

---

[3] *Ibid.*, 369; R. D. Hussey, "Spanish Reaction to Foreign Aggression in the Caribbean to about 1680," *Hispanic American Historical Review, IX* (August, 1929), 287–288; Germán Arcienagas, *The Caribbean: Sea of the New World* (New York, 1946), 132; Nellis M. Crouse, *The French Struggle for the West Indies, 1665–1713* (New York, 1943), 1.

[4] Diego González y Gutierrez, *Historia documentada de los movimientos por la independencia de Cuba, de 1852 á 1867* (Habana, 1939), 2–3, 4, contains a summary of colonial revolts.

pockets of local merchants. Before the departure of English occupation forces, almost a thousand ships visited the city's ports. The streets and market places knew the constant hubbub of sidewalk vendors. On the wharves, muscular Negroes unloaded the luggage of English visitors who came to bask in the tropical sunshine. Overnight, Havana seemed like a festival city with perpetual fairs. Momentarily, Cubans tasted the luxury of free trade, and they never forgot the lesson.[5]

The peace settlement, however, brought this commercial rejuvenation to a quick end. In England, the populace interpreted the capture of Havana as a guarantee of peace and as a Protestant victory over vile Spanish Catholicism. The commercial classes, who had longed for a permanent occupation, saw their dreams of a great Havana market vanish in the Treaty of Paris. In that convention, England obtained Florida and eastern Louisiana. Havana was returned to Spanish overlordship.[6]

II

Trade and commerce had aroused British interest in Cuba from the first conquests of the New World. Similarly, it was Cuban trade that attracted American merchants to Havana during the Revolutionary War. The politics of that struggle brought Spain and the American colonies into a voluntary alignment for the duration of the conflict. Cuban ports opened to the merchant vessels of Boston entrepreneurs, and they were closed just as quickly as they had been opened when peace came. To several American investors in the Cuban trade, such capricious colonial policy proved costly. Oliver Pollock, for instance, appointed commercial agent to Havana, had dispatched two of his own ships from New Orleans to Havana. On arriving at his post, Pollock discovered that his merchandise had been confiscated and that he had been accused of smuggling. The Spanish denied

[5] Richard Pares, *War and Trade in the West Indies, 1739–1763* (London, 1936), 593; Alan Burns, *History of the British West Indies* (London, 1954), 487–488; González, *Historia . . . Cuba*, 5; Arcienagas, *Caribbean*, 306–307.
[6] N. V. Russell, "The Reaction in England and America to the Capture of Havana, 1762," *Hispanic American Historical Review*, IX (August, 1929), 310–311; Pares, *War and Trade in the West Indies*, 601.

his recognition as a commercial agent for the United States. Crestfallen, Pollock filled out his report, predicting the complete cessation of the Cuban trade because of local arbitrariness. It was a sad commentary, wrote Pollock, on the ineffectiveness of Spanish colonialism.[7]

The American government favored free trade with Cuba but steadfastly opposed Cuban independence. The Federalist administrations of George Washington and John Adams, for instance, surveyed the rumblings of revolution in the Caribbean, particularly Haiti, and recoiled in horror. In 1804 the former slaves achieved political power in Haiti, and the prospects for similar upheavals appeared strong in the other Antillean islands, for France, England, and Holland, as well as Spain, had imported slaves to their Caribbean colonies. If these became black republics, Adams feared, the social, economic, and political impact on the slave South would be frightening to calculate. For that reason, he believed, the American government must discourage any independence movement in Cuba. Thus, in the formation of a Cuban policy, the American government distinguished carefully between *commercial* regulations in the island's ports and the *political* structure of Spanish rule.[8].

Revolution failed in Cuba but succeeded on the mainland. When Hidalgo raised the standard of revolt in Mexico in 1810, Cuba remained loyal to Madrid. Already Spaniards were lauding Cuba as the "ever faithful isle." In the midst of counterrevolution, however, the harmony was short-lived. As Spanish armies retreated from the mainland, rule in Cuba became more despotic. Foreign commerce, which had trickled into the colony and revived the economy, was closed again. By 1818, Spain's hold in Cuba (and Puerto Rico) was stronger than ever. An effort to reform the island's commercial system appeared in the form of a tariff, but it proved so absurdly complex and discriminatory that goods from the United States reached Havana only if trans-

[7] Robert Freeman Smith, ed., *What Happened in Cuba* (New York, 1963), 23.

[8] R. W. Logan, *The Diplomatic Relations of the United States with Haiti, 1776–1891* (Chapel Hill, 1941), 86; John Adams, Diary, 14 December 1779, in Charles F. Adams, ed., *The Life and Works of John Adams* (Boston, 1850–1856), III, 235.

shipped first to Spain. The dissident *Creole* element produced no Bolívar or San Martín. Madrid transformed the island into a military base to supply mainland armies. Suspected revolutionaries were dealt with in summary fashion. Loyalist émigrés from Mexico and Venezuela strengthened the cause of counterrevolution. Finally, the lower clergy, an important element in the revolutionary movement elsewhere, remained loyal in Cuba.[9]

A continuation of Spanish rule in Cuba fitted perfectly the Caribbean policy of the United States. Equally as alarming as racial conflict was the possibility that a Cuban independence movement might pave the way for British domination of the island. Albert Gallatin, Jefferson's Secretary of Treasury, foresaw that the loss of Spain's colonies was favorable to the United States except in the case of Cuba. Revolution there could bring British or French occupation, an eventuality that Gallatin considered dangerous. The President and other Cabinet members thought along similar lines. In late October, 1808, as news of the Spanish American unrest came to the attention of the administration, the Cabinet decided that American agents in Cuba should make it clear to influential Creoles that there would be no United States support of an anti-Spanish insurrection. More important was the corollary to this statement: any transfer of power in Cuba from Spain to France or England would encounter the determined opposition of the United States. Successive Presidential administrations never swerved from this position.[10]

Thus, as Madison succeeded Jefferson as President in 1809, the Cuban issue compelled a compromise with the legacy of the American Revolution. Jefferson's and Gallatin's thoughts on the

---

[9] Hudson Strode, *The Pageant of Cuba* (New York, 1936), 71; Philip Foner, *A History of Cuba and Its Relations with the United States* (2 vols., thus far, New York, 1962), I, 81–83; C. C. Griffin, *The United States and the Disruption of the Spanish Empire, 1810–1822* (New York, 1937), 278–288.

[10] Jefferson to Madison, 16 August 1807, in Paul Ford, ed., *The Writings of Thomas Jefferson* (10 vols., New York, 1892–1899), IX, 125; Gallatin to Jefferson, 10 May 1808, in Henry Adams, ed., *The Writings of Albert Gallatin* (3 vols., New York, 1960), I, 387; Record of Cabinet Discussion, 22 October 1808, in Ford, *Writings of Jefferson*, I, 334–335; John Logan, *No Transfer: An American Security Principle* (New Haven, 1961), 140–141.

independence of Caribbean colonies may serve as an illustration of the dilemma. Independence for all the Western Hemisphere was theoretically desirable, for it fulfilled the requirements of an historical destiny that demanded exclusion of European domination. The rejection of Old World rule was symbolized in the Declaration of Independence. Imminent revolution in Spanish America, however, brought Jefferson face to face with strategic imperatives. Upheaval in the Caribbean might erupt into political chaos or invite British intervention. Gallatin possessed similar opinions. Writing to Madison, he predicted that Great Britain prepared to rule the Latin American mainland through puppet governments and intended to occupy Cuba. American commercial and political interests in the island would doubtless suffer under British rule.[11] The only alternative seemed to be formal United States support of Spanish Cuba.

The acquisition of Florida, ratified by treaty with Spain in 1821, was important in the formation of a Cuban policy. With Florida safely in the national domain, there was no longer any need to placate Spain by withholding diplomatic recognition of the Latin American republics. John Quincy Adams, despite the importunings of Henry Clay, had opposed early recognition for fear that it would anger the Spanish government and, consequently, impede the Florida negotiations. The consummation of the Florida acquisition brought diplomatic approval of the mainland republics, but at the same time it did not lead to acceptance of Cuban independence. The reasoning once again was rooted in strategy rather than commitment to Cuban independence. In the upheaval of revolution, Spain's colonial grip might be loosened and replaced by a British protectorate. A weak Spain was no menace to American interests in the Caribbean; an expansion of British influence there appeared as a direct threat. Florida's absorption had brought Cuba closer to the political orbit of the United States. Simultaneously, that acquisition had alerted the British government, which looked with suspicion

[11] Gallatin to Madison, 17 September 1810, Adams, *Writings of Gallatin*, I, 490–491; Jefferson to W. C. C. Claiborne, 29 October 1808, Ford, *Writings of Jefferson*, IX, 212–213.

at the southerly course of American expansion. Havana was a gateway to the sugar islands of the Lesser Antilles. Both governments now saw benefit in the maintenance of Spanish rule in Cuba.[12]

III

When James Monroe assumed the Presidency in 1817, the Cuban policy was distinct and separate from a more general Latin American policy, which included the idea of independence for Spanish colonies on the mainland. Fear of the aftermath of Cuban revolution, whether British intervention or racial chaos, added a conservative hue to the Monroe administration's Caribbean view.

In late 1822, the Spanish government warned of possible revolution on the island. The leadership, Madrid claimed, lay in a branch of the society of Free Masons in Havana that had liaison with other Masonic groups in Philadelphia. John Forsyth, then American minister to Spain, commented on the Cuban situation in a long despatch to John Quincy Adams. The Peninsular authorities, wrote Forsyth, were accusing the American government of secret aid to the Masonic movement in Cuba. Condemning the Spanish logic, Forsyth warned that unsettled conditions on the island, as well as the political weakness of the Spanish government, provided the British with the opportunity to involve themselves more deeply in Spanish colonialism. The British navy had already sent a squadron to Havana. Now the British ambassador was applying diplomatic pressure in Madrid, ostensibly for a new commercial treaty. In reality, Forsyth went on, the British wanted Spain as a European ally, access to Peninsular commerce, the role of mediator between Spain and her former colonies, domination of the isthmian passage, and, finally, the possession of Cuba, which would allow British hegemony in the Caribbean. Havana in British hands, *Nile's Register* editorial-

[12] J. M. Callahan, "Cuba and Anglo-American Relations," American Historical Association *Annual Report, 1897* (Washington, 1898), 196–197; A. P. Newton, "United States and Colonial Developments, 1815–1846," *The Cambridge History of British Foreign Policy*, II, 226–227; "Cuba and the Floridas," *Nile's Weekly Register*, XVII (8 January 1820), 306.

ized, would mean a controlling influence over the trade of the Mississippi Valley.[13]

Actually, British motives ran along parallel lines, but Great Britain's Cuban policy showed restraint when confronted with the question of occupation. George Canning, who inherited the Foreign Office following the suicide of Lord Castlereagh, valued Cuba for its strategic and commercial utility and, for that reason, was apprehensive of American designs. In 1822, while alarming reports of British movements were flowing from the pen of Monroe's minister in Madrid, British diplomats sounded warnings of an American peril. Canning, for instance, believed that the American government would seize Cuba under the pretext of stifling the notorious pirate activity in Caribbean waters. American occupation in his mind would be disastrous for British interests, especially in war time, for trade with her West Indies possessions usually was chartered via Cuban waters. Frigates operating out of Havana would be able to strike almost any British base in the Caribbean. This explained why a British squadron had been dispatched to the area in 1822 to dispel pirate activities. Canning wanted to prevent any opportunity for the United States, or any other power, to exercise greater influence in Cuban affairs. More than other contemporaries, he recognized that the strategic and commercial interests of Great Britain and the United States were best preserved by the retention of Spanish rule in Cuba.[14]

The issue of Cuban revolution in the early 1820's compelled the administration, especially Secretary of State Adams, to state its Cuban policy in precise terms. During the negotiations with Spain for the acquisition of Florida, Adams had thwarted attempts in the Congress to recognize the Latin American republics on the assumption that hasty recognition would annoy Spain.

[13] Forsyth to Adams, 22 November 1822, in William R. Manning, ed., *Diplomatic Correspondence of the United States Concerning the Independence of the Latin American Nations* (3 vols., New York, 1925), III, 2025; "Cuba and the Floridas," *Nile's Weekly Register*, XVII, 306.

[14] C. J. Bartlett, *Great Britain and Sea Power, 1815–1853* (Oxford, 1963), 69–70; W. C. Ford, "John Quincy Adams and the Monroe Doctrine," *American Historical Review*, VII (July, 1902), 678; Dexter Perkins, *The Monroe Doctrine, 1823–1826* (Cambridge, Mass., 1927), 62.

In 1821, however, the Florida purchase was confirmed, and Adams no longer possessed any practical reason for refusing to support revolution throughout the hemisphere. When rumor of revolt came out of Cuba in that same year, the Monroe cabinet stood face-to-face with the question of aid to the independence movement, for the Cuban junta appealed to American sympathies and asked for material aid from the government. As was his wont, Monroe presented the matter to the cabinet and told them to thrash it out. John C. Calhoun, Secretary of War and a potential Presidential candidate in the 1824 election, argued forcefully for immediate annexation. Absorption of Cuba would forestall independence and prevent the establishment of a black republic at the doorsteps of the South. On this occasion, Adams evidently triumphed. Calhoun feared a black Cuba. Adams feared much more the prospect of war with Great Britain if the American government attempted to annex the Spanish colony. The nation was militarily weak in the Caribbean. When the others inquired as to what should be told to the importuning Cubans, Adams' answer was that no commitment should be given by the administration. Cuba would not become a state in the American Union; neither would the United States obligate itself to protect a Cuban revolution. The country enjoyed amicable relations with Spain, Adams continued, and there was no point in destroying this harmony as long as the interests of the nation were better ensured through the preservation of Spanish colonialism in Cuba.[15]

Adams' logic stemmed not from a cynical contempt for revolution or independence but from a thorough grounding in the tenets of international power politics. Like Canning, he saw that the balance of power between France, Great Britain, Spain, and the United States had been achieved in the Caribbean. Spanish colonialism, defeated elsewhere in Latin America, held on with dogged determination in Cuba and Puerto Rico. However oppressive and archaic, Spain's rule in these islands ap-

[15] Allan Nevins, ed., *The Diary of John Quincy Adams, 1794–1845: American Political, Social, and Intellectual Life from Washington to Polk* (New York, 1929), 289; Callahan, "Cuba and Anglo-American Relations," AHA *Annual Report, 1897*, 198.

peared superior to the disruption and anarchy that *might* follow in the wake of revolution. The other three powers were presided over by men who abominated the Haitian brand of revolution with its complementary horrors of racial warfare. Because they saw another potential Haitian bloodbath in Cuba, they accepted Spanish colonialism there. Because they recognized the strategic advantage that would accrue to any powerful nation in possession of Cuba, they blocked one another. Where Calhoun and Adams disagreed was on the timing and reason for Cuban annexation. Calhoun wanted immediate Cuban annexation because he imagined the spectre of a Negro republic, a haven for runaway slaves from the South. The Secretary of State looked into the future. Adams convinced his colleagues that a course of delay provided far greater advantages. In late March, 1823, he received evidence to justify his caution. From Madrid, the secretary of the American legation wrote that Spain and England were not negotiating for the transfer of Cuba and, if an offer were made, the Spanish government would refuse because of distrust of Britain and the loss of national pride that would accompany a voluntary surrender of the island. As for the Cubans, the despatch continued, they had little liking for British political overlordship.[16] A month after receiving these assurances, Adams wrote his views on Cuba in a despatch for Hugh Nelson, then Minister in Madrid. This letter, quoted often by diplomatic historians, illustrates the development of the Cuban policy of the United States from 1789 to 1823:

> . . . These islands [Cuba and Puerto Rico], from their local positions, are natural appendages to the North American continent; and one of them, Cuba, almost in sight of our shores, from a multitude of considerations has become an object of transcendent importance to the political and commercial interests of our Union. Its commanding position with reference to the Gulf of Mexico and the West India seas; the character of its population; its situation midway between our southern coast and the island of San Domingo; its safe and capacious harbor of the Havana; fronting a long line of our shores destitute of

[16] J. J. Appleton, American Legation secretary, to Adams, 20 March 1823, Despatches from American Ministers in Spain, National Archives. In 1820 the English had proposed the cession of eastern Cuba, but Spain considered such a move to be dishonorable. Appleton to Adams, 10 July 1823, *ibid.*

the same advantage [transform the island into a strategic bastion]. . . . It is scarcely possible to resist the conviction that the annexation of Cuba to our federal republic will be indispensable to the continuance and integrity of the Union itself. . . . Cuba, forcibly disjoined from its own unnatural connection with Spain, and incapable of self-support, can gravitate only towards the North American Union, which by the same law of nature cannot cast her off from its bosom.[17]

In this passage, the Secretary of State summarized the strategic and commercial utility of Cuba to the United States. His words revealed that he accepted the inevitability of American domination of the island.

Adams' concern about Cuba's fate in 1823 and the possibility of British intervention placed that issue somewhat outside the main course of events leading to Monroe's famous message of December. The Secretary deemphasized the likelihood of European military crusades to recover Spain's lost colonies on the South American mainland. Cuba was a different matter. Monroe's December utterance dealt with suspicion of Spain and the prospect of a New World counterrevolution by European absolutism. Adams' despatches regarding Cuba pointed directly at Great Britain. France, he believed, was too weak militarily to conquer the island; and any effort by the French government to dominate Cuban affairs would be thwarted by Great Britain. On the other hand, Great Britain possessed the naval strength either to seize the island or to pressure Spain through diplomatic channels to allow the establishment of a British protectorate.[18] While the cabinet grappled with the wording of Monroe's message, the Secretary of State busied himself also with the question of Cuban transfer to another power. The March assurances that Spain would never voluntarily cede Cuba now appeared as an insufficient guarantee. Adams had to know what the Cuban *Creole* class, which loomed as the potential leadership for any Cuban revolt, thought about British annexation. Thomas Randall, sent as a special agent to Cuba, was instructed by Adams

---

[17] Adams to Hugh Nelson, Minister to Spain, 28 April 1823, in W. C. Ford, ed., *The Writings of John Quincy Adams* (New York, 1917), VII, 372–373.
[18] Perkins, *Monroe Doctrine, 1823–1826*, 54–55.

to inform the *Creoles* that the American government wanted not only the continuation of Spanish rule but remained adamantly opposed to a transfer of the island to another power.[19] The no-transfer policy was not new; it had been applied by Congress in 1811 when Spain hinted that Florida might be transferred to another power. The Secretary of State resurrected the doctrine and utilized it in Cuba as a lever against British power. In 1823, no-transfer seemed to be the most logical approach to the preservation of American strategic interests. Even Thomas Jefferson, who admitted his fascination with the subject of Cuban annexation, conceded now that a perpetuation of Spanish colonialism was better than war with Great Britain.[20]

There was still the prospect that the *Creoles* might take action. The stifling of liberalism in Spain in the early 1820's was simultaneously a counterblow to Spanish colonial reform. In Havana, men had talked of Cuban representation within the Spanish assembly. But reaction had triumphed, not only in Spain, but in the major capitals of Europe. What the *Creole* program for Cuba was constituted something of a mystery. From Spain, John Appleton, American legation secretary, observed that affluent Cuban *Creoles* feared the consequences of Cuban revolution and looked toward the American government for protection. Even more comforting to them, wrote Appleton, was a joint Anglo-American announcement that would guarantee the tranquillity of Cuba in the event of an independence movement.[21]

Such a multilateral guarantee to Spain—not to Cubans—was proposed in 1825 by George Canning. The coincidence of Anglo-American interests in Cuba convinced him that each power would check the other. A war for control of Cuba, however, might be precipitated by an erratic and bellicose French foreign policy. The solution in Canning's mind was a tripartite pact between Great Britain, France and the United States. An agreement of that kind would be advantageous to each, for the signa-

[19] Adams to Thomas Randall, Special Agent in Cuba, 29 April 1823, in Manning, *Documents . . . Latin American Independence*, I, 185–186.
[20] Jefferson to Monroe, 24 October 1823, Ford, *Writings of Jefferson*, X, 278.
[21] Appleton to Adams, 10 July 1823, Despatches, Spain.

tories would disclaim any intention to occupy Cuba and strive to prevent its annexation.[22]

The purpose of Canning's proposal was obvious. By condemning the capriciousness of France's Caribbean policy, Great Britain could enlist the aid of the United States. This would block the absorption of Cuba by the United States and, at the same time, would tarnish the image of that nation as an independent force in Latin America. Similar logic had convinced Adams that Monroe's declaration in 1823 had to be a unilateral statement. As President, Adams was reluctant to ascribe accuracy to Canning's overtures. The danger of French pressure in Cuba was exaggerated by London. A convoy of French ships had sailed from Martinique carrying Spanish soldiers bound for Cuba. Once the British government protested the action as a violation of neutrality, the French apologized and explained that colonial authorities in Martinique had committed an error.[23] Canning's tripartite scheme failed to satisfy the President's anxiety. Instead, he looked toward the termination of revolution in Latin America as the most effective guarantee of stability in Cuba and the Caribbean. As soon as Spanish and republican armies ceased to fight, wrote Secretary of State Clay, the danger of Cuban upheaval would disappear.[24]

IV

The Monroe doctrine was an announcement of American opposition to the restoration of the Spanish empire in the New World. Conversely, the Cuban policy of the United States, as it had developed from Washington to John Quincy Adams, was not only antirevolutionary but promised to support Spanish colonialism.

Still, an absolutist government continued to doubt the promises of a nation whose traditions were marked by the "spirit of '76." Spanish officials watched with suspicion the activities of Americans in Havana. An outsider might be an *agent provoca-*

---

[22] Canning to Rufus King, American Minister, 7 August 1825, Manning, *Documents . . . Latin American Independence*, III, 1558.

[23] King to Clay, 9 August 1825, *ibid.*, 1555.

[24] Clay to King, 17 October 1825, *ibid.*, I, 244–255.

teur. When Alexander Everett, Minister in Madrid in 1825, argued impatiently for diplomatic recognition of American commercial agents in Cuba and Puerto Rico, the Spanish Minister of State refused on the assumption that these consuls would grant aid and comfort to Cuban revolutionists. The price of commercial concessions would have to be a pledge by the United States to preserve the maintenance of Spanish rule. At first reluctant to obligate his government, Everett recalled that a similar pledge had been made earlier in 1825. Once more, wrote the minister, the American government proclaimed a policy of peaceful intention in Cuba and supported Spanish rule there.[25]

The immediate threat to Spanish control came not from the United States but from two former Spanish colonies, Mexico and Colombia. With the final eradication of Spanish military strength on the mainland, the armies of these republics remained intact and stood ready to expel colonial rule from the Caribbean. The weakness of Spain and the exhaustion of its army, wrote Clay, provide the new nations an opportunity to strike at their former enemy. An expedition against Cuba and Puerto Rico was a logical plan of attack for Mexico and Colombia. Clay was especially concerned with the intentions of Guadalupe Victoria, a former guerrilla chieftain and now a Mexican general.[26] In Veracruz, his ardent followers combined with discontented Cuban exiles to promote the "Aguila Negra" conspiracy, which aimed at the obliteration of Spanish rule in Cuba and Puerto Rico.[27]

When John Quincy Adams was Secretary of State, Clay had directed a vigorous opposition in the Congress against the Monroe administration's reluctance to recognize the new republics of Latin America. As Secretary now, Clay found his earlier zeal had dimmed. Writing to Joel R. Poinsett, Minister to Mexico, he warned of unfortunate consequences in the event of a Mexican-Colombian expedition toward Cuba. His reasoning

---

[25] Alexander Everett, Minister to Spain, Memorandum, 24 September 1825, *ibid.*, III, 2060–2062; Everett to Spanish Secretary of State, 10 October 1825, *ibid.*, 2063–2064.

[26] Clay to Everett, 27 April 1825, *ibid.*, I, 242–243.

[27] González, *Historia . . . Cuba*, 15.

coincided with that expressed by Adams in 1823: Cuba's strategic and commercial importance was too crucial to the United States to allow any meddling by Mexico and Colombia. "In the hands of Spain," wrote the Secretary, "its ports are open, its cannon silent and harmless, and its possession guaranteed by the mutual interests and jealousies of the other maritime powers of Europe." Neither Mexico nor Colombia was militarily able to defend Cuba. If the island should become the protectorate of any nation, Clay believed, it should be the United States.[28]

Plans for a Mexican-Colombian venture soon faltered. Poinsett in Mexico City followed closely the political course of the government and noted that the Mexican legislature had discussed the entire project and concluded that any military venture at the present time was imprudent. British, rather than American, opposition to the plan was apparently a decisive factor, for Poinsett wrote that the Mexican government feared that London might interpret an expedition against Cuba as a strike at British rule in the Caribbean. Moreover, the Mexicans were jealous of the Colombian liaison and wanted to appear as the sole champion of Cuban revolution in order to facilitate the island's incorporation into the Mexican republic.[29]

Ironically, the American government, which had rejected the idea of European interference in New World affairs in Monroe's famous utterance, now appealed to the Old World powers to employ their moral and diplomatic efforts to maintain the *status quo* in Cuba. Clay disavowed American intentions to seize the island, reiterated the "no-transfer" policy, and condemned Mexico-Colombian republican aggressiveness. A crusade against oppression was theoretically just, but in Cuba an invasion and revolution might result in racial upheaval. The employment of American forces to aid the Spanish in stifling insurrection seemed equally repugnant.[30] For Clay, the solution to this dilemma was a warning to the Mexican government and a plea for

---

[28] Clay to Poinsett, 26 March 1825, Manning, *Documents . . . Latin American Independence*, I, 231.

[29] Poinsett to Clay, 15 June 1825, *ibid.*, III, 1627.

[30] Clay to Henry Middleton, Minister to Russia, 26 December 1825, *ibid.*, I, 266.

European support. If the capitals of the Old World exerted diplomatic pressure in Madrid to bring about a reconciliation between Spain and her former colonies, Caribbean security would be assured. Clay's appeals went out to St. Petersburg, London, and Paris. The entire episode appeared as a rejection of the Monroe doctrine, but as Dexter Perkins has observed, where strategic interests were imperative, an American Secretary of State was not hesitant in calling for Old World diplomatic leverage to redress the balance of power in the New World.[31]

By late 1826, Clay's plans for Caribbean stability had improved considerably. From Madrid, Everett wrote that the Spanish government had been shaken from its lethargy and had sent reinforcements to Cuba and Puerto Rico. In London, Albert Gallatin cornered the Mexican *chargé* and attempted to convince him that a Mexican-Colombia expedition would provoke the British to occupy Cuba.[32] What Gallatin needed was a firm commitment from Canning, but conversations with the British minister failed to produce anything except an unofficial opinion that the British empire was overburdened with colonies. At least the American minister had the opportunity to reiterate his government's "no-transfer" policy and its opposition to the Mexican-Colombian scheme. The overtures to European governments had met with little immediate success: Canning refused to disavow the possibility of British occupation of Cuba; the Spanish maintained a detached haughtiness towards their ex-colonies. At least, Clay's labors had brought delay in Mexico, for Poinsett reported that Guadalupe Victoria's presidential message to the national assembly had indicated postponement, if not abandonment, of the Cuban expedition.[33]

One reason for this postponement was the calling of the famous Congress of Panama in 1826. Simón Bolívar, whose

[31] Perkins, *Monroe Doctrine, 1823–1826,* 203–204.

[32] Everett to Clay, 5 April 1826, Manning, *Documents . . . Latin American Independence,* III, 2114; Gallatin to Clay, 16 December 1826, *ibid.,* 1584–1585; Jacobo de la Pezuela, *Historia de la isla de Cuba* (4 vols., Madrid, 1868–1878), IV, 184–185.

[33] Gallatin to Clay, 22 December 1826, Adams, *Writings of Gallatin,* II, 346; J. M. Callahan, *American Foreign Policy in Mexican Relations* (New York, 1932), 42–43.

dreams of a hemispheric union had laid the foundation for the Panama meeting, had refused invitations to the United States and Brazil because they had been neutral in the struggle against Spain. Great Britain, however, was welcome, for in Bolívar's mind British naval power offered a bulwark for the preservation of Latin American independence. When the United States did receive an invitation, it came from the governments of Central America, Mexico, and Colombia.[34]

American policy at the Panama Congress provided an excellent illustration of the manner by which the government approached the concept of hemispheric unity. Belatedly, the Adams administration accepted the invitations and sent agents southward. The history of this mission is well-known: one of the emissaries died en route; the other tarried and arrived late. They had been instructed to attend the conference not for the purpose of promoting some kind of Pan American federation but rather for the prevention of an attack against Cuba. Both Mexico and Colombia refused to ratify the proposals that emanated from the congress. They did sign an alliance, but it failed to provide any offensive measures against Cuba and Puerto Rico. Instead, each signatory agreed to aid the other in the event of Spanish counterrevolution in Mexico or Colombia.[35]

By the end of the Adams administration, the Cuban policy of the United States was clearly defined. Predicated on commercial and strategic interests, that policy called for the preservation of the *status quo* in Cuba as the most effective guarantee of Caribbean security. Revolution in Cuba, whether from internal roots or importation by other republics, was rejected in favor of the stability of Spanish colonialism. Any other course was too dangerous: the price of Cuban independence might be British occupation or racial war. Independence for mainland Latin America

[34] J. L. Mecham, *The United States and Inter-American Security, 1889–1960* (Austin, 1961), 33–34, reviews the Panama Congress. See also Francisco Cuevas Cancino, *Del congreso de Panamá á la conferencia de Caracas, 1826–1954* (2 vols., Caracas, 1955), I, 110.

[35] *Ibid.*, 65, 113–114; Callahan, *American Foreign Policy in Mexican Relations*, 34, 42–43. For an assessment of the Panama Congress see A. P. Whitaker, *The Western Hemisphere Idea* (Ithaca, New York, 1954), 43–44.

was both philosophically and politically desirable: the American Revolution served as a prototype of the rejection of Old World rule. Revolution in Cuba, although ideologically desirable, was strategically impractical. In the formation of a Cuban policy, power politics and strategic imperatives outweighed any commitment to an independent Cuba.

Cuba in Revolt, 1868-78, 1895-98
ATLANTIC OCEAN
Bahía Honda
Havana
HAVANA
Cárdenas
MATANZAS
Pinar del Río
PINAR DEL RÍO
Santa Clara
SANTA CLARA
Bahía de Cochinos
(Bay of Pigs)
Isle of Pines
CAMAGÜEY
Camagüey
ORIENTE
Yara
Sierra Maestra
Santiago
Bahía de Guantánamo
Caribbean Sea
0
50
100
150
200
Miles

CHAPTER II

The American Democracy and the Cuban Issue

By identifying its position clearly to Spain, Mexico, Colombia, and other European powers, the Adams administration had strived to prevent a republican invasion of Cuba. Momentarily, in 1827, there had been warnings from the American minister in Madrid that Simón Bolívar, a virtual dictator in New Granada, was preparing an attack against Spanish colonialism in Cuba. A Bolivarian coup in Cuba, wrote Alexander Everett, would mean a union of Bolívar's forces with the "coloured castes" of the island. A military depotism supported by a Negro army would be erected at the doorsteps of the slave South.[1] But the danger passed quickly, primarily because Bolívar's regime in New Granada was fragmenting. In 1829 Martin Van Buren, a Jacksonian stalwart, wrote with satisfaction that a liberal commercial program in Cuba seemed imminent. The United States stood waiting to take advantage of Cuba's excellent commercial opportunities.[2]

The Spanish overseers, however, failed to satisfy Van Buren's aspirations for a Cuba-American trade prosperity. In the 1830's American shippers complained constantly about discriminatory duties in Havana and the ports of Puerto Rico. Spain and the United States, wrote Edward Livingston in 1833, were on the verge of a tariff war. A program of retaliation against Spanish

[1] Everett to Clay, 7 January 1827, Manning, *Documents . . . Latin American Independence*, III, 2139–2140. In 1827 Clay instructed Daniel Cook, confidential agent in Cuba, to study Cuban population, agriculture, political parties, independence movements, and Spanish defenses. Clay to Cook, 12 March 1827, *ibid.*, I, 282–283.

[2] Van Buren to Cornelius P. Van Ness, 2 October 1829, *ibid.*, 306–307.

products in American ports was the only recourse for the Jackson administration.[3] Harassment of American shippers continued through the 1830's and 1840's. The evidence of discrimination was convincing: in Cuban ports American vessels paid $1.50 per ton duties compared with 62.5¢ for Spanish ships. The fact that Cuba was a Spanish colony was a minor consideration in the view of the Department of State. Throughout the decade, the Jackson and Van Buren administrations applied futile pressure in Madrid to force a reduction in Havana customs. It was hopeless, moaned John Forysth in 1840, and the only recourse appeared to be a system of high duties against Spanish products in American ports.[4]

The debate over commercial restrictions in Cuban ports pointed to still another facet of the Cuban policy of the United States. Years earlier, John Quincy Adams and Henry Clay had stressed the island's strategic utility. Their successors fought to obtain a larger share of Cuban commerce. (See Tables 1 and 2.) No American government wished to violate Spanish trade restrictions in Cuba and Puerto Rico, Forsyth wrote in 1834, but the United States could not tolerate the exclusion of its capital and industry from Spain's insular possessions. Cuba's commercial potential was for the enjoyment of all nations. Its geographic proximity to the American people and their produce transformed the island into an economic complement. Spanish colonialism with its rigid policy of commercial exclusion served only to damage the future prosperity of Cuba and Puerto Rico. An enlightened nation would not pursue such harmful economic policy.[5]

Forsyth's condemnation was actually a warning to the masters of Cuba's destiny. As a political force, Spanish authority served the strategic interests of the United States because it maintained the *status quo* in the Caribbean. Forsyth and his associates were rebuking the *economics* of Spanish colonialism. American com-

---

[3] Edward Livingston to Van Ness, 24 March 1833, State Department, Instructions, Spain, National Archives; Livingston to Van Ness, 12 April 1833, *ibid.*; Louis McLane to Van Ness, 30 May 1834, *ibid.*

[4] Forsyth to Van Ness, 29 August 1836, *ibid.*; Forsyth to Aaron Vail, 15 July 1840, *ibid.*

[5] Forsyth to Van Ness, 28 July 1834, *ibid.*

Table 1. Value of Exports from the United States to Cuba (1834-1836 and 1853-1855)[a]

Years	Value
1834	$3,690,101
1835	5,406,919
1836	6,553,281
1853	6,287,959
1854	8,551,752
1855	8,004,582

Table 2. Value of Imports into Cuba During the Years, 1826, 1829, and 1834[a]

	1826	1829	1834
National Commerce			
National vessels	$409,352	$1,460,041	$3,412,487 (National and Foreign vessels combined)
Foreign vessels	2,449,440	3,501,002	
Deposit	1,759,621	2,521,442	1,134,407
Foreign Commerce			
National vessels	314,683	844,826	4,970,013
From the United States	5,632,808	5,734,765	3,690,101
From France	1,169,451	1,245,947	906,414
From England	1,323,627	1,837,775	1,676,918

[a]U.S. Cong., House, 34th Cong., 1st Sess., *Executive Documents.*, No. 47, I, 180, 182.

mercial doctrines called for free trade and the introduction of Yankee capitalism into Cuba. From the decade of the 1830's, Spanish economic policy remained on trial. Spain was expected to reform Cuban commerce through the eradication of burdensome restrictions on American shipping. Failure would bring inevitable ruin to Cuba's economy and, eventually, to Spanish rule in Cuba.

II

Slavery heralded a vigorous expansionist effort to acquire Cuba in the 1840's and 1850's. In the last year of the Van Buren presidency, Secretary of State Forsyth expressed apprehension of British pressure on Spain to eradicate the external slave trade. The ending of the trade on the high seas had been the official policy of the American government since 1808, but Forsyth saw in these overtures from London a design to increase British influence in Cuba. He was determined, as determined as John Quincy Adams had been in 1823, to block any effort to establish British sway over Cuban slavery or the slave trade.[6] The immediate challenge came from the activities of British abolitionists in Cuba. In the early 1840's, the proselytizing of abolitionist thought was due primarily to the indefatigable labors of the British consul in Havana, David Turnbull. A resolute foe of the slave system, Turnbull hoped to employ the slave-trade issue as a lever to strengthen the cause of abolitionism throughout the island. He made grandiose promises to his listeners, one of which was a pledge that the Negroes of Cuba would receive the protection of the British empire. Finally, the Spanish captain-general tired of Turnbull's appeals and sought authority from Madrid and London to remove the offending agent, who carried on his activities under the protection of consular immunity. It was not Turnbull but the impact of British abolitionist thought in Cuba that frightened Forsyth and his successors.[7] If successful in its efforts to end slavery in Cuba, it endangered slavery in the American South. A nonslave Cuba would mean a gateway to escape and, perhaps in the future, another black republic (on the Haitian model) lying near the South. That prospect underlay the move to acquire Cuba by purchase and, peaceful methods failing, by force.

It was not Forsyth, however, but James Knox Polk and his Secretary of State, James Buchanan, who seriously considered annexation of Cuba. The President led a people who might welcome extension of the national domain southward into the Gulf of Mexico as well as westward to California. In mid-1848, several months after the end of the Mexican War, Polk received a visit

---

[6] Forsyth to Vail, 15 July 1840, *ibid.*

[7] Pezuela y Lobo, *Historia de la isla de Cuba,* IV, 358–359; Abel P. Upshur to Washington Irving, Minister to Spain, 9 January 1844, Instructions, Spain.

from Stephan A. Douglas and John L. O'Sullivan, a New York journalist who coined the phrase "Manifest Destiny." Both urged the President to initiate discussions with the Spanish government for the purchase of Cuba. Having listened to their arguments (O'Sullivan read a prepared statement on the benefits of annexation), Polk refused to commit himself, but later he wrote in his diary that he favored annexation and incorporation of Cuba as a state.[8] Like Adams more than two decades before, he emphasized national security. He approved preventive annexation to forestall eventual British absorption of the island. The sum mentioned in these discussions was $100 million.[9]

Buchanan was unable to restrain himself from extended analysis of the utility of Cuba: the ports of the island were vital to trade and defense. Under the aegis of the American economy, he was convinced that Cuba would prosper. New states strengthened the Union, and Cuba would be Americanized as Louisiana had been after the purchase of 1803. Anglo-Saxon precepts of frugality and competition, coupled with internal free trade, would destroy the cumbersome and outmoded economic structure of Spain. With revolution and chaos imminent in Cuba, Buchanan believed, now was the time to pressure Spain to sell.[10]

The offer to purchase Cuba, of course, had not taken into account two relevant factors: Spanish pride and European politics. Buchanan concluded that the proposal must succeed simply on the grounds that Madrid would recognize the huge expenditures for Cuba annually as an unwarranted drain on her colonial treasury. In the view of the Secretary of State, $50 million was a just payment for Cuba: How could twice that amount be refused?[11] He was overlooking that incalculable matter of pride. Certainly, the loss of Cuba would mean a solution to a nagging administrative and financial burden, but to any Spanish government the voluntary sale of Cuba signified something much more disastrous: the opposition would cry treason. As for England

[8] Allan Nevins, ed., *Polk: The Diary of a President, 1845–1849* (New York, 1929), 321.

[9] *Ibid.*, 326.

[10] James Buchanan to Romulus Saunders, 17 June 1848, Instructions, Spain.

[11] *Ibid.*

and France, each of these powers still harbored the idea of a Cuban protectorate, and they could be expected to prevent any cession of the island to the United States.

Buchanan's offer was rejected and, as his successor John Clayton noted, was accompanied with an indignant reply from Madrid. Clayton, Secretary of State in the Whig administration of Zachary Taylor, concluded that a renewal of the offer was unwise. In fact, Clayton favored a retraction of the old commitment to preserve Spanish Cuba, for that pledge, extended years before during the Monroe administration, had prompted counterproposals from other European nations.[12]

Too little attention had been given by these men to the likelihood of revolution within Cuba. In 1848 a three-man Cuban delegation had visited Polk in Washington to inform the President that revolution was near and that its ultimate purpose was annexation to the United States. Rejecting the idea of American occupation of the entire island, the emissaries asked instead for the concentration of troops at selected points in order to guarantee the lives and properties of American citizens in Cuba. It was a bizarre proposal, and had the President followed the advice, he would have alarmed the British and French governments and, doubtless, some members of his own party. Accounts of this visit are clouded in mystery, but one famous Cuban historian, Herminio Portell Vilá, has maintained that these advances by Cuban revolutionary elements were aimed solely at thwarting the ambitions of still another revolutionary leader, Narciso Lopez.[13]

Envious Cuban exiles might well have feared Lopez, for already he had earned a reputation as a charismatic hero. Lopez was born in Venezuela in the closing years of the eighteenth century (1798 or 1799). The son of a respectable plantation owner, the young Lopez proved to be a leader of men. During the Spanish American revolutions, the elder Lopez lost his ranch,

[12] John Clayton to Daniel Barringer, 2 August 1849, *ibid.;* Barringer to Clayton, 20 June 1850, Despatches, Spain.

[13] Herminio Portell Vilá, *Narciso Lopez y su época* (3 vols., Habana, 1930), II, 16.

and the family moved to Caracas when Narciso was a teenager. The father established his son in business, but the young Lopez had a taste for military life. On one occasion, he aided a small village in fighting off an attack by a royalist force. Later, captured by another Spanish army, he joined with it to avoid execution. As the Spanish empire slowly crumbled, Lopez proved himself to his superiors and rose to high rank in the Spanish military command. Transferred to Cuba, Narciso once again acquired a hatred of Spanish government. When revolt came in 1849, he organized the insurrectionists and wielded a direct influence in the drafting of the republican constitution. But he recognized the futility of insurrection without outside support and thus decided to carry the message of revolutionary Cuba to the United States.[14]

For several months in 1849, Lopez operated in New York, but he soon came into conflict with the leadership of another revolutionary group, the *Club de la Habana.* Together with the *Consejo de Organización y Gobierno Cubano* and *La Junta Promovedora de los Intereses Políticos de Cuba,* the *Club de la Habana* represented the strongest annexationist Cuban force in the United States. It sent money in modest amounts for the outfitting of expeditions to raid Cuba. Lopez's relations with the Club were strained, as his biographer relates, because its members suspected that he was another Latin American *caudillo* and, more importantly, because his goal was Cuban independence, not annexation. It is true that Lopez commanded annexationist forces, but Portell Vilá asserts that Lopez himself was not an annexationist.[15] In any event, following several frustrating military defeats in the summer of 1849, Lopez condemned the dilatory policies of the New York juntas and moved his command to New Orleans.[16]

Whatever his innermost thoughts about annexation, Lopez' move from New York to New Orleans was a stroke that guaran-

---

[14] W. F. Johnson, *The History of Cuba* (5 vols., New York, 1920), III, 23–26; Portell Vilá, *Narciso Lopez y su época,* II, 33; *ibid.,* III, 721.

[15] *Ibid.,* II, 64–65, 128, 154.

[16] *Ibid.,* 209.

teed some damage to the prestige of the Cuban juntas in New York and, at the same time, excited the restless slaveholders of the South. Publicity for his movement became more widespread as news circulated that the Cuban revolutionary was now operating from the South's largest commercial port. He knew that even the most ardent annexationists would flock to his banner. The existence of slavery in Cuba was viewed in the Southern states as a necessary defensive bulwark for the institution in the South. A slave Cuba formed a convenient buffer against the encroachments of British or New England abolitionism. It was, in fact, a defensive rather than a purely aggressive instinct that clamored for Cuban annexation. Southerners feared the activities of the British and French governments in stifling the slave trade as a prelude to the extinction of slavery throughout the Caribbean. Abolitionist congressmen damned the shrill cry of Cuban annexationists as a hollow pretext for the addition of more slave states to the Union. To Southern interests, however, annexation's benefit lay in the prevention of a free labor society in Cuba. The key word was "Africanization." "Africanization" of Cuba meant the erection of a labor system that would eventually supplant slavery through economic growth. Once destroyed in Cuba, the institution of slavery in the South would begin to crumble; men would escape to the Cuban haven; Southern society, a whole way of life, would disintegrate. Perhaps this was an unlikely eventuality, but the truth is that the Southern slavocracy believed it. All kinds of horrors were associated with "Africanization": racial war, instability, and, most dreadful, extermination of the whites on the island. In the ideology of the plantation masters, that would signal the demise of Christianity and civilization in Cuba and the erosion of Southern society.[17]

But the composition of Lopez' forces was decidely more heterogeneous and indeed more complex than the above passage sug-

[17] Stanley Urban, "The Africanization of Cuba Scare," *Hispanic American Historical Review*, XXXVII (February, 1957), 29–30; Foner, *Cuba*, I, 139–140. William Walker, a pro-slavery filibuster who dominated Nicaraguan politics in the mid-1850's, intended to invade Cuba and "regenerate" the island. W. O. Scroggs, "William Walker's Designs on Cuba," *Mississippi Valley Historical Review*, I (September, 1914), 199.

gests. For fear of Cuban "Africanization," the revolutionary cause gained widespread affection in the South. In abolitionist circles in New England, which scorned the conspiracy of the slavocracy, the Cuban movement found adherents simply because it professed a policy of liberation and an end to old world domination. In one expedition, for instance, Lopez' troops included many Hungarians, Poles, Irish, Germans, French, and Italians (immigrants who had struggled futilely in the European revolutions of 1848).[18] As for the sizable Cuban exile groups in the United States, some were for independence; others, for annexation. For years, prominent Cuban *Creoles* had sent their sons to the United States for education; in mainland schools these young men imbibed the lore of free enterprise and returned to Cuba convinced of the salutary effects of annexation. The educational exodus had become so embarrassing to the Spanish that colonial authorities outlawed such educational emigration after 1849.[19]

In the clamor of voices, it was sometimes difficult, if not impossible, to ascertain any uniformity in the attitude of the Department of State. The Taylor administration had announced in 1849, when the Lopez expeditions began, that the neutrality laws would be enforced against filibusters. And, on several occasions, invading forces departed from Southern coastal waters only to be turned back by the Navy. The enforcement of neutrality by a Whig administration resulted in intense criticism from Democratic periodicals and avowals that the successor of Taylor would be more sympathetic to the Cuban revolutionary movement.[20] While Taylor aroused the ire of the opposition for halting the expeditions, the Spanish government maintained a barrage of criticism at the Department of State for its laxity! From Madrid, Daniel Barringer, American minister to Spain, reported that Spanish authorities failed to comprehend how Narciso Lopez could lead 1000 men in an attack against Cuba, withdraw, be arrested for violation of neutrality laws, and gain freedom within

[18] Portell Vilá, *Narciso Lopez*, III, 490–491.
[19] Foner, *Cuba*, II, 11.
[20] "General Lopez, the Cuban Patriot," *United States Magazine and Democratic Review*, XXVI (February, 1850), 112.

a short time. Unless strict enforcement of the law was followed, Barringer warned, Spanish authorities were considering an appeal to other European states to protect Spanish colonialism.[21]

The explanation for this alleged failure of the Taylor administration lay not in its intentions but in the refusal of injuries to convict violators of the neutrality laws. Apprehended and charged, Cuban filibusters were usually placed on trial in Southern cities (Lopez once stood trial in Charleston) where sympathy for the revolutionary cause was so widespread that convictions were rare. John Quitman, a Mississippi governor who served with Lopez on one escapade, survived three mistrials; the prosecuting attorney finally dropped the charges of neutrality violation for want of convictions.[22]

Thus, the Taylor administration was caught between an aggressive South and an unconvinced Spain. Politically, the Whig administration of Taylor and Fillmore was not antiexpansionist but unwilling to annex Cuba through violent means (such as aid to Lopez and his forces) and to exacerbate the slavery issue. As Fillmore remarked later, Cuba's acquisition and incorporation as a slave state would revive the acrimonious debate that had plagued the nation since the Compromise of 1850.[23]

Even the Whigs expected Spain to prove that it was able to control and govern Cuba. In late summer, 1851, the opportunity came. Altering his plans for isolated raids along the coast, Lopez decided to launch a major thrust in western Cuba. The boats landed at Bahía Honda on August 11. Alerted, the Spanish army closed in. About 120 Americans who remained on the beach to guard supplies were surrounded and captured. Fifty of these made a break, were recaptured, taken to Havana, and after a farcical military trial, were publicly shot. At another spot, Lopez

---

[21] *La España*, 13 September 1851, clipping in State Department files; Barringer to Clayton, 19 June 1850, Despatches, Spain; Barringer to Webster, 3 October 1850, *ibid.*

[22] J. F. H. Claiborne, ed., *Life and Correspondence of John A. Quitman* (2 vols., New York, 1860), II, 55–57, 75.

[23] Foner, *Cuba*, II, 63. Portell Vilá contends that Fillmore and Webster refused to aid Lopez because they knew he would try to prevent Cuban annexation. Portell Vilá, *Narciso Lopez*, III, 713.

and approximately 150 men were taken prisoner. Justice was meted out in quick and summary fashion: Lopez was garroted in a grisly public execution.[24]

The fate of the Lopez expedition brought inevitable remorse and also some reappraisal of the Cuban policy of the nation. Because many American citizens had served with the Cuban revolutionary movement, their friends and families awaited the news of their death or execution. What made the final raid doubly tragic was the manner in which the condemned prisoners were executed: a quick trial, a fusillade, or, in the case of Lopez, the *garrote*. Such punishment appeared archaic, even medieval, raising again the spectre of the Inquisition to a generation of Americans already convinced of the inherent brutality of Spanish rule. Who could doubt now that the destiny of the western hemisphere decreed an independent or an American Cuba? men asked.[25] But, however brutal to sensitive minds, Spain had proved an ability to dominate Cuba, at least to extinguish a serious rebellion. The Taylor administration relaxed momentarily as the public vented its wrath at Madrid. Simultaneously, some of the avid annexationist publications reconsidered the Cuban revolutionary effort and now asked why the Cuban *Creole* class had not risen to aid Lopez. The unwillingness of many Cubans to assert demands for liberty reflected timidity, even cowardice, many suggested. Why, then, should Americans die for something that Cubans would not?[26]

Taylor and Fillmore had maintained an uneasy peace with Spain. They had rejected pleas for intervention and had endured caustic criticism in the Southern press. What critics overlooked, however, was the consistency of support rendered by the Whig administration to protect American lives and property in Cuba

---

[24] Basil Rauch, *American Interest in Cuba, 1848–1855* (New York, 1948), 160–161; Portell Vilá, *Narciso Lopez*, II, 145.

[25] "Narcisso [*sic*] Lopez and his Companions," *Democratic Review*, XXIX (October, 1851), 299. An American naval officer reported later that the bodies of the prisoners were mutilated by Spanish officers, who kept pieces of the skulls as souvenirs. Johnson, *History of Cuba*, III, 106–107.

[26] Barringer to Webster, 14 October 1851, Despatches, Spain; "Invasion of Cuba," *Southern Quarterly Review*, XXI (January, 1852), 6.

and, after Lopez's fiasco, to procure the release of Americans imprisoned in Spain. A year before Lopez met death, Secretary of State John Clayton had dispatched a strongly worded note to Madrid reciting the history of unjust treatment of Americans charged with conspiracy in Cuba and thrown into jail. Warning that such arbitrary confinement would only incite public antipathy, Clayton explained that his government had no desire to protect offenders of Cuban law but would not tolerate illegal imprisonment of its citizens. In one incident, several men were awakened at ten o'clock in the evening by Cuban officials, given no explanation nor charged with any offense. Arms tied behind, they were marched to jail and lashed back-to-back for the remainder of the night.[27] Article VII of the Treaty of 1795 (Pinckney's Treaty or the Treaty of San Lorenzo) guaranteed certain basic judicial privileges to American citizens facing trial in Spanish jurisdiction. Usually the Spanish government sought refuge in diplomatic niceties by contending that the Governor-General of Cuba possessed no diplomatic authority and, therefore, was not bound by the treaty's provisions. In the case of the men arrested in the night and bound in jail, the Spanish argued that they had violated the law by importing gunpowder for the use of the insurgents. Regardless of the offense, it was not uncommon for American citizens to spend days, sometimes weeks or months, in a Cuban prison at great physical discomfort and considerable financial loss.[28] Settlement through diplomatic channels seemed hopeless at times. The "gunpowder" episode, for instance, elicited a vigorous moral attack from the Secretary of State on Spanish justice: the Spanish had assumed the guilt of a man before he was tried by law.[29] Similar damnations of what was styled as Spanish bestiality or arbitrariness were not rare. The American government accepted Spain's legal right to

---

[27] Clayton to Barringer, 1 April 1850, Instructions, Spain; Barringer to Clayton, 2 May 1850, Despatches, Spain; Barringer to Minister of State, 8 May 1850, *ibid.*

[28] Johnson, *History of Cuba*, III, 20–21; Minister of State to Barringer, 6 May 1850, Despatches, Spain.

[29] Barringer to Minister of State, 10 May 1850, *ibid.*

rule Cuba but held the Spanish responsible for the *morality* of that rule.

In 1851, the immediate problem was the fate of the prisoners from the Lopez expedition. They had violated the neutrality laws, but certainly the administration could not refuse to answer their pleas for intercession. The public had been deeply shocked by the fate of the expedition and the subsequent sentences. Imprisoned first in Cuba, then transported to Spain, the captured American prisoners employed every psychological device in an appeal to the humanitarian instincts of the American minister. One letter to Barringer related how the men had been unwitting dupes of the Cuban movement. They had joined, the letter said, only to serve as bodyguards to General Lopez. Informed that the Cuban revolution was already a success, the men found later that they had been deceived. No revolt had occurred in Cuba. Already ashore, they could do little to disassociate themselves from Lopez' insurrectionists. Now, in a Spanish prison, they begged for mercy on the grounds of ignorance and for the sake of their families.[30]

However invalid their argument from a strictly legal position, the prisoners' importunings morally obligated the administration to procure their release. (In Springfield, Illinois, a year later, a speaker named Abraham Lincoln would tell his audience that the filibusters had lost the protection of their country whenever they signed up to invade Cuba.)[31] The plan of the administration in late 1851 was to stress humanitarianism and minimize legalities. The Spanish would release their prisoners, Barringer concluded, because such an act would promote friendly relations. But Spanish honor might demand an official apology.[32] Neither government wished to relinquish its position diplomatically for fear of admitting guilt in the eyes of the public. While the American press painted a horror picture of Spanish brutality, the politicos of Madrid cried out for the preservation of national honor.

---

[30] Prisoners to Barringer, October, 1851, *ibid.*

[31] Speech to Springfield Scott Club, 26 August 1852, in Roy Basler, ed., *The Collected Works of Abraham Lincoln* (9 vols., New Brunswick, New Jersey, 1953), II, 153.

[32] Barringer to Webster, 17 November 1851, Despatches, Spain.

The solution for this apparent dilemma was a lengthy disavowal of Lopez by the Fillmore administration. A dead man made a convenient scapegoat. Rejection of Lopez could be followed with a reiteration of the noble intentions of the Americans who served with him: starry-eyed wanderers, they had departed for Cuba in search of adventure, glory, and independence only to discover death and imprisonment. First came the repudiation of Lopez. He was a Spanish subject, wrote Daniel Webster, now Secretary of State, who abused the hospitality of the United States by illegal recruiting and unneutral activity. If Lopez had not arrived in the United States to arouse the public with stories of Cuban revolution, Americans would not be suffering in Spanish prisons. The prisoners? They were gullible and uninformed about the Cuban revolutionary movement. Although guilty from a strictly legal view, they deserved the protection of their government because of ignorance. Spanish clemency, Webster concluded, would reflect strength, not weakness.[33] Barringer was even more obsequious in conveying Webster's appeal to the Spanish government. The prisoners had been intoxicated with dreams of glory and rescue of the beleaguered Cuba. Deceived and disillusioned, they now recognized their folly and wished only to return home.[34]

A plea for humanitarianism was, in one respect, a legal admission of guilt. In any event, the Spanish government was preparing to release the prisoners. Delay had been prolonged for two reasons. One of these, as Barringer had guessed, was Spanish pride and honor; the other was the expectation of an indemnification for damage to the Spanish consultate in New Orleans by a mob angered over the arrest and executions after the failure of the last Cuban expedition. As weeks became months, however, the condition of many of the prisoners became so aggravated (many were destitute) that the Queen consented in December, 1851, to a pardon. By February, 1852, all had obtained release and arrived home.[35]

---

[33] Webster to Barringer, 26 November 1851, Instructions, Spain.

[34] Barringer to Minister of State, 28 November 1851, Despatches, Spain.

[35] Barringer to Webster, 8 December 1851, 12 December 1851, *ibid.*; Webster to Barringer, 12 February 1852, Instructions, Spain.

III

Throughout the winter of 1851-1852, while the public anxiously awaited news of Americans confined in Spain, the Spanish government sought European support to preserve its Cuban colony. Suspicious of imminent American designs, Madrid sounded the British government for a guarantee. The logic was simple: Great Britain possessed colonies and commercial interests in the Caribbean and would profit by a continuation of the status quo. British diplomats had similar aims but were reluctant to issue a unilateral statement. The episode of 1823 was now repeated. If France and the United States joined in a *tripartite* pact pledged to protect Spanish colonialism in Cuba, all would benefit. British West Indian possessions would remain secure; both Britain and France would impede the entrance of the United States as a political and commercial rival in the Caribbean.[36]

Although equally convinced of the need to contain the Yankee giant at the shores of the Gulf, neither France nor England was able in 1852 to fulfill that policy with military support. Cuba lay far from European shores. The French position in the Caribbean rested solely on a few minor islands in the Lesser Antilles. British influence was more formidable, but an attempt to discredit American diplomacy and commerce in Central America in the late 1840's had resulted in a draw. The Clayton-Bulwer treaty of 1850 recognized the emergence of the United States as a power in Central America. The key to the success of any tripartite Cuban agreement would be a strong self-denying ordinance from Washington.

The reply from the Fillmore administration was a quick denial of the pact's necessity and a reiteration of John Quincy Adams' famous dictum of 1823. Rejecting the Anglo-French proposal, Webster rephrased the commitment made by Adams more than a quarter of a century before. The United States, Webster wrote to British minister John Crampton, did not intend to annex Cuba and desired its retention by Spain. Any attempted transfer of

[36] Johnson, *History of Cuba*, III, 129–130; Newton, "United States and Colonial Developments," *Cambridge History of British Foreign Policy*, II, 269–270; Henry Blumenthal, *A Reappraisal of Franco-American Relations, 1830–1871* (Chapel Hill, 1959), 52.

the island to a European power, which had emerged as a fleeting consideration in Madrid, would be opposed vigorously.[37] Within the meaning of "transfer" the administration included the indirect influence obtained by Britain and France in the proposed tripartite pact. A more incisive analysis came from Edward Everett, who succeeded to the Secretaryship following the death of Webster in late 1852. Comparing Great Britain's and America's roles in the world, Everett argued that the nations of Europe must recognize the inherent right of expansion by the United States. In a famous analogy, he compared Cuba's strategic importance to the United States to that of an island lying near Great Britain. If Cuba lay a hundred miles from the British coast, Everett wrote, the British government would not hesitate to safeguard its national interests and security. Cuba was a crucial element in the national security of the United States.[38]

IV

During the darkest days of the Cuban revolution, the Whig leadership had strived to restrain any public impulse to seize the island by enforcing the neutrality laws and condemning Narciso Lopez. In 1852, it had held firm and resisted the diplomatic overtures from France and England to erect a three-power guarantee of Cuba. But, at the same time, Webster and Everett had extended the protection of the government to Americans in Spanish prisons. And Everett had issued a straightforward and vigorous reassertion of the Cuban policy laid down by John Quincy Adams.

In the robust era of "Young America" of the early fifties, such restraint often received scorn rather than praise. There was, after all, a legacy of manifest destiny. While Taylor and Fillmore rejected the clarion call of revolutionary Cuba, Democratic newspapers and magazines maligned the administration and predicted a resurgent burst of expansion with its successor. The opening salvos were fired by Franklin Pierce's Inaugural Address in

[37] Webster to John Crampton, British Minister, 29 April 1852, in William Manning, ed., *Diplomatic Correspondence of the United States: Inter-American Affairs, 1831–1860* (Washington, 1939), VII, 75.
[38] Blumenthal, *Reappraisal*, 55–56.

March, 1853. "The policy of my Administration," said the Democratic President, "will not be controlled by any timid forebodings of evil from Cuba." He specifically drew attention to "the acquisition of certain possessions not within our jurisdiction eminently important for our protection . . . ."[39]

There could be little doubt that the President was referring to Cuba when he spoke of "certain possessions." Similarly, there seemed to be little doubt of widespread popular support for positive action when it came to expanding the boundaries of the nation. Journal writers heralded the destiny of the Anglo-Saxon to colonize those portions of the hemisphere that still remained in the vise of Spanish colonialism. Spain, they maintained, was the citadel of oppression and the natural enemy of democracy as long as Cuba endured bondage. Democratic tenets called for the outstretching of arms to suffering Cuba, for only then would democracy be secure throughout the Western World.[40] Spain's failure in Cuba was evidenced by widespread graft and corruption among officials: the island produced some $25 million annually in revenue but Madrid received less than a fifth of this amount. Cuba deserved enlightened and progressive leadership to fulfill her productive capacities.[41]

That was one refrain in the litany of manifest destiny, and the Pierce administration could rely on general public approval if its Cuban proposals were couched in humanitarian and progressive overtones. The President certainly could count on the Southern wing of his own party, which spoke for the plantation masters and contributed its peculiar brand of progressivism. Cuba in the Union would mean an average increase in the price of slaves and an equalization in the cost of sugar production. Most importantly, Cuba as *a slave state* would constitute security, an added bulwark for the preservation of slavery as a social and

[39] James D. Richardson, ed., *A Compilation of the Messages and Papers of the Presidents, 1789–1897* (20 vols., New York, 1897), VI, 2731–2732.

[40] "Invasion of Cuba," *Southern Quarterly Review*, XXI, 11; "The Spaniards at Havana and the Whigs at Washington," *Democratic Review*, XXXI (October, 1852), 327; "Cuba and the Cubans," *North American Review*, LXXIX (July, 1854), 137; "Cuba," *Putnam's Monthly*, I (January, 1853), 4, 15.

[41] *Ibid.*, 6–7; W. J. Sykes, "Cuba and the United States," *DeBow's Review*, XIV, 63.

economic system. The last seemed all the more crucial, wrote *DeBow's Review*, for Spanish experimentation or flirtation with a free labor system in Cuba was detrimental to the preservation of Southern slavery.[42]

The architects of Pierce's Cuban policy, excepting the President himself, were the Secretary of State, William L. Marcy, and the ministers to Spain, France, and Great Britain: Pierre Soulé, John Y. Mason, and James Buchanan. Marcy and Buchanan had served together under Polk (Marcy as Secretary of War and Buchanan as Secretary of State) and had formed a friendship which matured in spite of the fact that Buchanan's political star was fast rising already and that his financial status, in comparison with that of the other cabinet members, was relatively secure. Buchanan, Soulé, and Mason were avowed expansionists and provided the Pierce administration with its bellicose overtones. Marcy was actually a moderate expansionist, and the meaning of that term was important to the understanding of the Secretary of State's thoughts on Cuba. He believed the enlargement of the nation through territorial acquisition was ultimately beneficial. Unlike the others, he had difficulty in committing the Department and himself to a policy of Cuban acquisition if that meant war with Spain. His hesitation placed him apart from the other members of this entourage who thought little about the long-range problems in the absorption of an alien culture. Marcy's religious convictions dictated that slavery was essentially a moral evil, but, unlike the abolitionist, he believed that the diversity and heterogenity of the nation, recognized by the Founding Fathers in the Constitution, allowed each state to control its domestic institutions.[43] Of the two remaining—Mason and Soulé—both were ideologues of the Southern slavocracy. Mason had served as Attorney–General under Polk. Soulé's roots were in the European revolutions of 1848 and Louisiana politics. In Louisiana, Soulé had carved an enviable reputation

[42] "Cuba as it is in 1854," *ibid.*, XVII (September, 1854), 222; J. S. Thrasher, "Cuba and the United States," *ibid.*, XVII (July, 1854), 46; "Cuba and the South," *ibid.*, XVII (November, 1854), 521.

[43] Ivor D. Spencer, *The Victor and the Spoils: A Life of William L. Marcy* (Providence, 1959), 138–139, 178, 223.

as a political dandy and skillful debater whose philosophy of politics was geared to the preservation and extension of slavery through espousal of revolution and annexation of Cuba. Less known to Pierce and Marcy were his ambition and vanity, two personality traits which would lead to the ruin of his ministry to Spain. The President assigned Soulé the Madrid post, perhaps the most sensitive in Europe. The Senate committee accepted his nomination unanimously, scarcely paying attention to the fact that Soulé was *persona non grata* to the governments of France (he had been a revolutionary activist there); Great Britain (his Anglophobia was notorious); Russia (his revolutionary views were suspect); and Spain (Soulé had openly espoused the annexationist cause). His appointment to Spain was a glaring error, but the President wished to placate the bellicose "Young America" wing of the party, and Soulé's nomination kindled a rejuvenation within the ranks.[44]

Marcy's initial step was a reiteration of the traditional Cuban policy by warning Great Britain and France against interference in Cuban internal affairs. In July, 1853, he sent instructions to Buchanan in London in which he reaffirmed the special position that Cuba occupied as a geographical and commercial adjunct of the United States. Any European combination designed to disturb what Marcy called the special relationship between Cuba and the United States was cause for alarm. Marcy followed these warnings with a restatement of the no-transfer prescription, only he expanded that doctrine to include noninterference by European powers to aid Spain in maintaining her domination of Cuba.[45] Heretofore, the American government had committed itself to a preservation of Spanish rule on the island. Now Marcy was saying that, if Spain recognized inevitable defeat for her colonial regime brought about by internal rebellion, there could be no appeal to Europe.

[44] "Cuba! Philosophy of the Ostend Correspondence," *United States Magazine and Democratic Review*, XXXV (June, 1855), 451; A. A. Ettinger, *The Mission to Spain of Pierre Soulé, 1853–1855* (New Haven, 1937), 101–119, 151, 163.

[45] Marcy to Buchanan, 2 July 1853, Manning, *Diplomatic Correspondence . . . Inter-American Affairs*, VII, 93–94.

Marcy's apprehension of a potential Anglo-French threat in Cuba echoed the diplomatic rigidity that had appeared a year earlier when the tripartite pact was proposed and quickly rejected by the Fillmore administration. Since that time, British and French strength in the Caribbean had weakened. Opposed to the Lopez expeditions and American pressure in Cuba, Britain and France had gambled that the tripartite proposal would prevent Yankee expansion southward. Ancillary to that diplomatic effort was a disenchantment with Spain because of the persistence of the slave trade in Cuba and the harsh measures employed by a colonial structure to suppress revolution. The British pledge to a *Spanish* Cuba had been joined with the stipulation that Madrid must enforce the provisions of existing slave-trade treaties and consider an abolitionist program for Cuba and Puerto Rico. In Spain the British ambassador explained that his government preferred a Spanish to an American Cuba but would not interfere in any Spanish-American confrontation unless Spain fulfilled her treaty obligations. The tripartite proposal was not a reaffirmation of faith in Spain but a calculated risk designed to forestall Cuba's absorption by the United States. The offer was refused. Britain was not prepared for an Anglo-American showdown over Cuba; the British government doubted the commitment of France to a Caribbean *status quo* and speculated that a confrontation with the United States in the New World would provide a simultaneous weakening of British power in the Old World.[46]

The Secretary of State made little distinction between the concept of a European protectorate in Cuba and outright occupation. He accepted the Cuban policy of John Quincy Adams but added to it the likelihood that 1853 was the year in which Cuba would become American territory. This reopened the possibility that Spain, if offered a fair price for the island, would recognize

[46] Portell Vilá, *Narciso Lopez*, II, 422; Foner, *Cuba*, II, 76; Crampton to Lord Clarendon, 7 February 1853, in Richard Van Alstyne, ed., "Anglo-American Relations, 1853–1857," *American Historical Review*, XLII (April, 1937), 493–495; Graham to Clarendon, 24 October 1854, *ibid.*, 497–498; William Miles to Marcy, 18 January 1854, Marcy Papers, Manuscripts Division, Library of Congress; "Cuba!" *Democratic Review*, XXXV, 448–449.

inevitable failure in Cuba and sell. He was leaning more and more to the "Young America" wing of the Democratic party. What set Marcy apart from the Soulé-Mason-Buchanan clique was the Secretary's conviction that the Spanish proprietors of Cuba would analyze the Cuban question and arrive at the conclusion that now was the opportune time to make a deal. Marcy's instructions to Soulé continued to show caution and restraint. It was better to avoid diplomatic pressure, he wrote, and instead to initiate discreet inquiries about the possibility of Cuba's sale. The Spanish had to be convinced that the American government desired a voluntary separation of the colony from the mother country.[47]

Unfortunately, Soulé's eagerness carried him far beyond the limitations laid down in his superior's instructions. The Minister to Madrid had departed from the United States determined to return with the deed to Cuba. Diplomatic success depended on immediate action, for in Soulé's mind there were deep fears of Cuba's imminent "Africanization."[48] Spain was old and weak; her empire was nearly destroyed. Spanish officials were inherently brutal, as the recent history of Cuba proved. They lacked determination and strength; their promises were unworthy of belief. The average Spaniard knew little of Cuba, and the island remained a colony only because of political favoritism granted by the monarchy to cliques and cabals. England and France? Soulé stated frankly that Spain could expect little support from these two powers. An historical process was unfolding, he wrote Marcy, and that was the inevitability of triumph for Cuban liberty and freedom (via annexation) and the demise of Spanish enslavement in the civilized world.[49]

From London, too, came glowing despatches that exaggerated Spanish weakness and called for immediate Cuban annexation. Soulé found unfailing support in Buchanan, who wrote of the *necessity* of Cuban absorption. Compared with Hawaii, which was vulnerable and unsuitable for an expanding population,

[47] Marcy to Soulé, 23 July 1853, Instructions, Spain.
[48] Ettinger, *Mission of Pierre Soulé*, 181; Soulé to Marcy, 23 December 1853, Despatches, Spain.
[49] Soulé to Marcy, 10 November 1853, 23 December 1853, *ibid.*

Cuba was a better prize. In February, 1854, Soulé wrote to ask for specific powers to buy Cuba. A spring insurrection, he was sure, would find the Spanish government in a state of desperation, ready to grasp at the first offer.[50]

V

Then, before Marcy had time to send Soulé specific authorization to purchase Cuba, word came of a serious incident between Cuban port officials in Havana and an American merchant ship, the *Black Warrior*. The ship and cargo were seized in mid-February, 1854, following a dispute over port regulations. Enraged over the confiscation, the *Black Warrior's* captain protested vehemently to local officers but finally surrendered his vessel. There followed the usual appeal to the Department of State.[51] Such events were not rare in the history of American trade with Cuba. Almost a year before this seizure, Marcy summed up his disgust with the Spanish colonial system for its annoying regulations and for the persistent confiscation of cargoes for the slightest violation of port protocol. These harassments, he had written, served only to impair the natural right of commerce between the United States and Cuba.[52]

The issue was serious because the seizure of the *Black Warrior* revived in Marcy's mind a score of related incidents in Cuban waters. Those who committed grievances against American commerce were in Cuba, but any redress had to be found in Spain. There the question would be an impediment to that other nagging problem of the purchase of Cuba. For that reason, the Secretary inclined once again to a cautious course. The press was calling for decisive measures. From Georgia, Marcy received a letter that labeled the seizure as official piracy and viewed the incident as a good excuse for the immediate acquisition of the island. In March, the Secretary wrote to Buchanan in London

[50] Buchanan to Marcy, 28 January 1854, Marcy Papers; Soulé to Marcy, 23 February 1854, Despatches, Spain; Johnson, *History of Cuba*, III, 138–139.

[51] *Ibid.*

[52] Marcy to Barringer, 19 April 1853, Instructions, Spain.

to state that, at least, the *Black Warrior* episode had disrupted the monotonous discussion in public circles of the Kansas-Nebraska bill. The British government should know, he instructed Buchanan, that Spain's obstreperous conduct was predicated on the false assumption that Madrid had the support of England and France in Cuba.[53]

Momentarily, in early spring, Marcy lost grip on Spanish-American problems. The February confiscation of the *Black Warrior* had resulted in a public outcry, and the President, sensing that it was opportune to fulfill his Inaugural promise, suddenly seized the issue as a means for satisfying his ultimate goal of Cuban acquisition. On March 15, Pierce sent a ringing message to the House of Representatives. In the account of the affair, he recapitulated past irritations involving Cuban port regulations but broadened the scope of the message to include a general indictment of Spanish imperialism. Especially an affront to justice, wrote Pierce, were the unnecessary and extensive privileges granted to Spanish officials in Cuba. It was Spain that was responsible for the blatant misuse of power, and it was Spain that owed prompt redress for the *Black Warrior* seizure. Two days later, Marcy's instructions to Soulé emphasized the President's impatience: Spain must satisfy the American people by paying $100,000 indemnity to the owners of the vessel.[54]

Soulé could scarcely have asked for a better opportunity to thrash away at his diplomatic counterpart. He was met with an equally emotional rebuff. In a memorandum for Soulé, the Spanish Minister of State complained that, whatever the merits of the American claim, his government was unaccustomed to the haughty and abusive attitude it now received because of the *Black Warrior* affair. Such vituperation, he warned, only prolonged a crisis. Soulé, as was his wont, responded in similarly

[53] Marcy to Soulé, 25 February 1854, *ibid.*; J. C. Wright, Savannah, Georgia, to Marcy, 12 March 1854, Marcy Papers; Marcy to Buchanan, 12 March 1854, *ibid.*

[54] Message to House of Representatives, 15 March 1854, Richardson, *Messages and Papers of the Presidents*, VI, 2767; Marcy to Soulé, 17 March 1854, Instructions, Spain.

intemperate letters. The greatest outrage, he wrote, was not the seizure of the ship nor the confiscation of its cargo but the indignity suffered by the United States and the insult to the flag. Reparation must include an apology for the affront to the nation's colors.[55]

Soulé's initial outburst appeared rash and immature, but his strategy called for employing the *Black Warrior* incident as a means of obtaining his ultimate goal of Cuban annexation. He tried to convince Marcy that the Spanish rebuff was a conspiracy to malign the United States. Calculated insults must be met with a reciprocal determination by the American government to reprimand Spain. A hard line now, Soulé believed, would convince Madrid once and forever that it could not rely on support from England and France in its quarrels with the United States. Hopefully, Spain would then reassess her Cuban position and, in a moment of crisis, finally conclude that sale to the United States was the only salvation from political and financial embarrassment.[56]

For a while, at least, Marcy seemed to acquiesce in the arguments emanating from his subordinates in London, Paris, and Madrid. He warned that England and France might intervene in Cuban affairs. Buchanan tried to allay these fears with assurances that neither London nor Paris possessed a secret protocol with Spain. Moreover, Buchanan wrote, he had made it known to the British government that the United States would not tolerate any interference from Britain in a future Cuban rebellion. He was certain that his skill in preparing the citizenry for the eventual annexation of Cuba was successful.

The Secretary's instructions to Soulé became more demanding. Spain's loss of Cuba, Marcy thought, was an inevitable consequence of arbitrary colonial rule and constant aggravation of American citizens and commerce. Employing the ideology of "Manifest Destiny," Marcy wrote of Cuba's "natural connection" with her northern neighbor. Under the aegis of Anglo-Saxon political institutions, Cuba would prosper and fulfill her economic potential. Now was the time, he instructed Soulé, to

---

[55] Minister of State to Soulé, 12 April 1854, Despatches, Spain; Soulé to Minister of State, 20 April 1854, *ibid.*

[56] Soulé to Marcy, 3 May 1854, *ibid.*

approach the Spanish with these arguments and attempt to purchase the island. That failing, Soulé was to announce discreetly the opposition of his government to any European combination designed to support Spain in a Spanish-American confrontation in Cuba. If anything prevented the sale, it would probably be Spanish pride, Marcy wrote; but Spain might be willing to accept Cuban independence as an alternative. Under the latter plan, the United States would guard Cuba's political interests, for in Marcy's opinion the island had no bona fide representation in Madrid.[57]

In Madrid, Soulé kept the pressure on the Minister of State, and each side sought stronger positions. The indemnity for the *Black Warrior* seizure was promptly increased to $300,000, following a reassessment of damages by the owners of the vessel. Soulé's bellicose despatches to his Spanish counterpart failed to soothe ruffled pride. The Minister reciprocated with pages of denials: the American flag had not been insulted, since the *Black Warrior* was a merchant ship; Havana port officials had not usurped their powers; and the captain of the *Black Warrior* had disobeyed harbor regulations.[58]

Soulé, Mason, and Buchanan interpreted these harsh protests not as the prelude to diplomatic crisis but as harbingers of success for the Cuban annexation scheme. Doubtless, Soulé wrote to Marcy in early April, the Queen was frightened at the prospect of American intervention and had concluded that Spanish rule in Cuba was doomed. Now she would become more disenchanted with the Cuban venture and agree to sell to the United States. France and Britain were of similar views. From Paris, Mason wrote that the Cuba prize would fall into the waiting grasp of the Pierce administration. And Buchanan? There was no danger of hostile public opinion, and he predicted a favorable response from capitalistic elements in Europe.[59]

From May to June, 1854, the three ministers talked in roseate terms and eagerly awaited news of consummation of the Cuba

---

[57] Marcy to Buchanan, 11 March 1854, Marcy Papers; Buchanan to Marcy, 31 March 1854, *ibid.*; Marcy to Soulé, 3 April 1854, Instructions, Spain.

[58] Minister of State to Soulé, 3 May 1854, Despatches, Spain.

[59] Soulé to Marcy, 7 April 1854, *ibid.*; Mason to Marcy, 5 April 1854, Marcy Papers; Buchanan to Marcy, 18 April 1854, *ibid.*

purchase. Marcy was already losing faith in the entire project. As Soulé's enthusiasm permeated the despatches from Europe, the Secretary was revealing serious doubts and dissatisfaction not only with Soulé but also with Mason and Buchanan. The Minister to Spain, Marcy wrote to a friend, was unpopular in the United States; the administration could no longer support his aggressive course. American prestige in European capitals, especially London, was embarrassingly low. Partly, Marcy blamed the ill tidings on Soulé's bluster; partly, on political opponents (unnamed in the letter) whose appointment he had protested. Judge Mason in Paris was also annoying with his repetition of sycophantic despatches and appended commentaries on the seizure of Cuba. A belligerent course in Cuba, Marcy concluded, was not in the offing.[60]

Soulé was unaware that what was at stake was not so much Cuba's sale as his ministry. In a succession of boastful despatches, he wrote Marcy that the Spanish were discussing publicly the sale of Cuba. Spain could not hope to triumph in a war with the United States.[61] Futilely, he attempted to exploit internal politics. In midsummer came news of an insurrection against the monarchy. Soulé was able to contact the leaders of the opposition and assess their program for the nation after the fall of royalist government. The unexpected upheaval and the weakness of monarchical government would certainly convince any doubters that Cuba must be disposed of to the United States. Once the antimonarchical forces were firmly in power, Spain would sell the island for a nominal price. If persuasion proved inadequate, Soulé believed, force of arms would be employed.[62]

VI

Soulé's optimism laid the groundwork for one of the most notorious incidents in the diplomatic history of the United States.

---

[60] Marcy to A. J. Thomas, 5 April 1854, *ibid.*

[61] Soulé to Marcy, 10 May 1854, 24 May 1854, Despatches, Spain; Buchanan to Marcy, 11 July 1854, Marcy Papers; A. Dudley Mann to Marcy, 24 August 1854, *ibid.*

[62] Mason to Marcy, 5 July 1854, *ibid.*; Soulé to Marcy, 15 July 1854, Despatches, Spain; Soulé to Marcy, 18 July 1854, *ibid.*

On August 16, 1854, Marcy instructed Soulé to prepare a conference with Buchanan and Mason in Paris in order to *discuss* once more the cession of Cuba. The Secretary added a warning that Spain's Cuban policy served only to exacerbate Spanish-American relations. Soulé was ridiculing the defeatist tones in the speeches of some ministers, who were referring to Cuba's imminent loss to the United States. From Paris, A. Dudley Mann, a subordinate on leave from the Department of State, gloried in the prospect that Spain was on the verge of ceding Cuba and that France and England could do little to prevent annexation.[63]

The conference was scheduled for October after considerable delay in arranging a site that was mutually acceptable. Soulé wanted to meet in Bâle because it was close to his Madrid post, but Buchanan complained of the long distance from London, and the possibilities centered on Belgium. Advance publicity of the meeting had appeared already in European newspapers. Marcy, infuriated, sent instructions to the major European capitals in an effort to locate the "leak" and, perhaps significantly, made a point of complaining bitterly to Mann, whose outspoken letters had aroused more attention. The notoriety, Marcy concluded, seriously damaged the conference's potentiality.[64]

Any hope of salvage was bleak in Marcy's view, but the same pessimism had not yet overcome Soulé, Buchanan, and Mason, who agreed to meet in Ostend, Belgium, but adjourned to Aachen (Aix-la-Chapelle). On October 15, the three contrived the infamous Ostend Manifesto. Inappropriately named since the document was not intended for public knowledge, the "manifesto" was bellicose in tone and self-defeating in its purpose. Restating the shopworn argument of Cuban security, the ministers warned of impending island rebellion and predicted dire consequences unless Cuba were annexed immediately. Spanish Cuba meant constant unease and alarm for the Union. An offer of not more than $130 million should be extended to Spain and,

[63] Marcy to Soulé, 16 August 1854, Marcy Papers; Marcy to Soulé, 16 August 1854, Instructions, Spain; Soulé to Marcy, 30 August 1854, Despatches, Spain; Mann to Marcy, 31 August 1854, Marcy Papers.

[64] Buchanan to Marcy, 30 October 1854, Marcy Papers; Marcy to Mann, 18 October 1854, *ibid.*; Mann to Marcy, 2 October 1854, *ibid.*

if refused, the United States would be justified in seizing Cuba.[65]

Marcy had been correct in his belief that unfavorable advance publicity would shatter the dreams of Buchanan, Mason, and Soulé. Antiadministration newspapers in the United States painted the conference as a Southern conspiracy. The three ministers and the entire Pierce administration underwent abusive criticism. It was unfair to Marcy. He had not expected the belligerent wording of the Ostend document. He had agreed to approve the conference only on supposition that Spain would be compelled to sell. In mid-November, it was obvious that the administration had reassessed its Cuban policy. Soulé was reminded that the President still approved purchase, but the American minister was not to pursue the question further in Madrid if his inquiries proved irritating to Spanish honor and pride. There was certainly no urgency that dictated Cuban seizure.[66]

Thus ended a sad story. The authorship of the Ostend Manifesto remained uncertain because each of the three ministers minimized his role in the conference. Buchanan's political calculations were reflected in the document, but the ablest account of the affair points to Soulé as the principal author.[67] Buchanan, in fact, tried to exonerate himself in unctuous despatches to Marcy. He denied that the ministers had called for Cuban seizure; their aim had been the peaceful acquisition of the island. The only reason for suggesting immediate action, Buchanan explained, was the imminence of Cuban "Africanization." [68]

The embarrassment suffered by the Pierce administration following the Ostend Manifesto meant the end of any intensive effort to acquire Cuba while Pierce served. It marked also the demise of Soulé's inglorious mission. Months before the Ostend meeting, Marcy had expressed serious doubts about the minister's ability and discretion. A few weeks later he received still another warning from Soulé's staff in Madrid. The informant,

[65] Foner, *Cuba*, II, 100.

[66] Marcy to Mason, 4 November 1854, Marcy Papers; Marcy to Soulé, 13 November 1854, Instructions, Spain.

[67] Ettinger, *Soulé*, 368.

[68] Buchanan to Marcy, 8 December 1854, Marcy Papers.

later labelled as Marcy's spy, was Horatio Perry, a secretary who valued his personal knowledge of Spain and Spanish affairs much higher than that of Pierre Soulé, James Buchanan, or John Y. Mason. In a lengthy despatch to Marcy, Perry related the repeated failures of Soulé's Cuban policy, noting that the minister's importunings for cession had fallen on deaf ears, that the democratic movement in Spain was a fantasy, and that no Spanish government would dare suggest the voluntary relinquishment of Cuba to the United States.[69] Similar castigations from Perry earlier in 1854 had been answered with a reprimand from Marcy. Soulé had remained at his post, but so had Perry. The Ostend meeting was Soulé's last chance. The President, torn between his loyalty to Soulé and his respect for Marcy's judgment, had to choose between removal of the Louisianan or disruption of the Cabinet. Soulé was expendable. It was the wiser choice, for his activities in Madrid had undermined seriously Spanish-American relations. In February, 1855, broken in spirit, he returned to the United States. Simultaneously, the Spanish government offered reparation for losses to the owners of the *Black Warrior*.[70]

VII

The settlement of the *Black Warrior* episode was only a minor diplomatic victory for the Pierce administration. It had failed to achieve Cuban annexation through the Soulé mission and the Ostend Manifesto, and in that failure the United States had alarmed the major European powers. Equally apprehensive of an aggressive Democracy and "Young America" expansionism was a growing number of citizens, primarily abolitionists and Free Soil Whigs, who suspected the handiwork of Pierce as a plot of the Southern aristocracy. Certainly the Southern wing of the Democratic party had promoted and championed the all-Cuba movement. The cry of immediatism for Cuban annexation reflected not so much a desire to possess another slave state or *Lebensraum* for slave society as it did the determination of the

[69] Ettinger, *Soulé*, 469; Perry to Marcy, 26 September 1854, Marcy Papers.
[70] "Cuba!" *Democratic Review*, XXV, 457; Minister of State to Perry, 21 February 1855, Despatches, Spain.

South to prevent the "Africanization" of Cuba. Buchanan had employed that word to describe his actions in the Ostend Manifesto conference. The danger that slavery could be replaced by some form of free labor in Cuba excited the slaveholders (and the Pierce administration) to take quick defensive measure. Abolitionist and Free Soil critics, of course, made no such distinctions, but these nuances were crucial for comprehending the motivations of slavery.[71] More than anything, slavery was an institution that jealously guarded its periphery by opposing the erection of "free territory" in peripheral areas. If Cuba became nonslave, the island would become a hideaway and refuge for fugitives from the South; Cuba's acquisition would prevent that possibility.

The era of the late forties and early fifties marked a point in the tone of the nation's Cuban policy that would not be achieved again until the nineties. The proponents of an expansionist Cuban policy in the nineties would be successful; their predecessors of the mid-nineteenth century were not. Polk and Pierce attempted to persuade Spain to sell the island and failed. And in the case of Pierce, a series of incidents were employed in blundering fashion to pressure Spain. The Cuban policy during this epoch reflected a heretofore unparalleled bellicosity. Polk and Pierce modified somewhat the dictum of John Quincy Adams whenever they broached the subject of immediate separation between Cuba and Spain. Until the time of Polk, the retention of Cuba by Spain formed an integral portion of national policy. In the minds of his predecessors there existed the belief that Cuba would free itself eventually, but that day should not be hastened through unwise intervention.

Largely, the most blatant attempts to wrest Cuba from Spain during the forties and fifties came from the Democratic party. Taylor and Fillmore accepted a policy of restraint and enforced the neutrality laws against filibusters operating from American bases. Energetically, they upheld the right of Americans to expect fair and equal justice in Cuban and Spanish courts. Under

---

[71] An excellent assessment is Urban, "Africanization of Cuba Scare," *Hispanic American Historical Review*, XXXVII, 44–45.

Fillmore's successor, the nation listened to rallying cries for Cuban annexation. Soulé, Mason, and Buchanan imbibed the spirit of a "Young America" and were determined to bring glory to the Union through territorial aggrandizement.

Why, after an unequalled expansionist furor in the Mexican War, did the Pierce administration, the "Young America" movement, and the Southern slavocracy fail in their efforts to add a Cuban star to the flag? Pierce's Inaugural promise of a dynamic foreign policy represented a calculated drive to divert public attention from the internal debate over slavery and the expansion of that institution into the territories. The public was not necessarily antiexpansionist, for it had thundered across the land to the Pacific during the previous decade. Continental enlargement fitted in with American precepts of national destiny and mission. In the wake of the Mexican War, there had appeared a crisis over the extension of slavery into the territories acquired from Mexico. The absorption of Cuba, a policy that Pierce believed would mitigate the slavery debate, was in fact a proposal that resurrected the dispute in its most virulent form. The abolitionist and Free Soil element who opposed slavery's expansion into the Mexican cession believed the Cuban scheme to be a devious plot to add more slave territory or another slave state. After all, the question of free territories was really a contest between two brands of imperialism, one representing the institution of slavery in a desperate attempt to create buffer zones around the South, the other representing the Free Soil forces who demanded an economic outlet to the West. Those who proposed Cuban annexation cried out the attributes of a superior civilization and demanded that Spanish authority be replaced with another brand of authority. The rhetoric appeared hollow when one considered that the annexationist movement was rooted in the South. How could the preservation of slavery through absorption by the United States improve the material and spiritual condition of Cubans any more than Spanish colonialism? What the annexationists wanted was not the betterment of Cuba but security to shore up the decaying hulk of slavery.

CHAPTER III

The Republicans and Cuba: The Ten Years' War

WITH RESOUNDING FREQUENCY IN THE 1850's, journalists had trumpeted the inevitability of Anglo-Saxon domination in the Caribbean. Even English statesmen who had traditionally opposed the emergence of the United States as a potent force in the Caribbean now seemed to acquiesce. Lord Palmerston, for years the giant of British foreign policy and a staunch opponent of American power in the Caribbean, complained bitterly to Lord Clarendon in 1857 that such diplomats as Lord Napier were ready to concede ground to the Americans in such strategic places as Cuba.[1] Arguing that the sway of Spain in the Western Hemisphere was doomed, periodicals wrote optimistically of future reward in the quest for Cuban annexation. When Pierce had presided in the White House, a sense of urgency had appeared in the Cuban policy. His successor, James Buchanan, valued Cuba's utility, but the Buchanan administration revealed no hurried determination to wrench the island from Spanish hands. Rather, Secretary of State Lewis Cass, an aging Democratic stalwart, authorized the American minister in Madrid to negotiate for the sale of the island but with discreet regard for Spanish pride. No longer was there need for immediate settlement of the Cuban question, wrote the *Southern Quarterly Review*, for the time would come when the American giant held dominion not only over Cuba but also over Santo Domingo, Mexico, and indeed, all of the West Indies. (In Illinois, Stephan Douglas received thunderous applause when he made the same

[1] Palmerston to Lord Clarendon, 6 June 1857, in Van Alstyne, ed., "Anglo-American Relations, 1853–1857," *American Historical Review*, XLIII, 499.

point during a debate with Lincoln.) Spain's oppressive reign in the world was collapsing slowing after three centuries of imperial rule, and no nation could save Cuba for Madrid.[2]

But the assumption of power by Lincoln and his party in March, 1861, had a profound effect on the Cuban policy of the nation. A fundamental tenet of Republicanism in the 1850's was the conviction that the Cuban annexationist movement of that decade was a Southern conspiracy to guarantee the preservation of slavery. Once in office, the Lincoln government rejected the aggressive views of their Democratic predecessors. Lincoln himself remained convinced of the Southern conspiracy thesis. Writing to James Hale in January, 1861, the President-elect predicted that the South, once the nation was dissolved, would demand the annexation of Cuba as a condition for maintaining the Union.[3] The new administration also showed an inclination to return to the judgments of John Quincy Adams. As long as Spain proved unaggressive and did not use her West Indian possessions as a base of attack against the United States, then the American government was content to allow Cuba to remain Spanish.[4] These views were, of course, rooted in the Monroe period. What was abruptly altered by the Republicans, once in command of the nation's Cuban policy, was a deep antagonism to Cuban slavery. In September, 1863, Seward reaffirmed the determination of the administration not to seek new territories but warned that the Union would strike a counterblow if the Southern slavocracy sought refuge in Cuba. Seward recognized a mutuality of interest between Southern and Cuban slavery. A similar philosophy had dominated Southern thinking in the 1850's, but now Seward was reversing the logic by declaring that Southern slavery was doomed and could not depend on the institution in Cuba as a last bulwark against inevitable extinction. Nor did Seward limit his views merely to politics or economics. In 1868, in an instruc-

[2] Lewis Cass to W. Preston, 3 January 1859, Instructions, Spain; "Invasion of Cuba," *Southern Quarterly Review*, XXI (January, 1852), 4; "Continental Policy of the United States: The Acquisition of Cuba," *United States Democratic Review*, XLIII (April, 1859), 9; Douglas' remarks are in Basler, ed., *Works of Lincoln*, III, 115.

[3] Lincoln to James T. Hale, 11 January 1861, *ibid.*, IV, 172.

[4] Seward to Carl Schurz, 27 April 1861, Instructions, Spain.

tion to John Hale in Madrid, the Secretary emphasized that the changed attitude towards Negroes in the United States obligated the American government to demand equal and just treatment for its Negro citizens in all nations. Specifically, he protested the arbitrary treatment of Negro seamen in Havana by Spanish officials.[5] In slightly more than a decade, a drastic alteration had occurred in the approach of the American government towards slavery. Internally, the abolition of slavery had served as moral justification for the Civil War. The Republican party was convinced that the eradication of that institution was a potent force in the moral and political rebirth of the Union. It was only logical for Seward and his successors to believe that Cuba, too, might be redeemed politically, economically, and socially if Spain abolished slavery there.

II

During the last year of Seward's service as Secretary of State, Cuba erupted once again in revolution. For a short time, there had appeared faint hope for reconciliation between the Peninsular masters and the Cuban *Creoles*. In 1865 a group of liberal Spaniards had joined together to form the *Partido Reformista,* a political organization established to bring administrative reform to Cuba and Puerto Rico. The Reform Party was partially successful, for in late November, 1865, the Spanish crown issued a royal decree whereby a special junta was formed in Madrid to study Cuba and Puerto Rican government. But the results were inconclusive and, in the opinion of Cuban *Creoles,* inadequate. Vague statements were issued from the junta, but they rarely matched the expectancies of the Cuban petitioners. Reform spokesman said little about the submerged masses of Cuba —the white proletariat, the mestizo, and the Negro slave.[6] The Cubans of the countryside viewed the *Peninsulare* in the cities as an oppressive master who reaped the economic bounty of the land. Spanish rule was perpetuated and enforced by military

[5] Seward to Horatio Perry, 3 September 1863, *ibid.*; Seward to John Hale, 9 July 1868, 19 August 1868, *ibid.*

[6] José L. Franco, *La revolución de Yara y la constituyente de Gúaimaro* (Cárdenas, Cuba, 1950), 10–12.

decree; its representatives were the merchant, the tax-collector, the soldier, and the cleric. The cause of revolution was just, the disenchanted shouted, and the rebellion was proclaimed at the plantation of Yara (where the Indian hero, Hatuey, had been slain by Spanish invaders 350 years earlier) in October, 1868.[7]

Politically, the manifesto of the revolution coincided almost exactly with the grievances of the thirteen American colonies in 1776. In a famous proclamation, Manuel de Céspedes, a renowned Cuban leader of the Ten Years' War, blamed the uprising on Spanish tyranny, excessive taxation and tribute, denial of political, civil, and religious liberties, and *Peninsular* contempt for reform petitions. Fears of social and economic upheaval colored the writings of José Antonio Saco, an eminent nineteenth century Cuban political thinker. Cuba must construct a civilization, Saco believed, that possessed political but not necessarily social liberty. The future of Cuba lay in the benevolent tutelage of the European. Spain was obligated to insure political freedom and prosperity to the island or Cuba would be lost forever by the force of revolution. Incorporation into the United States was unwise, for it would mean the extinction of the Cuban race. Spain's best opportunity to salvage her colony was by the application of liberal reforms and the establishment of autonomy, which would maintain the facade of a Spanish colony but would, in effect, grant Cuba a dominion status.[8]

Saco, however, represented only one element of Cuban political thought. Those who actually led the revolution desired much more than political change. De Céspedes, for instance, bore some resemblance to the Virginia landowning class which supported the American cause in 1776. But that same de Céspedes was a plantation master who manumitted his slaves, urging them to become guerrillas, and committed his fortune and two sons

---

[7] Ramiro Guerra Sanchez, *Guerra de los diez años*, 1868–1878 (2 vols., Habana, 1950), I, 38. See also R. M. Merchán, *La honra de España en Cuba* (New York, 1871), 127.

[8] Luís Marino Perez, *Estudio sobre las ideas políticas de José Antonio Saco* (Habana, 1908), 70–71.

to the revolution.[9] Similar beliefs were expressed by Máximo Gomez, another Cuban general, who abhorred class society and the slave system.[10]

From its inception the struggle went poorly for both the insurgents and their enemy. Fighting was confined largely to the eastern portions of the island where mountains and a difficult terrain imposed tremendous logistical obstacles for the Spanish regulars. This benefited, of course, the guerrilla operations conducted by the revolutionists. But the latter were handicapped by local jealousies, division of authority between their leaders, and deep animosity towards any brand of central authority. The Spanish army, at least, operated under a unified command.[11]

The insurgents tried to unify their struggle in April, 1869, by calling the famous constituent assembly at Gúaimaro, a few leagues from Puerto Principe. Reasserting the declarations of social equality and undying hatred of slavery, the leaders at Gúaimaro agreed to respect property rights of noncombatants, even Spaniards, in the war zone. From this conference came the Constitution of Gúaimaro, an assertion of revolutionary prescriptions for the future republic: independence, abolition of slavery, equality before the law, and denial of special privileges to particular groups, a notorious holdover from the Spanish empire. To settle the dilemma of leadership, the convention named Manuel de Céspedes as president of the republic and Manuel de Quesada as general-in-chief. In an emotional tribute to a fallen revolutionary, the members accepted the colors of Narciso Lopez.[12]

The war soon degenerated into a brutal, vicious struggle with rapine and pillage a common denominator for both sides. The insurgents forgot completely their earlier utterances to respect the property of noncombatants: whole areas were denuded by

[9] Guerra, *Guerra de diez años*, I, 40–42.

[10] Ramón Infiesta, *Máximo Gomez* (Habana, 1937), 29.

[11] Guerra, *Guerra de diez años*, I, 38; Franco, *Revolución de Yara*, 23–24.

[12] *Ibid.*, 17, 29–31; Francisco de Arredondo y Miranda, *Recuerdas de las guerras de Cuba: Diario de campaña, 1868–1871* (Habana, 1963), 54; Proclamation of Carlos Manuel de Céspedes, in Morales y Morales, *Iniciadores y primeros mártires de la revolución cubana*, II, 489–492.

raids and burning in an attempt to ruin the sugar economy and thereby the entire fabric of Spanish colonialism. On one night in March, 1870, wrote the American consul at Santiago, a sugar estate was raided by guerrillas who systematically set fire to the fields, kidnapped three employees, and murdered a clerk, watchman, a *mayordomo*, and the overseer. The plantation lay some six leagues from the city.[13]

The Spanish retaliated with equal ferocity. Because of a royal order, promulgated in 1825, the captain-general of Cuba possessed both military and civil authority: he could replace any official who failed to have his confidence. Intended as a temporary power, the order of 1825 remained as the fundamental source of authority for Spanish legal rule in Cuba. Once the fighting had erupted, the captaincy-generalship became, in effect, more powerful than the Spanish viceroyalties of colonial days. Drastic orders were meted out to Spanish officers. Any incendiary (or suspicious person) caught in the cane fields was liable to immediate execution.[14]

Even more rigid and unyielding in their animosities towards the revolution were the "Volunteers," who constituted a kind of Cuban militia that dedicated itself to preserving Spanish rule. The Volunteers conjured up all kinds of horror tales in their efforts to prevent liberal *Peninsulares* in Spain from granting reforms. The strife of the insurrection, wrote one Volunteer, would lead to the loss of Cuba or the erection of another Haiti (a black republic). As for autonomy, the most acceptable solution for the liberal Spanish element, the Volunteers rejected the Canadian example, arguing that the preservation of white civilization in Cuba depended on the perpetuation of colonialism. In the cities, where Volunteer and Peninsular strength was located, those who criticized the Volunteers often faced harsh reprisal. From Santiago de Cuba, the American consul reported that threats

[13] A. E. Phillips to Henry Hall, Vice-Consul-General, Cuba, 4 March 1870, Department of State, Consular Records, Cuba.

[14] Jose de Ahumada y Centurión, *Memoria histórica-política de la isla de Cuba, redactada del orden del señor ministro de ultramar* (Habana, 1874), 432; E. L. Plumb to J. C. Bancroft Davis, 4 November 1869, Consular Records, Cuba.

against his life had been made because of alleged favorable utterances about the revolutionary cause.[15]

Any decision for peace would have to satisfy the following groups: the insurgents, the Volunteers, and the Spanish government. The insurgents had no intention of accepting autonomy as long as they believed that a protracted guerrilla campaign would destroy the plantations of the countryside, create havoc and devastation, and compel a demoralized Madrid to concede independence. Equally unremitting in its determination to quash the rebellion was the Spanish government. The Spanish liberals, who achieved power in 1868, were reformers, but they, too, believed that Cuba needed order and stability before colonial change. When the insurgents stopped fighting and accepted the rule of Madrid, both Cuba and Puerto Rico would be rewarded, not with independence, but at least something approximating autonomy. The question of Cuba became a matter of honor. Spanish newspapers recited the chaos and barbarism of the conflict and clamored for the reestablishment of peace. After peace there would come reform.[16] The peace would be decided by arms. Revolutionary logic was the exact reverse: Spain must show good faith by granting reforms (even independence), or the insurgents would continue to fight. Neither side was willing to yield; the war gradually assumed grisly overtones; and the Grant administration became convinced that only the United States had the answer to prevent a Cuban bloodbath.

III

It was natural for the Cuban insurgents to look upon the United States not only as a source of sympathy but of material aid. From New York and Southern ports Narciso Lopez had

[15] Zaragoza, *Las insurreciones en Cuba. Apuntes para la historia política de esta isla en presente siglo* (2 vols., Madrid, 1872–1873), II, 653–654, 658; J. W. Parsons to Thomas Biddle, Consul-General, 9 March 1870, Consular Records, Cuba; Francisco V. Aguilera, *Notes about Cuba* (New York, 1872), 49.

[16] Spain. Ministro de Ultramar, *Cuba desde 1850 á 1873 . . .* (Madrid, 1873), 300; *La Época* (Madrid), 27 July 1869; *El Imparcial* (Madrid), 14 August 1869; clippings in State Department files.

directed the destinies of the "generation of '49." The Civil War had transformed the United States into a unified nation, and Cuban revolutionaries in 1869 gloried in the prospect that the humanitarian crusade that had eradicated Southern slavery would sweep southward to banish slavery in Cuba. The leaders of the insurrection believed that the vast arsenals of the Union would open to them and that scores of veterans would flock to the banner of insurgent Cuba.[17]

Most Americans in 1868 considered Cuba a potentially prosperous island that had been subjected to systematic pillage because of a corrupt and tyrannical Spanish colonialism. A degenerate and an oppressive oligarchy presided over the island's future. Recognizing Cuba's economic importance, writers complained of an onerous commercial system hamstrung with rules and red tape and dreamed of the time when a booming free trade would unite the Cuban and American economies. Everywhere in Cuba, one journalist noted, there existed abundant evidence that the Spanish had never developed the island by exploiting its natural resources. Cuban prosperity depended on "the control of an intelligent and free population." [18]

American commentary on Cuba usually expressed or implied a need for guidance and tutelage before the island merited complete self-government. A hostility to Spanish colonialism was joined with the conviction that Cubans were unprepared to be their own masters. Cubans were naturally proud and ambitious, character traits which were not necessarily liabilities for political power; but the prospective ruling class, the *Creole* landowners, unfortunately lacked a Puritan determination to labor and carve out a stable and prosperous state. Perhaps these habits of languor and satiety in the landowning elite, related one writer, were due to an enervating tropical climate; perhaps, to a disinclination to take life seriously. After all, dancing was the national pastime.[19]

---

[17] Guerra, *Guerra de diez años*, I, 166.

[18] "Something about Cuba," *Appleton's Journal* (14 August 1869), I, 617–618, II (21 August 1869), 3, 5.

[19] *Ibid.*, 2; "La Reina de las Antillas," *Lippincott's Magazine*, I (April, 1868), 424, 432; W. W. Nevin, "The Revolution in Cuba," *ibid.*, III (March, 1869), 340–341, 343.

The Cuban cause possessed formidable allies in Washington. In the Congress, representatives of both political parties received a deluge of letters and telegrams calling for immediate action to end the carnage of war. Clearly, those clamoring for such a drastic measure as outright intervention were in the minority, but most members of the legislative branch, in accordance with popular feeling on the Ten Years' War, at least believed that it was the duty of the executive to grant belligerent status to the insurrectionists and employ diplomatic overtures to mediate the conflict. That reasoning dominated President Grant, whose erratic conduct in the sensitive arena of diplomacy especially alarmed some men. Gideon Welles, a member of Lincoln's cabinet, wrote pessimistically in his diary that, with Grant in the White House, the nation was stumbling into a foolish war with Spain.[20] Even more effusive than the President in his devotion to the Cuban cause was John Rawlins, Secretary of War for six months in 1869. During the Civil War, Rawlins had served Grant ably as chief of staff. Rewarded for loyalty on the battlefield, Rawlins' determined electioneering almost brought about a rapid Presidential recognition of the belligerent status of the insurgents. Later revelations would show that Rawlins, an indebted man, had received some $28,000 in Cuban bonds from the New York junta of the republic. When this information came to the attention of the Cabinet, Rawlins' efforts to shape an open alliance with the Cuban republic, whose success guaranteed him financial reward, failed tragically. He died shortly after, a miserable and broken man, forgotten by Americans but not by Cuban nationalist historians, one of whom characterized the Secretary of War as the greatest American friend Cuba ever knew.[21] Finally, the Cuban revolution could rely for support on the American minister in Madrid, Daniel Sickles. Before 1861, Sickles had been a Democrat who served in the New York bar and legislature, but he committed himself to the Union and was named as the military governor of the Carolinas in 1867. His personal

---

[20] Gideon Welles, *Diary*, 7 April 1869 (3 vols., Boston, 1911), III, 572–573.

[21] Foner, *Cuba*, II, 204–205; James H. Wilson, *The Life of John A. Rawlins* (New York, 1916), 359; Emilio Roig de Leuchsenring, *Cuba y los Estados Unidos, 1805–1898* . . . (Habana, 1949), 103.

life always intruded into his politics. In one of the most sensational trials of the century, he was acquitted of the shooting of Philip Barton Key, who allegedly had been involved in an affair with Mrs. Sickles. Later, in a gesture of classic Victorian altruism, Sickles forgave his young wife. Appointed to the Madrid post in 1869, Sickles' Anglo-Saxon flair earned him the sobriquet "Yankee King of Spain." Like Rawlins and many others, he firmly believed that the Spanish empire was doomed in the Western Hemisphere, and he energetically pursued every opportunity to pressure Madrid governments to sell Cuba to the United States.[22]

More than anyone, Hamilton Fish, Grant's Secretary of State, dimmed the hopes of Rawlins and Sickles to extend belligerent status to the Cuban insurgents. An aristocratic New Yorker, Fish shared the public disgust with Spanish rule and slavery in Cuba. Yet he failed to recognize any leadership abilities in those who followed the banner of revolution; the *potpourri* of Indian, Negro, and Spaniard that he saw in Cuba was deemed insufficient to guide the island towards stable self-rule. He accepted the Spanish liberal antidote of gradual and evolutionary reform for the anarchy and chaos of rebellion. Fish was absolute in his refusal to extend belligerent recognition to the Cuban insurgents, because the revolution exercised no real control, possessed no real government, and supervised no real domination over the diverse guerrilla bands.[23]

The Secretary of State's initial problem was the wresting of the Cuban question out of the hands of Rawlins and the more belligerent congressmen. Fish suspected that Rawlins had purchased Cuban bonds in the prospect of United States intervention and guarantee of the insurgent republic. He also feared that Grant would act precipitately in recognizing the belligerent status of the revolutionaries. In a frenzied burst, the House of Representatives had rushed through a resolution of sympathy for the insurgents on April 10, 1869, and had pledged simultaneously to adhere to a Presidential extension of belligerent

[22] *Dictionary of American Biography*, XVII, 150–151; Edgcumb Pinchon, *Dan Sickles, Hero of Gettysburg and "Yankee King of Spain"* (Garden City, 1945), 227.

[23] Allan Nevins, *Hamilton Fish: The Inner History of the Grant Administration* (2 vols., rev. ed., New York, 1957), I, 180–181.

rights. To be sure, the Congress had expressed its partiality to the Fenian "republic" as well, but Fish recognized that forces were organizing both within and outside the Congress to force the President's hand. In Washington, lobbyists for the Cuban New York junta labored frantically. In May, an interventionist crowd gathered in New York to hear an emotional plea for action by Stewart L. Woodford, the lieutenant-governor. (In 1897, William McKinley would send Woodford to Spain as minister; then he would be a determined foe of intervention.) But inside the Cabinet, the arguments of Fish were slowly winning out: when the Secretary requested that American naval officers might visit Cuban ports, the President acquiesced and gave the order. Steadfastly, Fish refused to recognize the executive of the Cuban New York junta and, later when they would meet, the Secretary was reserved and avoided any official sanction of the insurgency.[24]

Simultaneously, however, Fish was preparing to steal the thunder from the pro-insurgent factions by offering a daring proposal to settle the Cuban conflict. In June, while Grant toured the country, the Secretary drew up an elaborate plan that was soon to be delivered in Madrid by Sickles and Paul Forbes, a businessman recently appointed as a special envoy to Spain. According to the Secretary's proposals, (a) Spain was to recognize the independence of Cuba; (b) slavery would be abolished there; (c) Cuba was obligated to pay Spain not more than $100 million (with the consent of Congress, the United States guaranteed that sum); and (d) each side was to recognize an armistice during the negotiations. In a stroke, the plan aimed at the settlement of the nagging Cuban issue: Spanish power would depart from a strategic place in the Caribbean, and a potential source of war would be erased. (Forbes himself represented a business elite that wanted stronger commercial ties with Spain and thus desired a thaw in Spanish-American relations.) A few days later, in a long letter to Sickles, Fish explained his reasoning for the abrupt offer to Madrid. He summed up the contention of earlier generations. The holocaust hampered Cuban-American

---

[24] *Ibid.*, 182, 184. For anti-interventionist views see also "The Cuban Insurrection," *The Nation*, VIII (15 April 1869), 288; and "Our Supposed Sympathy with Cuba," *ibid.*, IX (8 July 1869), 24.

commerce; violence in the island interrupted the natural economic union of Cuba and America; the insurgents appeared to be in a struggle for self-determination; a continuation of the war would mean the destruction not only of American property but of the island's potential wealth. It was imperative, wrote Fish, that the Spanish understand that a prolongation would result in a devastated island. As a bargaining lever, Fish threatened the recognition of Cuban belligerency if the Spanish government refused the good office tendered by the President of the United States. The Secretary of State had triumphed momentarily in his debate with the Secretary of War. If the Spanish procrastinated, Fish could always find another excuse to delay carrying out his threats.[25]

Both Sickles and Forbes left New York at the same time, but Forbes arrived sooner and, in mid-July, sent back word that the Spanish had agreed to United States mediation. The stipulations were that the insurgents must lay down their arms and pay a $150 million indemnity guaranteed by Washington. In return, Spain would grant autonomy to Cuba *and* Puerto Rico. Although Forbes seemed hopeful of imminent success, Sickles, who also had full powers to negotiate a settlement, was more pessimistic. The Spanish premier, General Prim, recognized the fantastic cost of the war and looked to a cessation of the fighting, but the insurgents had to surrender their arms before mediation. Expressing his own view, Sickles believed Cuban independence was inevitable because the struggle for freedom was intertwined with the destiny of the Western Hemisphere.[26]

What destroyed any prospect for quick mediation of the Ten Years' War was Spanish politics and pride. Sickles failed to appreciate that colonialism and imperialism had its own ideology and mystique and that often the most crucial decisions in Madrid were made, not on the basis of hard facts, but on the basis of something called national sentiment and honor. Spain would

[25] Nevins, *Hamilton Fish*, I, 191, 194–195, 245; Fish to Paul Forbes, 26 June 1869, Department of State, Special Missions; Fish to Sickles, 29 June 1869, Instructions, Spain.

[26] Nevins, *Hamilton Fish*, I, 199; Sickles Memo, 10 August 1869, Despatches, Spain; Sickles to Fish, 11 August 1869, 12 August 1869, *ibid.*

leave Cuba but only in an honorable fashion, which meant proving that her armies could conquer the insurrectionists. Mediation in Washington under the auspices of the American government was objectionable; it was better to have the rebels come to Madrid, where in the *Cortés*, Cuba was already represented. On receipt of these statements, Fish became irritated and replied to Sickles that the offer of mediation would be withdrawn on October 1. To frighten the Spanish, the Secretary predicted imminent anarchy in Cuba and blamed the Volunteers for the murder of American citizens. The threat was useless. Madrid newspapers championed the determination of the government to stand forthright against any foreign meddling in Spain's domestic affairs. One called for a war *à outrance* in Cuba; another castigated the dishonor inherent in the loss of the island. Fish's calculated planning had failed, and on September 28, 1869, Sickles withdrew the offer of good offices.[27]

The firebrands who looked to the President to shape a more bellicose anti-Spanish policy were soon disappointed. Grant seemed content to allow his Secretary of State to shape the administration's announcements regarding the Cuban insurrection and American intervention. In the successive drafts of the 1869 Presidential State of the Union message, Fish had been able to include several paragraphs that would conciliate Spain. Recounting the historical interest of the United States in the cause of Cuban freedom, the message read, the President recognized the widespread sympathy for the insurgent movement. Nevertheless, the revolutionary effort had failed to prove that it commanded a government and the loyalty of all the people. As for recognition of belligerency, the President went on, he intended to follow a policy of watchful waiting. Almost as a warn-

[27] Sickles to Fish, 21 August 1869, 29 August 1869, *ibid.*; Fish to Sickles, 1 September 1869, Instructions, Spain; *La Discusión*, 27 August 1869; *El Imparcial*, 5 September 1869; *La Época*, 6 September 1869; clippings, State Department files; Sickles to Spanish Minister of State, copy, 28 September 1869, Despatches, Spain. Representatives of France, England, and Russia attempted to convince the Grant Administration that Spain was able to crush the rebellion. The move aimed to head off American recognition of Cuban belligerency. See Jerónimo Becker, *Historia de las relaciones exteriores de España durante el siglo XIX* (3 vols., Madrid, 1924–1926), III, 38.

ing to Spain, he added that the United States would be the judge in determining the criteria for belligerent recognition. Denying any intention to interfere in Cuba, Grant emphasized that it was the dream of the Western World and the United States that Spain would allow its dependent subjects to emerge as independent governors of their own destiny.[28]

Still, the truculent elements in Congress were not quieted. Soon after Congress opened debate, there were launched vicious attacks on Spanish policy in Cuba. A well of resentment had built up over the arbitrariness of the captain-general, alleged brutalities committed by the Volunteers, and capricious treatment of American lives and properties. Championed by irate newspaper editorials, the anti-Spanish protest movement in the Congress soon proved to be a hindrance to Fish's project to achieve a satisfactory solution to the Cuban problem. On December 13, 1869, a representative from New York announced that he had 72,000 signatures on a petition condemning Spanish rule. From the Senate, there emanated declarations that the insurgents had earned the right to belligerent recognition. Grumbling in both houses gave credence to suspicions that Fish himself would be censured by the Congress. During February, 1870, the efforts to force recognition of Cuban belligerency continued apace. In the House, John A. Logan, a future vice-Presidential candidate, offered a resolution and delivered an emotional speech; in the Senate, Oliver Morton in shrill tones castigated the brutality of the Spanish counterrevolution. Morton linked the Monroe Doctrine to the Cuban war and demanded that Spain be told that her power existed in this hemisphere only because of American toleration. A few days later there came another resolution from John Sherman, usually restrained and cautious, who declared that the people were tired of waiting for action. To be sure, much of the Congressional clamor was rooted in sensationalism and chicanery,[29] but there could be no denial that many sincerely believed Spanish colonialism was corrupt, archaic, and tyrannical, that the Cuban

[28] Draft of speech, in Grant Papers, Series III, vol. II, Manuscripts Division, Library of Congress.
[29] Nevins, *Hamilton Fish*, I, 336, 348.

revolution was an expression of self-determination by oppressed masses, and that, sooner or later, the United States would have to end the carnage a hundred miles from her shores.

Equally enthusiastic in his determination to end the Cuban conflict under the aegis of American power was Daniel Sickles. As Minister Plenipotentiary and Envoy Extraordinary in Madrid, this Republican diplomat viewed the possible settlement of the war (and possibly the purchase of Cuba) as a personal triumph. His optimism often lead to an exaggeration of every utterance of the Spanish Minister of State, every debate in the *Cortés*, and every hint of internal political division within the Spanish state. In mid-March, 1870, Sickles wrote to Fish explaining that three Madrid dailies were advocating the sale of Cuba to the United States. These constituted a minority, of course, but informal comments of some ministers, he continued, also included references to cession of the island. Spanish politics, Sickles believed, was demoralized; the public sickened at the atrocities of Cuban Volunteers; news of insurgent shooting of prisoners brought additional opposition to recruitment of soldiers. Sickles hoped to magnify the spectre of imminent decay of Spanish colonialism in an effort to force the hand of the Spanish ministry. In early March, he read an unofficial memorandum to General Prim in which he alluded to the public dissatisfaction with the war and called for a Spanish-American *démarche* on Cuba while the legislatures of each nation were still in session. Explaining the American tradition of nonexpansion to noncontiguous territories, Sickles intimated that the American government would pay handsomely to facilitate such an understanding (the details here were not made clear). Spain's obligation would be to grant Cuban autonomy, a status within the empire similar to that held by Canada, and to abolish slavery.[30]

It was a futile undertaking. Sickles' interpretation of the strength of republicanism in Spain was distorted, and he apparently falied to appreciate the reluctance of *any* Madrid government, republican or monarchical, to yield a foot of Cuban territory without a fight. The idea of selling Cuba to the United

[30] Sickles to Fish, 16 March 1870, 30 March 1870, 31 March 1870, Despatches, Spain.

States, one journal editorialized, was the invention of New York periodicals. Madrid had negotiated on the subject but had committed no act that stained national honor. Volunteer opinion was even more nationalistic. The *Casino Español*, the voice of Volunteer Cubans, issued a manifesto called "To the Spanish People" that read, in part: "The Spaniards in Cuba will *never* be sold, traded away, or conquered; Cuba will be Spanish or we shall leave it abandoned in ashes!" The Grant administration was quick to condemn Spanish atrocities in Cuba, wrote one Volunteer historian, but was quick to forget the legacy of brutality left in the South by Ben Butler and William T. Sherman.[31]

A congressional report on the Volunteers and the war was soon in the offing. More strident in their counterinsurgency proclamations than the Spanish government, the Volunteers were stereotyped in the American press as vicious brutes who pursued devastation and rapine with malicious delight. In June, 1870, the House Committee on Foreign Affairs issued a report on the Cuban war that summed up popular attitudes about the Volunteers. They were responsible, the report read, for the introduction of war atrocities. Only 40,000 in number, the Volunteers necessarily held the balance of power in Cuba and compelled Madrid to adopt forceful positions. Their purpose in Cuba was the acquisition of wealth; their most salient trait, a complete disregard for law and order. The Volunteers lacked the normal cultural values of western civilizations.[32]

Citing the historical relationship between Cuba and the United States, the majority report of the House Foreign Affairs Committee appealed to the President to protest the inhumane conduct of the war. The sympathy of the Committee lay obviously with the Cuban insurgents, who were portrayed as warriors for independence, self-government, religious and commercial freedom, and material progress. Included in the report, however, was a resolution calling for the President to observe strict neu-

[31] Translation, *Diario de las Sesiones*, 12 March 1870; "Al Pueblo Español!" 23 March 1870, in Consular Records, Cuba; Zaragoza, *Las insurreciones de Cuba*, II, 460–461; Fish to Sickles, 20 April 1870, Instructions, Spain.

[32] House of Representatives. Committee on Foreign Affairs, *Cuba*, 14 June 1870 (Washington, 1870), 2–3, 11, 17, 32–36.

trality. The resolution carefully avoided a statement of belligerent rights but proclaimed faith in the rectitude of Cuba's struggle for freedom. Carefully segregated from the legal question of belligerency, which lay solely within the power of the President, was an inherent right of the American people to intervene in Cuba in the name of civilization. The majority report was not calling for immediate intervention but rather announcing that a *moral* or *humane* basis for intervention existed.[33]

Meanwhile, Grant was exhibiting the same restlessness that had already infected the House Foreign Affairs Committee. The warhawks outside the Executive branch were not reassured that the President was ready to yield to the popular will. At first, Grant did talk in increasingly bellicose tones as he prepared a special message on the Cuban situation. The thunder quickly departed from him once Fish got wind of what was happening. He threatened to resign in protest, and the gamble succeeded. The climactic episode occurred during a cabinet meeting during which Fish and a few associates launched a vigorous debate against Grant's first drafts of the message, which included condemnatory passages of Spanish atrocities and intimidation of American citizens in Cuba. None of the charges, Fish retaliated, had been proved. By delivering the message in its original form, the President was tantamount to asking for a declaration of war. Reluctantly, Grant and the remainder gave in, and the message was rewritten.[34]

Thus, the deletions in the message of June 13, 1870, were of far more importance in illustrating the deep and bitter division within the administration. In a sense, Grant's statements were anticlimactic, for the Congress had expected a strong anti-Spanish diatribe. Instead, the members were told that *both* warring factions in Cuba committed unmentionable atrocities. The question of recognition of belligerency received more attention. Before the encounter with Fish's firm protests, Grant had included a paragraph making the recognition of Cuban belligerency subject to American interpretation. In successive drafts of the message, however, this paragraph was omitted. And in

---

[33] *Ibid.*

[34] Nevins, *Hamilton Fish,* I, 353–360.

the final draft, the President concentrated on legal criteria, arguing that the rebels had not earned recognition because their armies held no cities and their leadership possessed no central authority. As a matter of fact, Grant went on, a recognition of belligerency would do damage to the insurrectionist cause by stopping American shipping in Cuban coastal waters.[35]

III

Having failed to mediate the Cuban conflict, the Grant administration nevertheless persevered in an effort to settle the "Cuban problem" by persuasion. The island knew bloodshed, the American argument stated, because of Spanish procrastination in extending reforms. Cuba experienced economic backwardness because of the preservation of slavery and an outmoded commercial system.

The relationship between abolition and reform was now emphasized in appeals to Madrid. In the view of American critics, Cuban slavery perpetuated the general political and economic *malaise* of the island. The insurgents, for instance, were actually an army composed of thousands of slaves struggling for freedom. Even Hamilton Fish, so quick to point out rebel brutality, sincerely believed that the war would continue so long as Spain delayed emancipation schemes for Cuba and Puerto Rico. Morally, more than politically, the Spanish were obligated to abolition. Failure to initiate emancipation legislation, Fish wrote in 1870, constituted "bad faith" of Spain's *moral* commitment to Cuban reform.[36]

Grant's minister in Madrid employed the historical experience of the United States as evidence of the inevitable demise of human bondage. Emancipation in the South, Sickles informed one Spanish minister, had brought political harmony, increased

[35] Message to Congress, 13 June 1870, in Richardson, *Messages and Papers of the Presidents*, IX, 4018–4023; A draft of the December 1870 annual message showed that Grant had marked out one paragraph that called for unilateral judgment by the United States in the recognition of Cuban independence. Grant Papers, Series III, vol. III.

[36] Nevin, "Revolution in Cuba," *Lippincott's Magazine*, III, 339; Fish to Sickles, 26 January 1870, 11 March 1870, Instructions, Spain.

productivity, and financial reward. Cuban emancipation would prove that labor possessed an inalienable right to freedom. The American public, Sickles contended, saw the future of Cuban prosperity dependent on an enlightened Spanish reform program. The last strongholds of slavery in the hemisphere were Cuba and Puerto Rico. An inexorable historical process—a law of civilization—commanded the destruction of slavery in Spain's possessions.[37] Similarly, Sickles saw the unfolding of another historical analogy in the 1868 triumph of Spanish republicanism. The Revolution of that year, which installed antimonarchical elements in power, was symbolic of the triumph of democracy and the principle of representative government. This democratic victory Sickles compared with the internal political experience of the United States, which had accepted the rule of the common man and had repudiated human slavery. The enemies of Cuban reform, the Volunteers and the slaveholders, were in his mind the enemies of western civilization.[38] Thus, political and economic betterment in Cuba meant to Sickles a transplanting of Anglo-Saxon concepts of self-government. A truly liberal and democratic change in colonial policy, he informed the Spanish government, would grant Cuban autonomy, embrace free trade, and eradicate slavery.[39]

The stress given to abolition as a necessary requirement in any political reform program for Cuba and Puerto Rico was a sign that the Grant administration, particularly Secretary Fish, had substituted persuasion for mediation in an effort to end the Cuban revolution. Belatedly, in June, 1870, the *Cortés* passed an abolition law, but it was not wholly satisfactory. Only aged slaves and infants gained freedom under the law, Fish observed, and they would be unable to survive without transitional aid. The measure doubtless would elicit contempt from the civilized nations that recognized "liberty as the universal law of nature . . . ."[40] Sickles, too, was dismayed at the law and criticized the

[37] Sickles to Fish, 27 February 1870, 8 March 1870, Despatches, Spain; draft of message, 31 May 1870, Grant Papers, Series III, vol. II; Sickles to Sagasta, 21 December 1870, Despatches, Spain.

[38] Sickles to Fish, 12 August 1870, 27 November 1870, *ibid.*

[39] Sickles to Fish, 28 March 1871, *ibid.*

[40] Fish to Sickles, 20 June 1870, Instructions, Spain.

impediments in the path of its execution. The government spoke often about reform, but delay in emancipating the slaves was another sign that colonial authorities were reluctant reformers. Fish was adamant. He instructed Sickles to continue his pleas for reform and fulfillment of the emancipation promises of Madrid. There was only slight success in these overtures. Two years following the announcement of the 1870 law found the Spanish *Cortés* still in debate about the justification of emancipation. An 1872 act, which was passed to supplement the earlier law, committed the freed slave to the jurisdiction of local boards, whose membership included slaveholders. Sickles complained that the new legislation added more complex and bureaucratic devices to impede emancipation. Again Sickles applied the American example. Slavery was abolished in the United States, not by war, but as a political act. The result was beneficial: a sizable body of ex-slaves had become citizens, and the Southern states had learned that free labor brought a more efficient and productive economy. Any Spanish minister who championed the emancipation of slaves in Cuba would be lauded as another Jefferson, Wilberforce, or Lincoln. The eradication of that abominable institution would be Spain's gesture of respect for the customs and laws of the civilized world.[41]

It is within the context of this plea for reform, especially the freeing of slaves, that Fish's Cuba policy must be interpreted. The Secretary of State was not insensitive to the cry of Cuban independence. Yet he looked at the insurrection from a legal stance and refused to approve recognition of belligerency without solid foundation. The insurgents had every cause to expect moral support from the American public, but they had no right to compel intervention because of exaggeration of some alleged grievance. On the other hand, Fish believed that Spain could not quell the insurrection solely by military means. The first step towards real reform lay in a meaningful emancipation law. When it became obvious in October, 1872, that the new membership of the *Cortés* was politically unwilling to produce anti-

[41] Sickles to Fish, 24 September 1870, Despatches, Spain; Fish to Sickles, 28 February 1871, Instructions, Spain; Sickles to Fish, 27 August 1872, 24 November 1872, Despatches, Spain; Sickles Memo, 30 November 1872, *ibid.*

slavery legislation, the Secretary sent a strongly-worded instruction to Sickles. The letter, which warned that Spanish inability to end the war *might* lead to American intervention, was also an indictment of Spanish colonial policy. The United States had emancipated the Southern slaves, Fish wrote, therefore emancipation was the logical answer for Cuban ills. A small minority of slaveholders in Cuba defied the moral duty of Spain. Was this not an admission that Madrid had lost control over her colonial dominion? In intemperate language, the Secretary instructed Sickles to remind the Spanish that a prolongation of the strife in Cuba might result in drastic changes in American policy. Spain was a great power, he wrote, and thus should not fear to do what was just. A month brought still another instruction, equally condemnatory, from Fish's pen. The Spanish refusal to facilitate promised reforms now left the American government with no choice but the withdrawal of its offer of "good offices." Spain should recognize that the rebels would continue fighting until colonial reforms became a reality. The President could not ask the rebels to cease hostilities until Spain pledged Cuba a provisional legislature, emancipation, municipal government, self-taxation, and autonomy.[42] Reform, particularly emancipation, had to be initiated, and the responsibility for reform lay in Madrid.

IV

The most dangerous incident in Spanish-American relations during the conflict was the *Virginius* episode. The *Virginius*, a blockade runner during the Civil War, had been sold to a private firm in 1870 and was leased out to the services of the New York Cuban Junta. The activities of the *Virginius* in transporting supplies to the insurrectionists had long annoyed the Spanish, and they were determined to put a stop to the ship's operations.[43] Its seizure in November, 1873, initiated a crisis that nearly resulted in war with Spain.

---

[42] Fish to Henry C. Hall, Acting Consul-General, Havana, 25 October 1872, Fish Letter Books, IV, 922–923, Fish Papers, Manuscripts Division, Library of Congress; Fish to Sickles, 27 October 1872, 16 November 1872, Instructions, Spain.

[43] Nevins, *Hamilton Fish*, II, 671.

The chase of the *Virginius* by the Spanish vessel *Toronado* began on October 31, 1873. Ordered to halt, the *Virginius* was boarded. To their delight, the Spanish found arms and supplies as well as several eminent revolutionaries, one of whom was Pedro Céspedes, son of the rebel general. Promptly the vessel and its prisoners were taken to Santiago de Cuba, and the men (including Americans) were summarily tried by a military tribunal for aiding the insurrection. On two days (November 7 and 8) the Spanish officer in charge ordered the execution of the captain, 36 crew members, and 16 of the passengers. All 53 were shot. Doubtless others would have died had it not been for the interference of Captain Lorraine of the British man-of-war *Niobe,* who learned of the trials, sailed into Santiago harbor, and threatened to level the city with his cannon if the shootings continued.[44]

The *Virginius* dispute involved not only the law of the sea but the law of humanity. Regardless of the legal status of the ship, the United States decried the executions as an insult to civilization and a flagrant example of Spanish brutality. If the vessel was American, Sickles wrote, then the Spanish had no right to seize it on the high seas. Momentarily, Fish forgot about legalities and instead centered on the Santiago executions. The shootings, he wrote to Sickles, were inhumane and barbaric, without regard to world conscience. In his opinion, the *Virginius* affair constituted another example of Spanish misrule in Cuba. Failure to punish the guilty, he warned, would be interpreted as Spanish inability to govern Cuba by law. In ringing tones, he laid down the minimum requirements for acceptable settlement: (1) restoration of the *Virginius,* (2) release of the prisoners to American custody, (3) salute of the American flag in the city of Santiago, and (4) punishment of the officers responsible for the executions. To Edward Pierrepont the Secretary wrote that he feared more public outcry and that the government had dispatched several warships to Cuban waters. In a more reflective mood, Fish wrote that the executions at Santiago signaled the demise of

[44] Becker, *Historia,* III, 163–168; Sickles to Fish, 7 November 1873, Despatches, Spain; John G. Ryan, ed., *Life and Adventures of Gen. W. A. C. Ryan . . .* (New York, 1876), 228–229, 244–245.

Spanish rule on the island. The bizarre episode convinced him that a colonial society that permitted such atrocities could not possibly survive. World powers should renounce Spain's domination of Cuba.[45]

The first Spanish reactions were angry, as if national honor had been insulted by the American demands. The *Toronado* had the right to stop the *Virginius* on the high seas if there was reasonable suspicion that the vessel carried arms for the Cuban insurrectionists, wrote an eminent Spanish historian years later. Since the *Virginius* was outside American waters, editorialized *El Imparcial,* the American government had no grounds for demanding an indemnity. The unreasonable denunciations of Spain, continued the same paper, were due in part to the well-known anti-Spanish biases of Mr. Sickles.[46]

Briefly, the contention of the Spanish government was that the stoppage of the *Virginius* was justifiable, that the Santiago executions were an unfortunate occurrence, and that the shootings ceased as soon as orders were sent to Santiago from the captain-general in Havana. No apology would be forthcoming until Madrid had completed an inquiry into the entire affair. As for reparation, if the facts proved that the American flag had been offended, then Spain would pay an indemnity. This reasoning, which would mean inevitable delay, was entirely unsatisfactory to Fish, and Sickles was instructed to demand an immediate apology for the "slaughter of Santiago." If refused, Sickles was to obtain his passports and prepare to return home. On November 26, almost three weeks after the Santiago incident, Sickles informed the Spanish government of his instructions. Apparently this threat to break relations convinced the Madrid officialdom of the angry shock in the United States caused by the shootings

---

[45] Sickles to Fish, 8 November 1873, Despatches, Spain; Fish to Sickles, 12 November 1873, 14 November 1873, Instructions, Spain; Sickles to Fish, 14 November 1873, Despatches, Spain; Fish to Edward Pierrepont, 14 November 1873, Letter Books, IX, 89–90, Fish Papers; Fish to W. C. Bryant, 17 November 1873, *ibid.*, 97–98.

[46] Becker, *Historia,* III, 186–190; *El Imparcial,* 14 November 1873, clippings in State Department files. On November 19, Sickles reported that an angry mob had gathered at the Legation. Sickles to Fish, 19 November 1873, Despatches, Spain.

of Santiago. Immediately, the government issued a proposal, obviously hastily drawn, but intended to placate Washington. The points included (1) a provision for ascertaining the legal responsibility of Spain in the seizure of the *Virginius;* if the ship was wrongfully seized, Spain would return the ship and salute the American flag; (2) an investigation of those authorities in Santiago who were responsible for criminal acts against foreigners; (3) settlement of reclamations by diplomacy; that failing, by arbitration; and (4) recognition of Spanish liability on December 25 if Madrid failed to substantiate her claims.[47]

Fish's demands had met with success. The Spanish offer of late November was, in effect, a capitulation to the American claim. After receiving the proposal, Fish wired Sickles his acceptance and added the stipulation that legal proceedings would be instituted against the *Virginius* if it was proved that the ship had no legal right to fly the flag. This was certainly a conciliatory approach compared to the bellicose protests of mid-November. On December 15, Sickles learned from the Spanish president that the survivors of the *Virginius* had been surrendered to American authorities. Five days later, Fish cabled the news that the *Virginius* had *not* been entitled to fly the flag and, therefore, there would be no demand for a Spanish salute of the colors.[48]

In effect, the incident was closed, because after December, 1873, there was no danger of hostilities arising from the seizure of the *Virginius.* The affair also terminated the mission of Daniel Sickles. An embittered man, his mission to Spain had proved largely a failure. Like Pierre Soulé, he believed the demise of Spanish rule in Cuba was imminent and longed for the day when the American flag flew above Havana harbor. The *Virginius* imbroglio was for him no isolated grievance: the seizure and executions represented another chapter in the catalogue of horrors in the history of Spanish rule in Cuba. Slavery and tyranny had produced a festering sore that only emancipation

---

[47] Sickles to Fish, 18 November 1873, 19 November 1873, 20 November 1873, *ibid.*; Sickles to Minister of State, copy, 26 November 1873, *ibid.*; Sickles to Fish, 26 November 1873, *ibid.*

[48] Fish to Sickles, 1 December 1873, Instructions, Spain; Sickles to Fish, 15 December 1873, Despatches, Spain; Fish to Sickles, 20 December 1873, Instructions, Spain.

and efficient administration could eradicate. While Fish was toning down his original *Virginius* notes, Sickles was recommending that the United States seize the island temporarily in order to provide civil government, emancipation, termination of the war, and free trade. Once reformed, the island would be returned as an autonomous entity to the Spanish empire. From 1895-1898, such an approach would attract widespread public support, but Sickles' design would not be accepted by Hamilton Fish in 1873. In February, 1874, Sickles' ministry ended. His successor was Caleb Cushing, who served as a diplomatic agent in China during the Tyler administration and as Attorney-General in the Pierce cabinet. Cushing, much more cautious than Sickles, was fearful of rushing headlong into a war with Spain. At his suggestion the *Virginius* negotiations were transferred to Washington, and, a year later, a final indemnity payment of $80,000 was authorized by the Spanish government.[49]

Sickles' departure from the Madrid post constituted a rejection of the man rather than his criticism of Spain. The administration, particularly Grant, continued to indict certain elements in Cuba as responsible for the war's duration. In his annual message for 1873, for instance, Grant blamed the proslavery faction in Cuba for prolonging the brutal conflict in Cuba. The Cuban slavocracy, he wrote, professed loyalty to the Spanish empire but was intent only in exhausting the island resources. In the name of humanity and civilization, the President appealed once more for an end to the fighting. Fish, too, expressed his disgust with Spanish rule. Cuba, he noted, was the largest of any European island possession in the Western Hemisphere. Lying near the United States, Cuba was commercially important as an outlet for American produce. Any internal dissension in the island had profound consequences for Cuban-American trade. These were familiar arguments dredged up from the writings and utterances of every President since Thomas Jefferson. But a curious transformation had occurred in the Cuban policy

---

[49] Sickles to Fish, 3 December 1873, Despatches, Spain; Nevins, *Hamilton Fish*, II, 692; Claude Fuess, *The Life of Caleb Cushing* (2 vols., New York, 1923), II, 361–362; Minister of State to Caleb Cushing, 15 February 1875, Despatches, Spain; Cushing to Fish, 17 March 1875, *ibid.*

of the nation. John Quincy Adams had contended that the commercial and strategic utility of Cuba was sufficient grounds for American support of Spain's hold on the island; now, Fish was using the *same* logic to arrive at the opposite conclusion. Writing to Cushing in February, 1874, the Secretary pleaded the cause of Cuban independence:

> In fine, Cuba, like the former continental colonies of Spain in America, ought to belong to the great family of American republics, with political forms and public policy of their own, and attached to Europe by no ties, save those of international amity, and of intellectual, commercial, and social intercourse. The desire of independence on the part of Cubans is a natural and legitimate aspiration of theirs, because they are American. And, while such independence is the manifest exigency of the political interests of the Cubans themselves, it is equally so that of the rest of America, including the United States.[50]

In the early years of the insurrection, the policy of the Grant administration had sought to arrange a Cuban-Spanish settlement under the aegis of the United States. Following the Spanish-American understanding of the *Virginius* seizure, the administration continued its condemnation of the war but appealed to other powers in an effort to bring about Spanish negotiation with the Cubans. The Spanish had become accustomed to American demands; they had been made again and again, and Madrid had avoided a head-on clash each time. Too cautious to force Spain's hand as he had done in the *Virginius* affair, Fish turned more to the idea of international pressure. His famous despatch No. 270, November 5, 1875, was a bitter denunciation of the war's persis-

[50] U. S. Grant, Message, 1 December 1873, in Richardson, *Messages and Papers of the Presidents*, IX, 4194–4195; Fish to Cushing, 6 February 1874, Instructions, Spain. In a memorandum apparently never sent, Cushing listed the reasons why the United States should incorporate Cuba: (1) geography, and (2) military and political. The peaceful cession of the island would not be dishonorable, he wrote. Spain at least must allow the United States to aid in bringing social harmony to Cuba. Cushing Memo, 27 April 1875, Cushing Papers, Manuscripts Division, Library of Congress. Earlier, he had expressed serious doubts about the leadership capabilities of the *Creoles* and predicted that the Cuban Negro would be unable to exercise the vote intelligently. As an example, Cushing used the post-Civil War record of the South Carolina Negro. Cushing to Fish, 23 November 1874, Despatches, Spain.

tence and a warning to Spain that, unless the conflict ended rapidly, *other* nations might have to intervene. The next month, he informed Cushing that information regarding the Cuban situation had been sent to Russia, Italy, and Austria, in the hopes that their opinions would facilitate a settlement. In January, 1876, Fish learned that the Russian minister in Madrid intended to protest the prolongation of the Cuban insurrection.[51]

It would be almost impossible to ascertain the effect of these veiled threats of intervention. Certainly, by 1874, the Spanish government recognized that the United States would not intervene unilaterally in Cuba. Fish's ready acceptance of the *Virginius* settlement had proved that the American government would avoid almost any pretext for war in Cuba. At the same time, the continuation of the war only increased Madrid's commitment to win out over the insurrection. Certainly Spain had lost heavily in Cuba, but the insurgents had lost men and matériel to the point of exhaustion. By 1876 the rebels barely possessed an organized government or army, and their fighting consisted largely of desultory raids on sugar cane plantations. The insurrection, according to the Spanish Minister of State, would soon face annihilation. Spain was now willing to listen to American pleas to the insurgents to lay down their arms, but if the United States attempted to block Spanish destruction of the revolution, national honor would compel Spain to fight. That was the inference drawn by Cushing from the remarks of the Minister of State.[52]

---

[51] "The Cuban Scare and the Press," *The Nation*, XXI (25 November 1875), 335–336; Dexter Perkins, *The Monroe Doctrine, 1867–1907* (Baltimore, 1937), 109; Fish to Cushing, 20 December 1875, 21 January 1876, Instructions, Spain. Fish recognized that he could obtain no aid from Great Britain in an attempt to compel Spain to end the Ten Years' War. On the other hand, the British government was gradually moving towards the American position that Spain would lose Cuba inevitably. See J. C. Bartlett, "British Reaction to the Cuban Insurrection of 1868–1878," *Hispanic American Historical Review*, XXXVII (1957), 312.

[52] Ahumada y Centurión, *Memoria histórica-política*, 3; *El Diario Español*, 8 December 1874; *La Política*, 9 December 1874; "State of Cuba," *The Nation*, XXII (17 February 1876), 110; Cushing to Fish, 16 January 1876, Despatches, Spain.

By 1878 the Ten Years' War was over. In January, all of the insurrectionist chieftains, except Maceo and Vincente García, surrendered their weapons. Random fighting continued for a few years, but the Spanish army had already shattered the revolutionary dream of an independent Cuba. The cost of peace was high for both victor and vanquished. Spain lost 150,000 men and spent 700 million pesos in defeating the insurgent army. In February, 1878, the major revolutionary leaders, with a few important exceptions, agreed to sign the treaty of Zanjón. By its provisions, Spain was obligated to extend political and administrative reform to Cuba and to grant amnesty to those who fought in the war.[53]

American policy during the Ten Years' War mirrored a deep ideological commitment to Cuban reform. The United States, as Fish explained in 1876, expected Spain to replace the old colonialism in Cuba with political, social, and economic change. Revolution in Cuba was produced by the inherent flaws in Spanish mercantilism. Peace, prosperity, and stability depended on good government, emancipation, and commercial freedom. Believing in Spanish willingness to alter Cuba's government and society, Fish now related what the United States expected Spain to accomplish there. The historical experience of the Western Hemisphere, he wrote, showed that peace, order, and honest government opened the way to prosperity. This had proved true in Canada and would doubtless prove true in the case of Cuba.[54]

Thus it was Hamilton Fish, a Secretary of State who has been criticized as a reactionary and an enemy of Cuban independence,[55] who altered the Cuban policy of the United States more than anyone between 1823 and 1898. In 1823 Adams had supported a Spanish Cuba but had warned of the inevitable gravitation of Cuba to the American Union. A half-century later, one of his successors forecasted the inevitable triumph of Cuban

[53] Royal Decree, 20 October 1877, in *Gaceta de Madrid*, 22 October 1877; José de Alcazar, *Historia de España en América* [*Isla de Cuba*] (Madrid, 1898), 173; Johnson, *History of Cuba*, III, 299–300.

[54] Fish to Cushing, 1 March 1876, Instructions, Spain.

[55] Roig, *Cuba y los EE. UU.*, 99; Portell Vilá, *Historia de Cuba en sus relaciones con los Estados Unidos* (4 vols., Habana, 1938), II, 247–248.

independence. Adams had argued that Cuban independence would impair the island's commercial and strategic utility to the United States. Fish observed that Cuban self-rule was both commercially and strategically practical. But, much more important in the evolution of a Cuban policy, the twin forces of *Realpolitik* and Revolutionary ideology no longer collided. Adams rejected a revolutionary commitment to Cuba because he believed it conflicted with the nation's Caribbean interests. Fish's commentaries, however, showed not only a disgust with Spanish rule but an optimistic faith in the eventual success of Cuban revolution. This fanciful dream he united with the hallowed strategic doctrine of his illustrious predecessor.

The South and the Caribbean, 1823

CHAPTER IV

The Decision to Intervene

For some of the Cuban revolutionists, the pact of Zanjón marked only a momentary cessation of the conflict to obtain Cuban independence. Calixto García, exiled in Paris in 1878, learned of the treaty's provisions, rejected the agreement, and proclaimed his unchanged hostility to the Spanish regime. For a few more years, he and other faithful adherents engaged in sporadic raids in Cuba, trying to keep alive the spark of revolt.[1] Known as the Guerra Chiquita, or "Little War," this minor struggle following the Ten Years' War was more a nuisance than a threat to Spanish power. In time, however, the exiled Cuban revolutionary juntas would renew their combat against Spanish Cuba. As the insurrectionists had done during 1868-1878, the revolutionists would employ every psychological and political device to involve the United States.

American interest in the fulfillment of Spanish reform pledges did not conclude with the signing of the Zanjón pact. The Madrid post remained one of the most sensitive and important in Europe; Spanish policy in the New World still attracted a great deal of attention from Washington. General Martínez Campos, newly appointed Captain-General of Cuba in 1879, impressed American minister James Russell Lowell as sincere, honest, and committed to Cuban reform. The most important question, in the view of the American government, was the Spanish commitment to abolish slavery in the island. For half a decade, the Spaniards vacillated between gradual and complete emancipation. The initial plan of 1870 for gradual emancipation provided for an

[1] Juan José Casasús, *Calixto García* (Habana, 1942), 106–107.

interim eight-year period of guardianship of the ex-slave by his master. Lowell found this measure objectionable, but Secretary of State William Evarts noted that the law was at least an important step in the progress toward complete emancipation. The abolition of an immoral institution would signify that Spain had achieved conformity with the dictates of modern civilization. Those landowners who predicted industrial depression and chronic conflict as the aftermath of abolition (an antebellum Southern contention), wrote one observer, were in error, for those dire forecasts had never proved true in the postwar American South. Thus, abolition would eventuate in economic growth for Cuba.[2]

Table 1. *United States Investments in Cuba, 1896*[a]

District	Amount (Dollars)
Cienfuegos	12,000,000
Matanzas	9,000,000
Sagua	9,229,000
Santiago	15,000,000

[a]Estimate of Secretary of State Richard Olney, in December, 1896 (*Foreign Relations, 1896,* lxxxv). The investment was primarily in sugar estates, except for that near Santiago, which was in mining.

Table 2. *Trade Between the United States and Cuba, 1892-1898*[a]

	Imports from Cuba (Dollars)	Exports to Cuba (Dollars)
1892	77,931,671	17,953,570
1893	78,706,506	24,157,698
1894	75,678,261	20,125,321
1895	52,871,259	12,807,661
1896	40,017,730	7,530,880
1897	18,406,815	8,259,776
1898	15,232,477	9,561,656

[a]From *Commercial Relations of the United States with Foreign Countries During the Year 1901* (Washington, 1901), I, 33, 37.

[2] Lowell to Evarts, 19 August 1879, 11 November 1879, Despatches, Spain; Evarts to Lowell, 10 December 1879, Instructions, Spain; C. C. Andrews, "Our Commerce with Cuba, Puerto Rico, and Mexico," *Atlantic Monthly,* XLIV (July, 1879), 91.

More than ever in the previous history of Cuban-American relations, the years from 1878 to 1898 saw increased involvement of American capital in Cuba (see Tables 1 and 2). By the end of the Ten Years' War, the volume of trade between the United States and Cuba was greater than the total amount of United States trade with the remainder of Latin America. The destructiveness of the war had compelled many Cuban and Spanish plantation owners to sell out, and American investors moved in to buy land. Edward Atkins of Boston, for instance, rapidly acquired land holdings in Cuba and by 1895 the Atkins company became an economic giant in Cuban sugar estates. Foreigners residing in the island obtained United States citizenship as a precautionary measure in the event of another rebellion.[3]

It was no surprise, then, that the volume of complaints cabled to Madrid from Washington centered on Spanish commercial and economic policy in Cuba. Official favoritism to Peninsular economic interests came in the form of monopolies and tariffs designed to impede the augmented American trade. The "ever faithful isle" constituted a logical market for American exports, but these products were blocked from the island because of an oppressive and backward mercantilistic policy. Duties on flour, cheese, lard, and butter—products of the American heartland—were excessively high. At the slightest pretext, complained one writer, the Havana revenue officers levied imposts on American shippers. Fines were often meted out for trivial errors: hoops not listed as "wooden hoops," or nails not named as "iron nails" in the cargo manifest.[4]

The demands made by American capital in Cuba conflicted directly with Spanish economic policy. Foreigners were required to pay a burdensome twenty-five percent tax. European governments issued a constant barrage of protests against the tax imposed on their citizens by Madrid, but the United States was the most persistent critic. Excessive taxation of Americans, wrote Secretary of State Evarts, was unjust, since the American market consumed seventy-five percent of Cuba's sugar, sixty

[3] Portell Vilá, *Historia de Cuba*, II, 532; Walter LaFeber, *The New Empire: An Interpretation of American Expansion, 1860–1898* (Ithaca, 1963), 38.
[4] Andrews, "Our Commerce with Cuba," *Atlantic Monthly*, XLIV, 81–84.

percent of her tobacco, and fifty percent of her manufactured products. Perhaps heavy taxation was necessary during the Ten Years' War, the Secretary continued, but its peacetime imposition created a serious obstacle to the future prosperity of the island, which could better be served through the exemption of American capital from taxation. The fact that salaries for Spanish officials depended in part on the taxes they collected, wrote one of Evarts' successors, was characteristic of the arbitrariness of Spanish officialdom. The conclusion was that American economic interests were arbitrarily barred from the island.[5] Indictment of the Havana port authorities for alleged capriciousness was an old grievance voiced by numerous American shippers. In 1882, Secretary of State Frederick Frelinghuysen protested a Spanish royal order transferring such questions from consular jurisdiction in Cuba to Madrid. A year later he blamed the Spanish government for tardiness in restoring embargoed American property in Cuba. Some of the American-owned estates had been embargoed during the war, but the owners had failed to receive satisfactory compensation or redress half a decade following the Zanjón settlement. As for the tariff, after the passage of the McKinley tariff in 1890, the American government consistently demanded most-favored-nation treatment for American products in the ports of Cuba.[6]

Cuban-American trade had fluctuated throughout the nineteenth century, but the years from 1878 showed a steady upsurge in commerce and, simultaneously, a consistent augmentation of American capital in Cuba. Leland Jenks later estimated that the Cuban trade of the 1880's was approximately one-fourth of the total world trade of the United States. Six shipping companies offered regular commercial service between Cuban and American ports. The products carried by these shippers to Cuba were the same products whose entrance into the island's

---

[5] Evarts to Lowell, 1 May 1879, Instructions, Spain; Evarts to Lucius Fairchild, 1 May 1880, *ibid.*; F. T. Frelinghuysen to John W. Foster, 19 December 1883, *ibid.*

[6] Frelinghuysen to Hannibal Hamlin, 15 February 1882, *ibid.*; Frelinghuysen to Foster, 3 May 1883, *ibid.*; Hannis Taylor to Walter Q. Gresham, 17 December 1894, 4 January 1895, Despatches, Spain.

market had been demanded by the American government during Jackson's day. In return, Cuba paid for these imports with sugar. The stimulation to Cuban-American trade came in large part from a corresponding increase in demand for sugar from the American public. American capital sought outlets in the Cuban sugar-producing industry. The influence of American business organization and technology was extensive; under the pressure to produce more sugar, the industry adopted the *central* system, which eliminated the local plantation mill in favor of the huge mill of the *central*. American engineers and technicians came to the island to construct rail lines from the plantations to the *central*. A tenancy system accompanied this transformation. Local or small proprietorships disappeared as more and more Cubans found themselves in the status of *colonos*, individuals who worked the land, took the risks, and delivered the cane to the *hacendado* or owner of a *central*. This process, which resulted in part from the incorporation of American capital, was to continue into the twentieth century and breed a host of social-economic problems.[7]

II

Meanwhile, those revolutionary elements exiled in the United States and European cities waited expectantly for the opportunity to strike once more for Cuban independence. They placed little faith in Spanish promises for political reform. General Martínez Campos, appointed captain-general in 1879, emerged as another Peninsular villain in the eyes of the former insurrectionists. Liberty of the press, right of assembly, and political privileges still depended on the whim of the captain-general. The revolutionary exiles had no intention of readjusting to Spanish rule as long as there existed the slightest hope for independence. The key figure was José Martí, Cuba's legendary patriot, who was kept busy organizing in New York City. Martí established the Cuban Revolutionary Party, and he aided other exiles to establish leagues for the dissemination of revolutionary propaganda.

---

[7] Leland Jenks, *Our Cuban Colony: A Study in Sugar* (New York, 1928), 21, 31–32, 39.

During these difficult years before the outbreak of the 1895 revolt, the exile movement was overshadowed by the rise of an autonomist party in Cuba. The autonomists feared the recurrence of violent revolution and resulting destruction of property and, thus, hoped to arrange a peaceful settlement with Spain whereby the island would enjoy autonomous status within the empire. Martí rejected autonomy as a futile effort and strived instead to turn attention, especially the gaze of the American public, to the Cuban revolutionary party. He distrusted the United States because of its nineteenth century expansionist record, yet he recognized the American giant as a potent weapon in the struggle against Spain. His appeal was directed to all Cuban exiles and a sympathetic world. The world, he wrote, was divided into two groups: those who loved liberty and those who did not. Spaniards and Cuban *Creoles* naturally fell into the first category; Cubans, into the latter. These were times for personal sacrifice, he wrote to Máximo Gomez in 1892, and under the risk of death, the Cuban Revolutionary party prepared for its war of liberty and the absolute independence of Cuba.[8]

The year 1895, which saw a resurrection of the Cuban insurgency, also witnessed a serious incident in Spanish-American relations. Early in March, the mail steamer *Aliança,* proceeding from Colón to New York City, was fired on by a Spanish patrol boat some six miles from the Cuban coast. Apparently the reason for the firing was a recent order from the Spanish ministry authorizing visit and search of suspicious vessels near Cuba. Such logic was rejected, of course, by Secretary of State Walter Q. Gresham, who demanded prompt indemnity for damages to the *Aliança* and the ship's cargo. A month passed without a Spanish apology, and Gresham dispatched a stronger note to

[8] Infiesta, *Máximo Gomez,* 145–6; Foner, *Cuba,* II, 318–319, 336–337; Félix Lizaso (E. E. Shuler, trans.), *Martí: Martyr of Cuban Independence* (Albuquerque, 1953), 221, 227–228; José Martí, *Cuba: Hombres* (2 vols., Habana, 1938), I, 93; Martí to Gomez, 13 September 1892, in Máximo Gomez y Baez, *Diario de campaña del mayor general Máximo Gomez* (Habana, 1941), 569; *ibid.,* 431–432; Emeterio S. Santovenia, *Estudios, Biografías, y Ensayos* (Habana, 1957), 156–157; Henry L. De Zayas, "The Causes of the Present War in Cuba," *Catholic World,* LXII (March, 1896), 812–813.

Madrid. The President, he wrote to Hannis Taylor, Minister to Spain, recognized the seriousness of the present Cuban revolution, but that situation afforded no excuse for the violation of maritime rights. Three days later, Taylor cabled to announce the Spanish apology and explanation that the firing was an error committed by the Spanish patrol boat's commander.[9]

Unfortunately, the efforts of the Cleveland administration to settle the *Aliança* dispute quietly failed to satisfy a growing truculent mood in the Congress. Cleveland accepted the Spanish apology, but several senators sought to employ the incident as an excuse for intervention in the Cuban revolution. From the Foreign Relations Committee came opinions that the nation prepare itself to annex more territory. Senator Frye, also a member of the Committee, was even more explicit: "I had almost hoped," he stated, "that Spain would assume such an arrogant tone that it would be necessary for the United States to go over and take possession of Cuba." [10]

Observers compared the revolt of 1895 with that of 1868–1878. Both parties engaged in a struggle of devastation; both disregarded recognized laws of combat; both promised early success. Spanish pledges of reform (there was more talk of autonomy for Cuba), pledges made to Fish and Grant two decades before, were now repeated. In September, 1895, the former mayor of Havana, writing in the *North American Review*, predicted that the army would ground out the insurrection as quickly as the rainy season ended. Most Cubans, he went on, opposed the revolution, which differed from the Ten Years' War. That struggle of a decade had been justified by political grievances, but the revolt of 1895 possessed no basic of legitimacy. Moreover, Cubans feared annexation to the United States,

---

[9] Gresham to Taylor, 14 March 1895, Instructions, Spain; Taylor to Gresham, 16 March 1895, Despatches, Spain; Gresham to Taylor, 16 April 1895, Instructions, Spain; Taylor to Gresham, 19 April 1895, Despatches, Spain; Minister of State to Taylor, copy, 16 May 1895, *ibid.*

[10] Edwin Uhl, Acting Secretary, to Taylor, 5 June 1895, Instructions, Spain; Walter Millis, *The Martial Spirit: A Study of our War with Spain* (Boston, 1931), 29.

because absorption into the American Union would eventuate in a loss of Cuban identity.

These utterances failed to convince the public. The large public dailies, hardly examples of mature journalism, portrayed every statement that came from Madrid as prevarication. Each day the press carried atrocity stories that depicted in lurid detail one repeated theme: Cuba was drowning in blood in a desperate fight to overpower a tyrannical and unyielding Spanish overlordship. Even Richard Olney, who succeeded Gresham as Secretary of State in 1895 and who usually viewed foreign problems with calculating logic, refused to believe Spanish assertions that the insurrection was defeated and that Cubans were incapable of self-government. From his sources, Olney wrote to Cleveland, the rebellion was winning adherents all over the island. Ninety percent of the population sympathized with the insurrection. The Secretary of State depended for this judgment on a large American plantation owner. Other property holders, he wrote, had concluded that Spain was no longer able to rule Cuba in a just manner. Confiscation, heavy taxation, and personal insecurity now troubled the more stable elements of the island. The insurrectionists would triumph because the Spanish deceived the 1868 rebels with reform pledges that had not been honored. Olney foresaw horror and destruction in the war and the likelihood of Cuba's sale to the highest bidder.[11]

Neither Cleveland nor Olney remained unmoved by the brutality of the insurrection, but neither was willing to rush headlong into war with Spain. Cleveland's obstinancy has been portrayed by his biographers as an example of sternness and courage in the face of Congressional and public fervor. From mid-July, 1895, the administration confronted the possibilities of (1) intervention, leading to war with Spain, or (2) strict maintenance of neutrality and American rights. Olney was in-

---

[11] John H. Latané, "Intervention of the United States in Cuba," *North American Review*, vol. 166 (March, 1898), 361; Don Segunda Álvarez, "The Situation in Cuba," *ibid.*, vol. 161 (September, 1895), 362–364; Millis, *Martial Spirit*, 43; Olney to Cleveland, 25 September 1895, Olney Letterbooks, VII, 230–234, Olney Papers, Manuscripts Division, Library of Congress.

clined towards the latter course, yet he, too, contended that the insurgents had a right to their day in court and recommended the sending of an agent to Cuba. The agent would investigate the rebellion and determine whether or not the rebels were marauders or patriots. If the causes of the insurgency proved justifiable, then Olney suggested that the administration protest the conduct of the war and consider the possibility of recognition of belligerency or, as a last recourse, recognition of Cuban independence. Reports from Cuba were conflicting, and he predicted a long winter of debate in the Congress.[12]

The Cleveland administration was equally hard-pressed to satisfy a burgeoning number of claims from American citizens who suffered property losses in Cuba. For years, foreign property owners in the island had been acquiring American citizenship as a future safeguard for property protection. Once the insurrection resulted in heavy losses (by both revolutionary and Spanish forces) the State Department received a constant stream of complaints. Diplomatic procedure committed Olney to satisfy these claimants, and he issued periodic protests to Madrid. In effect, Spain was asked to respect not only Article VII of the Treaty of 1795 but also the rules of civilized war. In one instance, Olney wrote angrily to Ambassador Dupuy de Lôme, Spanish soldiers camped on the estate of an American citizen. Subsequently they killed his hogs, took his food, and appropriated personal belongings. These random destructive acts violated the rights of private property as well as the credos of civilized nations. He demanded immediate punishment. But it was not easy to afford protection to American property, except by diplomatic protest. In a personal letter to Cleveland, Olney complained of the disastrous consequences of the insurrection for property owners. However, he went on, it was the misfortune

[12] Henry James, *Richard Olney and his Public Service* (Boston, 1923), 166–167; Olney to Cleveland, in Allan Nevins, ed., *Letters of Grover Cleveland* (New York, 1933), 410; Olney to Cleveland, 25 September 1895, Olney Letterbooks, VII, 235–237, Olney Papers; Olney to Cleveland, 8 October 1895, *ibid.*, 248–249; *Literary Digest*, XII (18 January 1896), 335–336, showed that the public wanted immediate recognition of Cuban belligerency.

of American investors to own property in a land devastated by war, and he was pessimistic about the ability of the government to protect them from the consequences of battle.[13]

No matter how much the Secretary of State regretted the presence of American capital and property in Cuba, the Cleveland administration held Spain responsible not only for property losses but also for the personal rights and safety of American citizens in the island. Early in the rebellion, the captain-general proclaimed martial law and dealt severely with suspicious persons. In mid-July, 1896, he announced that all aliens must register or lose the right of diplomatic appeal to their own governments. The American response to this pronouncement was a vigorous rebuttal based upon international obligation. As W. W. Rockhill, Acting Secretary of State, wrote to de Lôme, each nation was empowered to demand protection for its citizens in other lands, and this right might not be usurped by martial law. Proclamation of a state of war, or a state of siege, by Cuban authorities, Rockhill explained, did not infringe the treaty rights of American citizens. Those Americans arrested must be guaranteed protection by civilian, not military, tribunals.[14]

These problems served also to burden the President's policy in Cuba. Like Grant, Cleveland saw the tragedy of the Cuban insurrection, but, unlike Grant, he resisted public and Congressional pressure to force Spain into a corner. Instead of recognizing Cuban belligerency, the President enforced the neutrality laws against filibustering and simultaneously tried to convince the Spanish government that it must reform Cuba's administration. Often, however, his quiet but forceful diplomacy was lost amidst the jingoism of Congress. In April, 1896, the legislature passed a concurrent resolution recognizing insurgent belligerency, and proposed that the President extend good offices to

[13] James, *Olney*, 157–158; Olney to Taylor, 5 March 1896, Instructions, Spain; Olney to de Lôme, 13 March 1896, Notes to Foreign Legations; Olney to Cleveland, 21 March 1896, Olney Letterbooks, X, 83–84, Olney Papers.

[14] W. W. Rockhill, Acting Secretary, to de Lôme, 25 July 1896, 9 September 1896, Notes to Foreign Legations; Olney to Taylor, 14 October 1896, Instructions, Spain.

settle the war. When Cleveland refused to accept the Congressional mandate, he was portrayed as an antihumanitarian who refused to aid suffering Cuba. The administration was increasing its pressure on Spain, but Congress and the public were already openly discussing intervention. Across the land, spontaneous demonstrations drew crowds who listened to ministers, newspaper editors, and local officials denounce Spain's conduct of the war and the immobility of the administration. The public demanded that something be done about Cuba.[15]

The administration stood firm. In April, Olney wrote a long note to de Lôme in which the Secretary rejected Spain's claim that the revolt would be speedily suppressed. In fact, Olney observed, the insurgents numbered more than 60,000, were well-disciplined, and controlled most of the countryside. Outside the towns, anarchy and lawlessness prevailed. He emphasized the ruinousness of the *productive value* of the island: Cuba was capable of producing eighty millions in a year, but in 1896 that had been reduced to twenty. Matters would inevitably worsen. If the struggle is shorter than the Ten Years' War, he predicted, its briefness will be due to Spanish exhaustion rather than triumph. If Spain withdrew, racial and factional bickering would result. The American government, Olney continued, did not presently accept a policy of intervention, but the American public were committed to any cause that demanded a free political society. The United States "cannot contemplate with complacency another ten years of Cuban insurrection. . . ." It was Spain's obligation to reform Cuba and prove to the insurgents that reforms were forthcoming.[16]

There is strong evidence that illustrates the administration's determination to find a factual basis for recognition of belligerency. In June, 1896, Olney requested Fitzhugh Lee in Havana to ascertain if the insurgents possessed a *de facto* government. If so, did that government pass laws, possess a legislative or court

[15] E. R. May, *Imperial Democracy: The Emergence of America as a Great Power* (New York, 1961), 80; Nevins, *Grover Cleveland: A Study in Courage* (New York, 1932), 714–719.

[16] Olney to de Lôme, 4 April 1896, Notes to Foreign Legations; Becker, *Historia*, III, 829–831.

system, and was it capable of protecting life, liberty, and property? Apparently, the inquiry produced a negative response, at least in Cleveland's mind, because a month later he expressed serious doubts of Cuban capability of self-government. It would be ridiculous, he wrote to Olney, to buy Cuba and place the island in the hands of its inhabitants.[17]

Unmoved by Spanish promises to stifle the rebellion and unyielding to the public and Congressional plea for intervention, Cleveland maintained his earlier skepticism. His annual message in December concluded that neither Spain nor the insurgents had established definite authority in Cuba. Most of the island was in a state of anarchy; the American people felt a deep humanitarian compassion for the suffering; American commerce and capital (thirty to fifty millions) were being damaged. Yet Cleveland's recommendation was not a policy of action but of caution. In time, if the carnage continued, the nation might be drawn closer to intervention. The public reaction to the President's statements was generally unfavorable. Newspapers criticized him for a policy of procrastination and for insensitivity to the travail of Cuba's fighters for freedom.[18] In an angry mood, Congress passed shortly the Cameron resolution, which constituted a Congressional recognition of Cuban independence. But Cleveland and Olney survived this onslaught by abruptly declaring that only the executive was empowered to conduct foreign policy. Acceptance of the resolution's proposal, Olney wrote later, would have meant a declaration of war against Spain. At that time the Secretary argued that his logic rested on an interpretation of the Monroe doctrine: if the nation recognized Cuban independence, then Spain's role in Cuba was a conquest of hemispheric territory by a European power. Later, however, Olney

---

[17] Cleveland to Olney, 16 July 1896, in Nevins, *Letters of Cleveland*, 448; Olney to Fitzhugh Lee, 29 June 1896, Olney Letterbooks, X, 338–340, Olney Papers.

[18] Cleveland, Message to Congress, 4 December 1896, in *Literary Digest*, XIV (19 December 1896), 194–195; Hartford *Post*, Chicago *Tribune*, Philadelphia *Times*, New York *World*, all quoted in *Literary Digest* (19 December 1896), 196–197; Mayo Hazeltine, "What Shall be Done About Cuba," *North American Review*, vol. 163 (December, 1896), 737–738.

asserted that his press statements rejecting the Cameron resolution had represented a hasty effort to prevent a financial panic. Fearing the impact of the Cameron resolution on the economy, Olney had calculated that a strong and vigorous reassertion of executive prerogative in foreign policy was the best answer.[19]

The final months of Cleveland's administration brought a glimmer of hope for Cuban reform. In mid-January, Olney wrote to Fitzhugh Lee in Havana that a *de facto* home rule plan would be forthcoming within a week. The opportunity existed now for the insurgents to demonstrate some faith in Spanish promises. By writing to the governor-general, Madrid, or the Spanish minister in Washington, leaders of the revolt perhaps would be able to use the promise of home rule as a basis for suspension of hostilities. Obviously, Olney thought, the Spanish government was unable to shoulder full responsibility for peace; the insurgents, too, had an equal obligation to conciliate.[20]

III

On March 4, 1897, the Presidency passed to William McKinley. Detractors of McKinley's Cuba policy have characterized him as a President personally committed to peace but publicly compelled to adopt a belligerent stance. To some observers, he appeared as an executive who was more fearful of offending a truculent public than keeping the peace. McKinley's definitive biographer, however, portrays the President as a humanitarian who was shocked by the savagery of Cuban war yet whose conservative and cautious politics searched for every channel of peaceful settlement. Where Cleveland was unbending in his determination to avoid hostilities with Spain, McKinley was flexible and accepted war as an alternative if conciliation and

---

[19] New York *Times*, New York *Sun*, quoted in *Literary Digest*, XIV (26 December 1896), 226–227; Olney to Miss A. M. Straw, 24 December 1896, quoted in James, *Olney*, 169–170; Olney to E. B. Whitney, Asst. Attorney-General, 26 December 1896, Olney Letterbooks, VIII, 59–65, Olney Papers; Olney to C. R. Breckenridge, Minister to Russia, 25 January 1897, *ibid.*, 178–179.

[20] Olney to Fitzhugh Lee, 18 January 1897, *ibid.*, 144–146; *Literary Digest*, XIV (27 February 1897), 485, 531–532.

compromise failed.[21] With McKinley in office, it was clear that the attitude of the American government towards the Cuban war would become much more critical.

No Spaniard received more scorn from the American public than Governor-General Valeriano Weyler, who now loomed as the symbol of brutality in Cuba. When the revolution erupted in 1895, the state of the Spanish army in Cuba was deplorable. Only 14,000 soldiers and four warships stood ready to defend the colonial regime. Still in command in Havana was Martínez Campos, who suffered a humiliating year as the insurrection crept closer to the western provinces. Out of favor with Madrid and loyal Cubans, he was succeeded in February, 1896, by Weyler. (During the Ten Years' War Weyler had commanded a group of Volunteers and, ironically, he had fought at one time in Santo Domingo alongside Máximo Gomez, the insurrectionist general.) Arriving in Cuba, Weyler energetically reorganized the army in an effort to instill loyalty and dynamism to the counter-revolution. In order to deprive the guerrillas, he divided the countryside into zones and removed the inhabitants into fortified places. *Reconcentrados* was the name given to those who were forcefully moved. The American people were emotionally unprepared to accept such devices of modern war. When correspondents journeyed to Cuba, they visited the *reconcentrados* and returned with harrowing stories. "These people will starve," wrote Stephan Bonsal, "unless some intelligent, organized effort is made to save them from starvation." Accommodations were woefully inadequate, since the movement of *reconcentrados* only added to the already crowded interior towns.[22]

Weyler was also condemned by the American government. Writing to de Lôme in June, Secretary of State John Sherman claimed that Weyler had ordered the burning of houses, destruc-

[21] Millis, *Martial Spirit, 124–125;* H. Wayne Morgan, *William McKinley and His America* (Syracuse, 1963), 335.

[22] Becker, *Historia,* III, 806, 827–828; Julio Romano, *Weyler: hombre de hierro* (Madrid, 1934), 45–50, 97, 115–116; Fitzhugh Lee, "Cuba Under Spanish Rule: Personal Impressions of the Island, the People, of the Government and the War for Freedom," *McClure's Magazine,* XI (June, 1898), 106; Stephen Bonsal, *The Real Condition of Cuba Today* (New York, 1897), 23–24, 111–112.

tion of crops, and creation of garrisoned towns. The governor-general seemed bent on destroying the productive labor force of the island. President McKinley, Sherman wrote, protested the loss of property and intimidations of Americans, but, more than these, he blamed Spain, particularly Weyler, for conducting an "uncivilized and inhumane" struggle in Cuba. In the administration's view, Weyler was not only responsible for unforgivable bestiality towards civilians but also for the *destruction of Cuban productiveness.* Plantations and estates, ordered burned by the governor-general, constituted a portion of the productive potential of the island. Spain was dutifully bound, thus, to follow the principles of civilized war, which meant in American terms a respect for human as well as property rights. The United States would not tolerate a war policy that utterly disregarded the "principles of humanity" or the material interests of the island.[23] Capitalism and humanitarianism had joined hands.

While McKinley organized his Cuban policy, late summer 1897 saw two changes of importance in Madrid. The first was the assassination of Prime Minister Cánovas, and the second, increasing public disillusionment with Weyler's command. From his post, Hannis Taylor noticed greater support for Weyler's recall and pressure on the Queen to conciliate the United States by granting autonomy to Cuba. Taylor, who had served Cleveland as ambassador to Spain, would soon be replaced with McKinley's special envoy, Stewart Woodford. During the Ten Years' War, Woodford had spoken out against the noninterventionist policies of Fish; in 1897 he searched for a peaceful settlement with Spain. Woodford was, in fact, the personal representative of the President. Unlike Daniel Sickles, who exaggerated his instructions, Woodford dutifully carried out the requirements for conciliation as established by the President. By early fall, those requirements encompassed the following.

1. The President wanted peace with Spain.

2. Cuba had suffered from rebellion and discord since 1868. The present struggle was unlike the previous insurrection, for in 1895 the

[23] Sherman to de Lôme, 26 June 1897, 6 July 1897, 14 July 1897, Notes to Foreign Legations.

Cubans revolted for self-determination. In September, 1897, they controlled areas all over the island.

3. Spain's relationship to Cuba could never remain what it was in 1895, even if Spain stifled the insurrection.

4. American capital and industry, which entered the island after 1878, would suffer by a continuation of the present revolt.

5. During October Spain would have to prove her intentions to reform Cuba, for the United States could no longer tolerate a rebellion that was destructive of life and property.

Woodford wrote McKinley the next day after he had presented these points to the Spanish government. He predicted that Spain was now inclined to adjust her relations with Cuba along lines proposed by the American government. The President's envoy recommended patience: kindness, justness, and firmness would compel a Spanish grant of reform and an end to the Cuban war. If the resolution of the United States weakened, however, Spain would adopt once again the old repressive policy that had failed so miserably in the past. McKinley's prescription for Cuban peace was a summing up of similar proposals that reached as far back as the Grant administration. But there was one crucial distinction between McKinley's ideas and those of prior administrations: if Spain declined the good offices of the United States on the bases enumerated above, then the administration "must then be free to take such action thereafter as may be dictated by the situation. . . ." [24]

The next month the Spanish government committed itself to a program of reform for Cuba. Attempting to coordinate military and political action, the plan offered a grant of autonomy to the island but retained sovereignty and the domination of military, judicial, and foreign policy by Madrid. Militarily, the program of pacification would have to be continued, the plan read, but it

[24] Taylor to Sherman, 7 June 1897, 8 August 1897, Despatches, Spain; Woodford to Minister of Foreign Affairs, copy, 23 September 1897, *ibid.*; Woodford to McKinley, 24 September 1897, *ibid.*; William R. Day, Asst. Secretary, to Woodford, 1 October 1897, Instructions, Spain; *El Correo*, 28 September 1897, clippings in State Department files. Hannis Taylor, representative to Madrid under Cleveland, agreed substantially with McKinley's Cuban policy. See Taylor, "A Review of the Cuban Question," *North American Review*, vol. 165 (November, 1897), 610–611.

would be continued with regard for life and property of civilians. As for American mediation, the Spanish believed that the pledge of reform was sufficient, and that the United States should allow Madrid a "free hand." At the same time, Washington was obligated to stop filibustering expeditions and to suppress the movement of aid from the United States to the insurrectionists. In Woodford's analysis, the Spanish *démarche* offered hopeful prospects. Spain was now obligated to alter the political and military situation in the island. If she violated that pledge, or if the move "too late," then the President was still unencumbered and "free to act." [25]

The failure of the autonomist movement was not so much the fault of the United States, or even Spain, as it was the fault of the insurrectionists. Two months before the announcement of Spanish reforms, the rebellion chieftains Máximo Gomez, Calixto García, and Domingo Méndez Capote had disseminated a manifesto that refused autonomy as an unworkable scheme for Cuban ills. Another manifesto, coming a month later, proclaimed to the people of North America that autonomy was a ruse that could not be accepted by those who were struggling for Cuban freedom. When the press circulated the reports of reform in November, Galixto García distributed a condemnatory circular to the various guerrilla bands. In the circular, he ridiculed the proferred autonomy as a device by which Spain hoped to divide the insurrectionists. The *only* basis for negotiation was the independence of Cuba, and only the officials of the Cuban Republic were empowered to negotiate with Madrid. Anyone in the revolutionary movement who entertained communication with the enemy would be declared a traitor of the republic.[26]

Notwithstanding the absolute rigidity of the insurrectionists, Woodford related to the Spanish Minister of Foreign Affairs in

[25] Woodford to Sherman, 26 October 1897, Despatches, Spain; Sherman to Woodford, 6 November 1897, Instructions, Spain; Woodford to McKinley, 14 November 1897, Despatches, Spain.

[26] Manifesto of Cuban Insurrectionists, 20 September 1897, State Department files; Becker, *Historia*, III 856–857; "Al Mundo que Contemple Nuestra Guerra, A La Gran República Norte Americana, y a los Patriotas de La Emigración Cubana," 25 October 1897; Casasús, *Calixto García*, 204.

late December the President's expectation that political and military reform provided a key to the restoration of Cuban productivity and peace. The American government stood willing to aid in the rehabilitation of the island by sending aid to the suffering *reconcentrados*. A substantial effort was now made on behalf of private relief organizations to enter the island and succor the ill and impoverished. As early as February, 1897, Clara Barton of the Red Cross had tried to gain access to Cuba and extend aid to dispossessed civilians. But it was not until December, after the Spanish government had reconciled itself to accepting McKinley's suggestion, that large-scale relief got underway.[27]

The story of these relief endeavors formed a logical part of the administration's program for "civilizing" the Cuban conflict. Daily, American readers were stunned by a catalogue of horrors emanating from the garrison towns. Doubtless many of the lurid details were fabrications and exaggerations by the yellow press, yet the consular correspondence from Havana was filled with revelations of suffering. In one Havana *reconcentrado* there were

> . . . 460 women and children thrown on the ground, heaped pell mell as animals, some in a dying condition, others sick and others dead, without the slightest cleanliness, nor the least help, not even to give water to the thirsty; . . . each one dying wherever chance had laid them. . . . Deaths ranged 40 and 50 daily. . . .

The same report noted the sighting of a baby clinging to the breast of its dead mother. Crowded into old buildings, the *reconcentrados* found little relief or comfort, except from a few local charities. Life, gaunt and necessitous, became a day-by-day struggle for survival. During October, approximately 100 *reconcentrados* received funds from the Cuban Relief Fund, which was channeled through the Havana consulate. But it was hopelessly insufficient, and McKinley requested that Spain allow huge importations of food, provisions, and clothing from the American people. This was soon followed by appeals on behalf of the Red

[27] Woodford to Minister of Foreign Affairs, copy, 20 December 1897, Despatches, Spain; Olney to de Lôme, 5 February 1897, Olney Letterbooks, VIII, 235–236, Olney Papers.

Cross, which had been trying for a year to overcome bureaucratic hurdles in order to establish stations throughout the island. Spain finally agreed to these appeals in late December.[28]

IV

If, for most Americans, the Cuban question elicited condemnations of Spanish misrule, for a small but vocal element the issue held vital strategic importance. During the two decades since 1880, the frontier was declared officially closed, industrial output was increased at a fantastic pace, and a new modern navy was born. To some maturing politicians and military thinkers, these phenomena gave the Cuban question a world-wide significance. The United States stood prepared to assume its rightful military and economic stance on the globe. From its ports, commercial vessels would carry industrial products to the markets of the world. The new modern navy would provide not only coastal protection but would extend American influence into the Caribbean periphery, scene of a future isthmian canal, and into the vast Pacific. Thus, Cuba and the demise of Spanish rule in Cuba opened a new era, an era when the United States would begin to look outward.

These ideas influenced greatly such dynamic rising Republicans as Theodore Roosevelt and Henry Cabot Lodge, but the ideologue of this "large policy" was Alfred Thayer Mahan. Critical of the post-Civil War naval retrenchment, Mahan argued that the future of the nation's strength rested on a commercial and military adaptation to industrialism. Later historians would erroneously characterize Mahan as a mercantilist, but he differed from the mercantilistic theoreticians of earlier centuries. In his view, it was unnecessary for a prosperous nation to own a commercial fleet in order to become a world power. Thus a national merchant marine was less crucial than a strong naval force that

---

[28] Enclosure, Consul-General of Cuba to Day, 20 October 1897, 23 October 1897, 27 November 1897, Consular Records; Day to de Lôme, 1 December 1897, 18 December 1897, Notes to Foreign Legations; de Lôme to Day, 24 December 1897, Notes From Foreign Legations; Clara Barton, "Our Work and Observations in Cuba," *North American Review*, vol. 166 (May, 1898), 554.

had been adapted to technological advancements in military science. Moreover, where the mercantilists championed the possession of colonies as markets or raw material suppliers, Mahan saw the accumulation of colonies as a means to open up the markets of Asia and Latin America. Cuba was valuable, Mahan wrote, because the island possessed superior strategic value for a nation that wished to dominate the Caribbean. The Roman empire had centered on the Mediterranean, Mahan wrote, and the empire of the New World rested logically on control of the Caribbean.[29]

Within this context of international power politics, the historical nineteenth century role of Europe, especially England and France, in the Caribbean had been to check American acquisitiveness. John Quincy Adams had predicated his statements about Cuba on the assumption that British power stood as a bulwark protecting Spanish colonialism. From the Ten Years' War, however, the role of Great Britain and France in the Caribbean weakened considerably. At mid-century, the population of Great Britain was 27 million; that of France, 35 million; but the population of the United States did not exceed 25 million, and Germany had not yet been born as a state. Four decades later, however, the population of Great Britain and France was near 38 million, and the United States and Germany had forged ahead in population at 63 million and 50 million, respectively. The historic balance of power between American, British, and French power in the Caribbean was disappearing in the 1890's, and Spain no longer was able to rely on that protection for the continuation of Spanish Cuba. Before, the maintenance of Spanish rule in Cuba had been a decisive factor in British and French policy; now, in the 1890's, these powers placed less emphasis on that criterion.[30] The relative power advantage in the Caribbean had shifted dramatically in favor of the United States.

[29] LaFeber, *New Empire*, 90–91; Allan Westcott, ed., *Mahan on Naval Warfare* (Boston, 1941), 108; Captain W. D. Puleston, *Mahan: The Life and Work of Captain Alfred Thayer Mahan, USN* (New Haven, 1939), 94–95; Mahan, "Influence of Sea Power on History," in Westcott, ed., *Mahan*, 27–28.

[30] Élie Hálevy, *Imperialism and the Rise of Labour* (New York, 1961), 10–11; Becker, *Historia*, III, 840.

Yet, even though Theodore Roosevelt wrote exuberantly to Mahan that the United States ought to remove Spain from Cuba as quickly as possible, the McKinley administration labored diligently to justify its Cuban policy in European courts. Woodford, sent to London to ascertain opinion there, concluded that Great Britain expected Cuba to become an American protectorate. Similar attitudes found acceptance in France and Germany. The American ambassador wasted no effort, however, to convince the British that American motives in Cuba centered on humanitarian and economic redemption. Stressing Spanish inability to end the conflict and the constant losses to the Cuban market for wheat, corn, meat, and manufactures, Woodford contended that Britain, too, would feel a deep responsibility to end a terrible war if Cuba lay near her shores. To the French ambassador, Woodford expressed antiexpansionist sentiments but contrived a similar analogy. These were explanations of American pressure on Spain. At the same time, the McKinley administration closed the door to any European interference by warning Madrid in October, 1897, that the United States would prohibit any Continental political or economic combination to intrude into the Cuban scene.[31]

V

As the first three months of 1898 passed, the prospects for Cuban-Spanish conciliation faded. Through press revelations, the public learned of recent failures to end the war. One of the most fantastic involved the scheme of a group of financiers who had devised in late 1897 the purchase of Cuba by the insurgents. Briefly, the plan called for negotiations, under the aegis of a New York financial syndicate, by which the Cuban revolutionaries would buy the island with the economic support of these American interests. Reputedly, one of the financiers had close contact with the White House, and the expected profit of the

[31] Theodore Roosevelt to A. T. Mahan, 3 May 1897, in Elting E. Morison, ed., *The Letters of Theodore Roosevelt* (8 vols., Cambridge, 1951–1954), I, 607; Woodford to Sherman, 30 August 1897, 13 September 1897, 11 October 1897, Despatches, Spain; Woodford to President, 20 October 1897, *ibid.*

enterprise was open to conjecture, but presumably sufficient to attract these financial magnates.[32]

By the time the public knew something of this bizarre proposal, the Cuban situation had changed dramatically. McKinley became more pessimistic about the reform measures of Madrid and Spanish promises to end the war. A forewarning had come in December, 1897, from the consul-general in Havana, who had written Secretary of State Day to predict that Spain could not win in Cuba by military means, nor by a grant of autonomy, nor by financial remuneration to the insurrectionist leaders. In fact, there was *no* way that Spain could settle the rebellion in a manner satisfactory to all factions. There existed only one solution, wrote Consul General Fitzhugh Lee. Peace could provide encouragement to those who still lived and shelter to those who were homeless. Weyler's removal in January was accompanied by a gradual worsening: businesses closed their doors; mobs gathered to protest against the new governor-general, Blanco. From Madrid, Woodford wrote that the Queen believed that Weyler's recall and the grant of autonomy were sizable concessions by Spain, and that now the American government should take punitive action against the New York insurgent junta. But, looking at events in Cuba, these were no longer satisfactory answers. Not only had the insurgents condemned autonomy, but the Spanish elite of the island stood opposed to it. Lee warned that the governor-general could not enforce autonomy in a hostile political climate. "If, therefore, Autonomy is a failure," he wrote, "and it is impossible to return to the Weyler or similar methods, the living question would seem to be—*what next?*" [33]

Confronted by this prophetic question, the administration seemed content to wait when, in February, the entire nation was jarred by two unfortunate occurences: the *Maine* disaster and the de Lôme letter. These phenomena, the details of which are gen-

[32] David Healy, *The United States in Cuba, 1898–1902* (Madison, Wisconsin, 1963), 14–15.

[33] Consul-General, Cuba, to Day, 13 December 1897, 8 January 1898, 13 January 1898, 18 January 1898, Consular Records; Woodford to McKinley, 17 January 1898, Despatches, Spain; "Death to autonomy. Death to the americano!" exclaimed a pro-Spanish handbill in late January 1898, clippings in State Department files.

erally well-known, involved a tragic (and inexplicable) explosion of an important ship and some embarrassing revelations by the Spanish ambassador. The *Maine's* presence had been requested by Lee as protection for the Americans in Havana in the event of full-scale riot. De Lôme's letter was a piece of personal correspondence purloined from the Havana mails in December by an insurgent sympathizer. When the contents were revealed, few criticized the invasion of the ambassador's private affairs, for the letter was a diatribe against the President. At the time, few contemporaries read closely other portions, for de Lôme not only condemned McKinley but admitted that only a military victory in Cuba would satisfy Spanish policy. The ambassador implied that the grant of autonomy was a ruse, and the letter's substance, as H. Wayne Morgan has observed, revealed Spanish bad faith in pledges of reform.[34] The public was, of course, shocked at both incidents, and both were viewed in the context of the Cuban war. De Lôme's letter had the effect of deepening the public's disgust with Spanish failure in Cuba and solidifying the conviction that the Spanish were perfidious scoundrels. De Lôme had clearly revealed that his ministry was practicing deception and hypocrisy in its diplomacy with the American government. As for the *Maine* explosion, one military periodical doubted any Spanish connivance in the disaster; another Midwestern newspaper maintained that it was no excuse for war. The Atlanta *Constitution*, a Democratic journal, called for a declaration of war, not on the basis of the *Maine* destruction but on the humane demand that the United States end the Cuban "butchery."[35]

March, 1898, was the most crucial test for the administration. On the first day, an aging John Sherman sadly recounted the recent frustrations. Two months had passed since autonomy was

---

[34] Lee to Day, 4 February 1898, Consular Records; de Lôme to Don José Canelejas, n.d., State Department files; New York *Journal*, in *Literary Digest*, XVI (19 February 1898), 212; Morgan, *McKinley*, 356.

[35] New York *Tribune*, Hartford *Post*, Philadelphia *Times*, *Literacy Digest*, xvi, 212; Milwaukee *Journal*, St. Louis *Republic*, Philadelphia *Times*, in *ibid.* (26 February 1898), 242–244; Atlanta *Constitution*, in *ibid.* (12 March 1898).

granted and Weyler was removed, he wrote to Woodford, yet the Spanish counterrevolutionary effort remained in the doldrums. Autonomist government existed only in Havana and in the principal cities, and thus it was impossible to judge any amelioration in the countryside. Apparently the insurgents had refused autonomy. Little had improved: the Spanish were still unable to alleviate the economic crisis; the *reconcentrado* system depopulated the rural areas; labor could not be supplied for the harvests. In Madrid, Woodford concentrated more on a sketchy timetable that called for suppression of the insurrection by April 1. Spanish arms failing, he predicted, what followed would be famine and disease brought on by the rainy reason. March 3: the *Maine* disaster, the de Lôme letter, Spanish ineffectiveness, the loss of commerce—these things created a "grave" situation, wrote William Day. Other men were more certain of the future. The Spanish Minister of Marine: "Our flag is still flying there [Cuba], and the Government, to meet the sentiments of the people, even at the cost of many sacrifices, desires that this Spanish colony should not be separated from our territory. . . ." Theodore Roosevelt: Cuban independence is the only solution. Whitelaw Reid, newspaper friend of the President: Spain is compelling us to act.[36]

Midway in the month, Woodford summed up the despondency of Madrid. The advent of the rainy season in Spain would mean military stagnation throughout the summer, and during this lull the insurgents doubtless would ravage the island. Businessmen in Spain were pessimistic about peace. The Spanish government had been stunned by the hasty $50 million appropriation granted by the House of Representatives for the President's use, Woodford related, and the consternation might provide a solution. Why not offer to buy the island? he recommended. After all, the Cubans were hardly able to govern themselves. The next day the minister cabled to relate that he had offered "unofficially" to

[36] Sherman to Woodford, 1 March 1898, Instructions, Spain; Woodford to McKinley, 2 March 1898, Despatches, Spain; Day to Woodford, 3 March 1898, Instructions, Spain; Minister of Marine to Cervera, 4 March 1898, in Pascual Cervera (translation), *The Spanish-American War* (Washington, 1899), 32; Theodore Roosevelt to Henry White, 9 March 1898, in Morison, *Letters of TR*, I, 790–791; Whitelaw Reid to McKinley, 8 March 1898, Series I, McKinley Papers, Manuscripts Division, Library of Congress.

purchase Cuba and at the same time guarantee the Cuban debt and the establishment of a "practical protectorate" for the future.[37]

McKinley, however, was working out his own plans, and these did not include the purchase of Cuba. Charles G. Dawes, who kept a diary record of these days, related the mood of uncertainty in the State Department. Roosevelt came in today (March 19), Dawes wrote, and urged war with Spain before the arrival of more Spanish naval forces. Dawes was sure that war was likely, but he trusted the President's judgment. The final weeks of the month were decisive. While the Spanish pleaded for time (until the beginning of the rainy reason), Woodford warned them that the President was preparing to act within a few days. Neither McKinley nor Sagasta (the Spanish premier) wanted war, Dawes wrote again in his diary, but the Cuban conflict must be stopped. McKinley's demand was already being delivered by Woodford in Madrid. Expressing a desire to maintain peace, the note reiterated American concern for the plight of the *reconcentrados* and blamed Spanish modes of war. The central theme of the message, however, was the conviction that Spain could not quell the insurrection. "We do not want the Island," the note continued, but Spain must prove its good intentions by (a) revoking the *reconcentrado* order, and (b) granting Cuba self-government and an indemnity. The third point obligated Spain and the insurgents to appeal for mediation by the President of the United States.[38]

The Spanish response to these conditions was officially conciliatory but concealed a prideful resentment. On March 30, the governor-general of Cuba rescinded the *reconcentrado* order and authorized the return of farm laborers to the countryside. To the question of a joint appeal for an armistice came an abrupt refusal. If the government unilaterally extended an armistice to the insurgents, Woodford cabled, it would face revolt at home. Instead, the Spanish restated the old autonomist provisions and

---

[37] Woodford to McKinley, 17 March 1898, 18 March 1898, Despatches, Spain.

[38] Charles G. Dawes (Bascom Timmons, ed.), *A Journal of the McKinley Years* (Chicago, 1950), 146–147, 149; Woodford to McKinley, 24 March 1898, Despatches, Spain; Day to Woodford, 26 March 1898, Instructions, Spain.

appealed to the insurgents to stop fighting. The autonomy offer, now repeated once again, was a hopeless gesture. Apparently, the Spanish government was reconciled to a war—a foolish, insane war that Spain could not possibly win with a decrepit navy and a demoralized army. Is it possible, a Spanish historian wrote years later, that a nation faced with such military disadvantages believed it could sustain a war? [39]

During the first week of April, the President prepared his message for Congress, which would certainly elicit a declaration of war. The Spanish searched frantically for support in European capitals, but none was willing to send military aid to Cuba or challenge the United States. These countries did make a final appeal to McKinley to avoid hostilities, but his reply of April 6 was a firm defense of the necessity, indeed justification, of American intervention. What emanated from Congress was technically not a declaration of war but an authorization to employ military forces to end the Cuban insurrection. McKinley's arguments for intervention stemmed logically from his Cuban policy: the firm reiteration that, unless Spain ended the insurrection and reformed Cuban administration within a reasonable amount of time, the United States might enter the conflict. Intervention was now justified, McKinley argued, in order to end the horror, to salvage Cuban-American commerce, and to terminate the military crisis to the hemisphere. The most important of these reasons to the President was the humanitarian contention that the United States must terminate a destructive and ravaging war.[40]

Thus, war seemed to be the only satisfactory solution to the Cuban dilemma. The jingoes, who had inundated Cleveland with demands that the United States recognize the Cuban republic, represented by a New York junta, sought to achieve that goal in

---

[39] *Gaceta de Habana*, 30 March 1898, clippings in Consular Records; Woodford to McKinley, 31 March 1898, Despatches, Spain; Day to Woodford, 4 April 1898, Instructions, Spain; Becker, *Historia*, III, 864.

[40] Reply of McKinley to representatives of Great Britain, Germany, France, Austria-Hungary, Russia, and Italy, 6 April 1898, in William McKinley, *Speeches and Addresses of William McKinley* (New York, 1900), 79–80; Day to Woodford, 14 April 1898, Instructions, Spain; Morgan, *William McKinley*, 342–343, 377.

April, 1898. Late in March a band of dissident Republicans and Populists had introduced a resolution in Congress calling for the diplomatic recognition of the Cuban republic. McKinley opposed the resolution because the republic was not a de facto government and, more importantly, because such action might restrict future policy in Cuba. An important issue in the debate was the control of foreign policy. McKinley contended that Congress must provide the President with the necessary military authorization to end the Cuban insurrection but should not restrict Presidential policy. Accusing McKinley of trying to usurp traditional Congressional powers, his Democratic opponents introduced (on April 13) a House resolution that called for recognition of the republic. Faithful Republicans defeated it, but the Senate adopted another resolution proclaiming Cuba's freedom and authorizing the President to employ military force to remove Spanish rule from the island. Significantly, in spite of McKinley's strenuous objections, the Senate approved the Turpie-Foraker amendment to this resolution, which stated that the United States should recognize the Cuban republic as the rightful government of the island. During the debate Senator Henry Teller (Rep., Colo.) suggested a substitute for the Senate resolution. Teller's proposal was defeated, but several of his colleagues noticed its special self-denying ordinance, which assured the world that the United States had no intention of annexing Cuba and would return control of the island to the people when they were able to manage their own affairs. A deadlock ensued, but McKinley exerted powerful political pressure on wayward Republicans who had voted against him. On April 19, Congress finally provided the President with the necessary authorization to conduct war against Spain. Teller's famous qualifying clause became a part of the Congressional mandate. The Cuban republic was not recognized, and McKinley, often belittled as a weak executive, retained his domination of Cuban affairs. The episode was important not only for the future of Cuba but also for the future of Presidential control of foreign policy.[41]

[41] For an excellent account of the intricacies of the debate leading to the Teller amendment, see Paul S. Holbo, "Presidential Leadership in Foreign Affairs: William McKinley and the Turpie-Foraker Amendment," *American Historical Review*, LXXII (July, 1967), 1321–1335.

VI

The Spanish-American War was the most popular foreign crusade in the nation's history. Men from North and South forgot old grievances of civil war and reconstruction in the hubbub of excitement that was generated by the launching of a crusade to vindicate Cuba's struggle for self-determination. Much of the ballyhoo, of course, soon disappeared once the troops encountered death from Spanish bullets or from the yellow fever. A cult of jingoism found new adherents as more and more people disregarded antiimperialistic caveats and accepted American expansion as a natural product of strategic necessity, free trade, and the white man's burden.

Since 1895, the public had believed the proposition that military intervention in Cuba constituted a moral commitment, not necessarily to revolution, but to the principles of good government and commercial freedom. The twin concepts of political self-determination and *laissez-faire* economics provided the solution to Cuban ills. Newspaper editors, politicians, clergymen, and civic leaders spoke loudly against Spanish maladministration and predicted in roseate terms the beneficence of Anglo-Saxon institutions that must be incorporated into Cuban life. In the agricultural Midwest, still emotionally attached to Populism, country editors wrote in belligerent tones about the nation's duty to save Cuba from Spanish mercantilism.[42]

The idea of mission helped unite such diverse elements as social reformers and the Lodge-Roosevelt imperialists. Very rarely did the former condemn foreign expansion or war; in fact, the progressive factions believed that the Spanish-American War would result in the transforming of Cuba along the lines of social and democratic reform at home. Lodge, who imbibed the teachings of Alfred Thayer Mahan, logically related the strategic

---

[42] Clarence King, "Shall Cuba be Free," *Forum*, XX (September, 1895), 57–58; H. D. Money, "Our Duty to Cuba," *ibid.*, XXV (March, 1898), 17–24; H. H. Beck, *Cuba's Fight for Freedom* (Philadelphia, 1898), 313–314; George W. Auxier, "Middle Western Newspapers and the Spanish-American War, 1895–1898," *Mississippi Valley Historical Review*, XXVI (March, 1940), 533; T. G. Shearman, "International Law and the Cuban Question," *The Outlook*, LVIII (16 April 1898), 987; "Support the President," *ibid.*, 903–905.

and commercial importance of the island to the humanitarian credos of the day. To Lodge, the uncivilized character of the insurrection provided justification for immediate intervention. Roosevelt's thinking paralleled that of his Republican associate. Writing to Brooks Adams in March, 1898, Roosevelt called for interference in Cuba on the basis of humanitarianism and self-interest. Mahan, reflecting on the 1898 crusade, wrote later:

> . . . In the island of Cuba, a powerful military force,—government it scarcely could be called—foreign to the island, was holding a small portion of it in enforced subjection, was endeavoring, unsuccessfully, to reduce the remainder. In pursuance of this attempt, measures were adopted that inflicted immense misery and death upon great numbers of the population. Such suffering is indeed attendant upon war; but it may be stated as a fundamental principle of civilized warfare that useless suffering is condemned, and it had become apparent to military eyes that Spain could not subdue the island, nor restore orderly conditions. The suffering was terrible, and was unavailing.[43]

Spain's vain appeal to the Pope and European powers on the eve of war not only showed that the New World balance of power was shifting in favor of the United States but illustrated also the acceptance by Europe of American domination in the Caribbean. Germany, whose rate of growth since 1870 had equalled that of the United States, supported the collective plea to the Vatican for arbitration of the Cuban war but refused to support Spain in war. Fearing the prospect of a rising power in the New World, the German government feared even more the possibility of alienating the United States. Nowhere was the acceptance of Anglo-Saxon mission in Cuba stronger than in Great Britain. John Hay, a diplomat in Britain, wrote in April, 1898, that the London government was the only one in Europe that supported McKinley's policies. Arthur Balfour, who presided at the Foreign Office, rejected Spanish overtures because he wanted fu-

---

[43] W. E. Leuchtenburg, "Progressivism and Imperialism: The Progressive Movement and American Foreign Policy, 1898–1916," *MVHR*, XXXIX (Dec., 1952), 485–486; Lodge, "Our Duty to Cuba," *Forum*, XXI (May, 1896), 286–287; T. R. to Brooks Adams, 21 March 1898, in Morison, *Letters of TR*, I, 797–798; Mahan, *Lessons of the War with Spain* (Boston, 1918), 225–227; J. B. Foraker, *Notes of a Busy Life* (2 vols., Cincinnati, 1916), II, 25.

ture American sustenance for British interests in the Far East. But British attitudes towards the Spanish-American War were shaped also by a religious conviction of the "divine mission of the Anglo-Saxon peoples as agents of world civilization." America's plan for Cuba was interpreted as the Anglo-Saxon cultural response to backward Spanish colonialism. Expansion of the United States posed no threat to British interests, as American intrusion into the Caribbean formed part of the "white man's burden."[44]

The relationship between ideology and economics helps explain the heterogeneity of support for intervention. In view of the longstanding American policy of demanding free trade with the island, the role of business interests in the Spanish-American War was not conspiratorial. Business interests staunchly defended McKinley's policy of watchful waiting. A. B. Farquhar, whose company had a substantial trade in Cuba, wrote to the President in February, 1898, and noted that he would profit if the war ended soon but believed peace must be preserved with Spain. When the war message was delivered in April, as Walter LaFeber has pointed out, businessmen who had heretofore opposed hostilities now accepted war, and the general business conditions of the nation improved considerably.[45] Historians of a later generation would condemn this transformation as a portent of the future economic exploitation of Cuba by American

[44] L. B. Shippee, "Germany and the Spanish-American War," *American Historical Review*, III (July, 1925), 758–759, 763; John Hay to H. C. Lodge, 5 April 1898, in Hay, *Letters of John Hay* and *Extracts from Diary* (Washington, 1898), III, 119–120; Hazeltine, "Possible Complications of the Cuban Question," *North American Review*, vol. 162 (April, 1896), 413; J. A. S. Grenville, *Lord Salisbury and Foreign Policy: The Close of the Nineteenth Century* (London, 1964), 202; Geoffrey Seed, "British Reaction to American Imperialism Reflected in Journals of Opinion, 1898–1900, *Political Science Quarterly*, LXXIII (June, 1958), 258–259; C. C. Campell, Jr., *Anglo-American Understanding, 1898–1903* (Baltimore, 1957), 149–150. For French and Latin American interpretations see Jacques Crokaert, *La Méditerraneé Americaine: L'Expansion des Etats-Unis dans la Mer des Antilles* (Paris, 1927), 213; Francisco Cuevas Cancino, *Del congreso de Panamá á la conferencia de Caracas, 1826–1954* (2 vols., Caracas, 1954), II, 30–38.

[45] A. B. Farquhar to McKinley, 12 February 1898, in McKinley Papers, Series I; LaFeber, *New Empire*, 406.

capital. Actually, the American government had pressured Spain throughout the century to open Cuban ports to the products of the American farm, had warned Spain that she must reform Cuba economically by dismantling the mercantilistic structure, and had consistently propounded the ideological concept that only free trade could salvage and revive Cuban productivity. The criticism that the insurrection was "inhumane" referred as much to war's *destructiveness of economic potential* as it did to loss of life. Implicit in the nineteenth century Cuban policy of the United States was the concept of a rich land whose growth had been stunted by Spanish political and economic maladministration. When the nation waged war against Spain in 1898, it did so in the conviction that the replacement of Spanish by American political and economic theories would lay the foundation for a democratic and prosperous Cuba.

CHAPTER V

The Years of Paternalism, 1898-1933

THE ROOTS OF AMERICAN PATERNALISM IN CUBA in the twentieth century emanated from nineteenth century judgments and attitudes. A recurring argument from 1868 was that the island was naturally rich, commercially attractive, and politically misgoverned. Under Spanish supervision, the "pearl of the Antilles" had suffered want and spoliation. The intrusion of American capital had been viewed as beneficient, since in the wake of investment, stability and responsible government would follow. With the demise of Spanish power, one writer predicted, an increasing Cuban-American commercial intercourse would lead to a marked improvement in Cuban society and politics; Cuba would progress under Anglo-Saxon civilization.[1] A corollary to these assumptions was the unfitness of the Cuban to govern himself without enlightened supervision. The island in 1898 was one-third Negro, two-thirds illiterate, and had undergone four centuries of political misrule. Revolution brought forth military but not political leadership, for an entire generation of Cubans had known little except violence. A lack of political preparation and an "inherited disposition . . . towards faction and indiscipline" made self-government risky. The experience of war in 1898 not only failed to erase these views but added a certain contempt for the Cuban's ability as a soldier and governor. From 1895, the American public imagined a heroic Cuban army holding out against terrible odds and symbolizing native resistance to Spanish oppression. Once the American and Cuban

[1] J. K. Reeve, "A Glimpse of Cuba," *Lippincott's Magazine*, LV (March, 1895), 404, 406–408.

soldier fought side by side, however, the commentary was far from favorable. During the Santiago campaign the capability of insurgent troops was questioned. Americans learned that the Cuban army had alienated itself from a substantial portion of the civilian population. The consequence was that Americans now began to doubt the prospect of immediate self-government and leaned towards the protectorate idea.[2]

Even the most steadfast foe of imperialism admitted the need for some transitional order in Cuba. The revolution of 1895 afflicted the agricultural and industrial production of the island, destroyed huge areas of territory, and left much of the population unsheltered and unfed. Sugar, the base of the economy, declined in production steadily from the initiation of the insurrection. Even in 1900, the severe economic dislocation and continued political uncertainty prevented a rapid postwar surge of production. The loss of population during the insurrection was staggering; approximately 200,000 lives were consumed by the revolution either directly from hostilities or indirectly from starvation, disease, and movement to the garrisoned towns. Equally alarming was the revelation in 1899 that only 8.32 percent of the Cuban population came from the age group 0 to 4 years. Cuban independence began with a population deficit. No Cuban government in 1898, it was argued in Washington, could overcome these obstacles. The Spanish left the island's colonial treasury bankrupt. For years a steady debt, much larger than the real estate values of the island, accumulated against the Cuban colony. The Spanish not only charged the costs of the Ten Years' War to the Treasury but also attached the charges from the Mexican expedition of 1862, the Santo Domingo experiment of 1861-1865, the Peruvian war of 1866, the Carlist wars in Spain, the yearly financial burden of the consular and diplomatic corps of the *entire* hemisphere, a pension paid to Columbus' heirs, and finally the administration of the island. In 1898, Cuba's debt was $500 million. Predictably, then, a delegation of Cuban revolutionaries appeared in Wash-

[2] Sydney Brooks, "Cuba," *Fortnightly Review*, XCIV (November, 1910), 801; Millis, *Martial Spirit*, 361–362.

ington in November, 1898, to obtain funds for paying the army and satisfying the creditors of the insurrection.[3]

Establishment of American rule in Cuba formed a crucial portion of peace discussions with Spain. While hostilities continued, the Spanish government sought a commitment from McKinley regarding the preservation of order in Cuba once Spain departed. The terms of peace, which were sent by Day in late July, required abandonment of sovereignty and evacuation of the island by Spain and the outright cession of Puerto Rico and "an island in the Ladrones" as indemnity for the cost of war. In reply, the Spanish agreed to evacuate Cuba but expected the United States to exercise authority in place of Spain. Little was said about the erection of an independent Cuba. The treaty ending the conflict stipulated that Spain would relinquish title to Cuba and that the United States would occupy the island and assume the subsequent obligation of government. During the treaty discussions, the Spanish tried vainly to attach the Cuban debt to the United States, but William R. Day, the aging Secretary of State, countered with an indignant refusal, arguing that the debt was the legacy of Spanish misrule. The United States, Day contended, performed a singular feat by intervening and thus ending the mounting cost to property and life.[4]

Aside from the treaty commitment to Spain, the legal foundation of American rule in Cuba rested on the law of conquest, not on a mutual agreement with the revolutionaries. As commander-in-chief of a conquering army, McKinley became the heir to Spanish authority. The President delegated his ruling powers to General John Brooke, who became Cuba's first mili-

---

[3] J. J. Le Riverend Brusone, "Historia Económica, " in Ramiro Guerra Sanchez, ed., *Historia de la nación cubana* (10 vols., Habana, 1952), IX, 287, 299–300; Jenks, *Our Cuban Colony*, 59–60; Healy, *U. S. in Cuba*, 44–45.

[4] Spanish government to McKinley, 22 July 1898, *Foreign Relations, 1898*, 820, hereinafter cited as *FR;* Day to Duke of Almodovar del Río, July, 1898, *ibid.*, 821; Duke of Almodovar to Day, 7 August 1898, *ibid.*, Treaty of Peace between the United States and Spain, *ibid.*, 832; H. Wayne Morgan, ed., *Making Peace with Spain: The Diary of Whitelaw Reid, September-December, 1898* (Austin, 1965), 105–106.

tary governor. The purpose of American rule, McKinley wrote in his instructions to Brooke, was to provide order and government in the island until Congress passed superseding legislation or until the Cubans established their own government. Brooke was to be a transitional figure who was supposed to gain the affections of the natives, mitigate their political rivalries, keep them from starving, protect the unfortunate, and promote local reforms.[5]

Brooke's instructions initiated a paternalistic program that characterized Cuban-American relations for a generation. Since the Spanish had provided few public services, Brooke began a regimen of "cleaning up" Cuba's cities. Sanitation in the towns, Elihu Root wrote in a War Department *Report* for 1899, was unbelievably backward: garbage littered the streets, animals were kept in dwellings, and disease was rampant. The solution to these problems lay in a thorough overhauling of local services. Under Brooke's command, soldiers were dispatched to inspect homes, a sanitary corps was established, the sewers and streets were cleaned, water sources were bettered, and both private and public structures were disinfected. To prevent the recurrence of such conditions, the military governor declared rules and punishments for those Cubans who failed to comply. In Santiago, Leonard Wood, the commanding officer in eastern Cuba, provided material improvements and dispensed relief. From July until December 1898, Wood's command disseminated an estimated 25,000 rations daily. The number occasionally leaped to 50,000 daily. In Matanzas, General Wilson distributed aid in the form of food and animals required for farm families. The prescription of relief and rehabilitation was followed in other cities throughout Cuba.[6]

Brooke served as military governor until 1900. When he departed Cuba, he left a population that had been kept from starving but which resented his methods. With the Spanish defeat,

[5] Healy, *U. S. and Cuba*, 55–56.

[6] Elihu Root, *The Military and Colonial Policy of the United States*, edited by Robert Bacon and James B. Scott (Cambridge, Mass., 1916), 189–190; Le Riverend Brusone, "Historia Económica," *Historia nación cubana*, IX, 290; John Brooke, *Report, 1899* (3 vols., Havana, 1899), I, 6–7.

Cubans expected a mass exodus of Spaniards, but many pre-1898 appointees in the lesser bureaucratic posts were retained by Brooke's administration. The military governor saw his role as that of a pacifier between Cuban and Spaniard. Brooke and his lieutenants were inclined to accept the Spanish opinion that the Cubans made better subjects than rulers. As one of Brooke's associates reported in 1899: ". . . The natives are naturally a sober, orderly, and inoffensive people, who willingly obey the constituted authority, and rarely give violent cause for arrest . . . ." Cubans, the military governor believed, were better off when they labored for material improvement and refrained from political strife. What Cuba needed was development of her natural resources, for these would lay the basis for progress and stability. American rule in the island was an experiment in apprenticeship for Cubans, who, once graduated, would assume command of their own destinies. What Brooke overlooked, and the former revolutionaries pointed out, was that American rule in Cuba seemed to violate the spirit of 1898 and the reason for intervention. For the old insurgents, Brooke's administration represented a denial of self-determination.[7]

Brooke's replacement as military governor was Leonard Wood, who had served as commander in Santiago but who had voiced severe criticism of his superiors in Havana. The choice of Wood satisfied such men as Theodore Roosevelt, who saw in Wood a firm but courteous administrator who would guide the Cubans towards responsible government with parental care. Elihu Root, too, doubtless found in the new military governor the embodiment of *noblesse oblige*. The first generation of Americans in Cuba had fed and clothed the people; the second generation would educate them in the fine art of good government. Writing to Paul Dana of the New York *Sun*, Root expressed the basic guidelines of future American policy in the island. These aims were political instruction to bring about conservative Cuban leadership and thus avoid internecine fac-

[7] Special Report of Brig. Gen. James Wilson, Department of Matanzas and Santa Clara, in *ibid.*, III, 3–4, 8; Brooke, *ibid.*, 14–15; Gomez, *Diario de campaña*, 424.

tional strife, electoral training to create a respect for the ballot, and financial tutelage to teach the Cubans how to balance the budget. Education was the key to American guardianship, Root wrote, for an illiterate people could not long remain free. He was convinced that a large Negro element in Cuba posed no insurmountable barriers to educational advancement, as several cynical observers had said. The erection of public schools throughout the island would herald a new era for the Cuban republic: its citizenry, instructed to respect law and order by American guidance, would then assume the reins of power.[8]

Wood's career as a soldier overshadowed his professional training as a doctor, and in Cuba he represented more the medical missionary carrying material progress to the natives than the iron-fisted soldier occupying the land. As commander in Santiago province he had imposed a regimen of cleanliness. Squads of soldiers were sent out to scrub the privies and cesspools, to inspect the markets and slaughterhouses, and to sterilize the hospitals. In the water supply, the soldiers found animal bones, pieces of clothing, and various discarded items of bygone generations. All the inhabitants were ordered to clean up their homes and businesses or suffer the consequences of enforcement. The recalcitrant found their doors battered down and homes invaded by Wood's sanitation officers. Still others suffered public whippings for having dumped garbage in the street in violation of the new civic code.[9]

To Wood, postwar Cuba constituted an excellent opportunity to carry out the credos of American middle-class progressivism: schools, roads, hospitals, and public works. His criticism of Brooke was for leniency, not harshness; his prescription for Cuban ills was material progress, not politics. Wood admitted

---

[8] Root to Paul Dana, 16 January 1900, quoted in Philip Jessup, *Elihu Root* (2 vols., New York, 1938), I, 305; Roosevelt to Leonard Wood, 9 April 1900, Morison, *Letters of TR*, II, 1252.

[9] Hermann Hagedorn, *Leonard Wood: A Biography* (2 vols., New York, 1931), I, 190–191; Wood, "The Military Government of Cuba," *Annals of the American Academy of Political and Social Science*, XXI (March, 1903), 153.

that the function of his administration was a temporary paternalism until the Cubans learned the prerequisites for stable government. Good government was founded not in political theory but in the minutia of day-to-day public services. The rural police would have to be trained; the lower courts would have to be reformed, and the lesser bureaucrats would have to be imbued with a sense of public duty. Under Wood's direction, the American occupation lost much of its strictly military character, for the army was now empowered to supply law and order and train the rural guards, and civilians were given charge of building a new Cuba. The Cubans themselves found employment in the civilian branch of the occupation, but Wood, unlike Brooke before him, was careful to place an American supervisor over them. The judicial system, for years a corrupt structure, was remodeled to facilitate judgment and to avoid bribery. Judges who had served for a lengthy term in one city were arbitrarily removed to another in order to prevent favoritism. Political and legal maturity in Wood's view was rooted in economic development. He stressed the importance of public works in transforming the island into a stable and orderly civilization. Public works projects were undertaken everywhere: roads and bridges went up in Matanzas, Cienfuegos, and Guantánamo. In Havana, teams dredged the harbor and converted old military barracks into schools and hospitals. The Spanish educational system, which had glorified Hispanic culture, was rejected by Wood in favor of a schooling that taught nationalism and instructed students in the practical and agricultural skills.[10]

With missionary zeal, Wood routed out corruption and graft wherever it tainted his work. He lashed out furiously against American adventurers who had ventured south to obtain sinecures in Cuba. In 1900, when scandals in the Havana post office were revealed to an incredulous public, Wood began an investigation to punish the offenders. The military governor reacted to these intruders in the same manner as middle-class pro-

[10] Hagedorn, *Leonard Wood*, I, 251, 273–274, 285–286, 319–320; R. L. Bullard, "Education in Cuba," *Educational Review*, XXXIX (April, 1910), 381; Wood, *Report, 1900*, in *House Documents*, 56th Cong., 2nd Sess., Serial Set 4080, pp. 3, 5.

gressives back in the states viewed the backroom bosses. Everywhere Wood saw enemies who despoiled his work: promoters searching for economic concessions; jingoists crying out for a perpetuation of American rule; and Havana businessmen intriguing with big New York corporations.[11]

When Wood departed Cuba in 1902, he was convinced that his two-year regimen had instructed the Cubans in the benefits of material progress and the principles of good government. Under his hand, the numerous municipal administrations had been either abolished or merged with others. By 1901 the rural guard, designed to keep law and order in the countryside, stood ready to assume the role carried out by occupation forces. In the cities, the police forces, heretofore subsidized by Havana, received payment from local governments. For coastal defense, Wood ordered the training of several companies of Cuban soldiers to man the armaments. Political training had appeared in 1900 in the form of a general election, in which Cubans who were twenty-one, had no criminal record, and possessed either literacy, $250 in property, or an honorable discharge from the Cuban army were allowed to vote. Writing later, Wood reflected on the occupation and lauded its accomplishments: administrative competence, treasury surplus, fair judicial system, police courts, marital equality to all denominations, local self-government, public schools, hospitals, asylums, railways, and a rural guard. The Americans had built a new Cuba, Wood believed, by importing Anglo-Saxon culture.[12]

The Teller amendment constituted a self-denying ordinance that prevented the erection of a *de jure* Cuban colony and a spiritual pledge to allow the creation of a republic. Justification for American occupation from 1898 derived from the belligerent rights and the contention that Cuba required a transitory supervision in the wake of a terrible war. Those elements opposed to granting the island full control of its destiny reiterated familiar arguments: the Cubans were unprepared for self-government, and the inevitable weakness of the first administrations would

---

[11] Healy, *U. S. in Cuba*, 139; Hagedorn, *Leonard Wood*, I, 282.

[12] *Ibid.*, 376; Wood, *Report, 1901*, Serial Set 4269, pp. 36–37; "Military Government," *Annals*, XXI, 160–161, 181–182.

pave the way for foreign pressure. The disciples of Mahan especially emphasized the need for strategic sites. They rejected, however, large-scale annexation of colonies in favor of naval bases and protectorates in the Caribbean. This combination would ensure an adequate American military presence as well as politically stable administration in the smaller republics of the Gulf-Caribbean periphery.[13]

Cuba obviously loomed large in the formation of hemispheric strategy. Root constantly stressed that the function of the occupation was to provide order and public services until such time as the Cubans themselves were willing and able to carry out their domestic and international obligations. What Root sought in Cuba was some device by which the United States would be allowed to continue the role of guardian, yet without the structure of an occupation force. In his view, Germany appeared as an external threat to traditional American interests in the Caribbean. Outright annexation of Cuba would have solved this fear, but Root opposed that method in favor of a protectorate. His experience with the Boxer rebellion led him to the conviction that Cuba must have a stable government capable of protecting foreign lives and property.[14]

The compromise between annexation and complete independence was the Platt Amendment. Although the amendment bore the name of Senator Orville Platt, the ideas came from a series of letters between Wood and Root on the eve of the occupation's termination. Interpreting the Treaty of Paris, Root argued that the United States inherited an obligation to protect Cuba. This obligation, manifest during the years of occupation, continued on after the departure of American troops. To depart from Cuba without some legal authority to intervene would mean reliance on the Monroe Doctrine as the lever to forestall European encroachment in the island's affairs. But the Monroe Doctrine, Root admitted, was not law but a *policy* of the United

[13] C. W. Currier, "Why Cuba Should be Independent," *Forum*, XXX (October, 1900), 144; J. Fred Rippy, *The Caribbean Danger Zone* (New York, 1940), 242; Russell H. Fitzgibbon, *Cuba and the United States, 1900–35* (Menasha, Wisconsin, 1964, orig. pub., 1935), 2–3.

[14] Root, *Military and Colonial Policy*, 171; Jessup, *Root*, I, 314–315.

States, and European nations might try to interfere in Cuba in order to test the doctrine. As for the prospective Cuban government, its duty resided in the protection of foreign lives and property and a fulfillment of international obligation. What Root was arguing was that the United States intervened in 1898 with the moral responsibility to end the insurrection but, in the defeat of Spanish authority, assumed a duty to maintain stability in Cuba.[15]

Thus, the salient features of Root's plan included provisions that Cuba was to incorporate into her new constitution. Briefly summarized, these points were (1) a commitment not to sign any treaty that impaired Cuban independence or to grant foreign powers special concessions without American permission, (2) a pledge to keep the Cuban debt at a low level, (3) an extension of authority to the United States to intervene to protect Cuban independence and maintain stability, (4) a ratification of the acts of the military occupation, and (5) a grant of sites for naval bases on the island. From the Cuban point of view, the most objectionable of these points was that allowing for intervention. In late April, 1901, Root received a delegation from the Cuban constitutional convention, which had rejected the intervention proposal as an unnecessary limitation of Cuban independence. In these conversations, Root assured the members that the President's utterances interpreted the intervention article as a step short of interference in internal affairs. For added support, he quoted a letter from Senator Platt contending that the wording of the article was changed several times to avoid any impairment of Cuban independence. Indeed, Root stressed that the right to intervene was important as a guarantee of the island's independence. For six hours on two successive days, the committee and Root thrashed out the issue with Root reiterating the historical interest of the United States in Cuba and pledging that interven-

[15] Root, quoted in Harry F. Guggenheim, *The United States and Cuba: A Study in International Relations* (New York, 1934), 63–64; Root to Wood, 9 February 1901, quoted in *ibid.*, 69; Albert Beveridge, "Cuba and Congress," *North American Review*, vol. 172 (April, 1901), 543–544, 549; Dana G. Munro, *Intervention and Dollar Diplomacy in the Caribbean, 1900–1921* (Princeton, 1964), 25, 34.

tion would take place only in case of foreign attack or in the event of anarchy. Unfortunately, no record remained of these conversations, and later officials employed the Amendment as legal basis for intervention in less extreme situations. Root's assertion that the naval stations would not be used to send troops into the republic was quietly forgotten in the future.[16]

In 1902, Wood turned over the reins of power to the newly elected Cuban president, Tomás Estrada Palma. Daringly, the Cuban constitutional convention had rejected the contention that the new constitution should be framed with American interests in mind. The clauses allowing American intervention and cession of naval bases were viewed suspiciously as infringements on national integrity. But, under the circumstances, there was little choice except to protest and incorporate the Platt Amendment into the fundamental law. Without that act, the military occupation doubtless would have continued. With its acceptance, an era of Cuban-American relations ended.[17]

II

The three decades following the signing of the permanent treaty between Cuba and the United States and the incorporation of the Platt amendment into Cuba's constitution witnessed continued interference in Cuban affairs. The Platt amendment obviously clashed with the spirit of Senator Teller's famous expression of April, 1898. But a great many things had changed since that time. The Spanish had been defeated, Cuba had been occupied, and the American government had assumed responsibility for the Cuban republic. In 1898, as McKinley's war message implied, Americans viewed the eradication of Spanish rule as the sole necessity for Cuban prosperity. The war and the subsequent occupation had led many to change their minds and to assert that an independent Cuba would require American supervision. Even though Root

[16] *Ibid.*, 26: Fitzgibbon, *Cuba and the U. S.*, 75–76; Wood to Root, 19 February 1901, in Root, *Military and Colonial Policy*, 187; Jessup, *Root*, I, 318–319.

[17] Committee of the Cuban Convention, Report on Cuban-United States Relations, 19 November 1902, in *FR 1902*, 360–364; *Treaty Series 437*, 6–8; Healy, *U. S. in Cuba*, 211.

pledged a strict limitation on intervention in Cuban affairs, the Platt amendment established a juridical framework that allowed the American government a wide degree of latitude. More and more the Cuban issue, so intertwined with humanitarianism in the 1895–1898 period, now fell logically into the broader spectrum of security in the Caribbean. On the assumption that strategic imperatives were better guaranteed if stability was the keynote of Caribbean republics, the United States took up the job of policing the "American lake," making sure that internal revolts did not succeed, that budgets were balanced, and that respect for elections was general. If this meant enforcement, either by dispatching a warship to troubled waters or hurrying the marines into a "banana republic," it was looked upon as the necessary price for law and order. Somehow, it was justified on the basis of isthmian security and political indoctrination. For Cuba, however, the distinction between the Teller and Platt amendments was crucial: the Teller amendment constituted a moral obligation to secure Cuban independence; the Platt arrangement was not only a spiritual violation of the 1898 pledge but a symbol of colonialism. The United States merely replaced Spain as the arbiter of Cuba's destiny.[18]

The first attempt at "stable" politics lasted only a few years. Cuba's first president, Estrada Palma, had served with distinction in insurrectionist causes all the way back to the Ten Years' War, had been jailed in Spain, and had resided as an exile in the United States. There he imbibed American educational ideas and assumed command of the Cuban Revolutionary Party after Martí was killed in 1895. Under the Wood administration, he labored slowly to build up a political following and achieved substantial support from the nuclei of emerging political parties. Estrada Palma accepted the reality of American power in the Caribbean and recognized that Cuba would have to endure several years of Anglo-Saxon paternalism before it achieved *de facto* indepen-

---

[18] *Ibid.*, 208; Doris Graber, *Crisis Diplomacy: A History of U. S. Intervention Policies and Practices* (Washington, 1959), 132; Munro, *Intervention and Dollar Diplomacy*, 531; Ramiro Guerra, *Cuba en la vida internacional* (Habana, 1923), 13; Luís Machado y Ortega, *La Enmienda Platt: estudio de su alcance e interpretación y doctrina sobre su aplicación* (Habana, 1922), 31.

dence. As president, he symbolized a transition between the occupation government and the new era of independence. He believed that Cuba must sign a commercial reciprocity treaty with the United States and grant that nation the necessary authority to protect Cuban independence. At times, the Cuban president disagreed with Washington's opinion, especially when he charged that the concession of naval bases merited the return of the Isle of Pines to the Cuban republic.[19]

Despite notable achievements in the signing of treaties with the United States, Estrada Palma's political obstinacy was in part responsible for the second intervention. In 1905, on the eve of the presidential election, the President threw his support to the Moderate Provisional Assembly, which had agreed to aid his reelection. Two other parties—National and Republican—proposed two other choices for executive, Alfredo Zayas and José Miguel Gomez, respectively. When the president announced his intentions to run again, the opposition parties coalesced into a Liberal alliance, voiced their unwillingness to accept the reelection of Estrada Palma, and proclaimed their refusal to abide by the electoral choice if he won. (The political problem was infinitely more complex than a mere clash of personalities. For months, the President had tried to influence Congress to alter the laws regarding elections and parties, the organization of the judiciary, and the control of local government. The political *malaise* of 1905–1906 stemmed also from legislative inadequacies.) When he was declared elected, the Liberals engaged in open revolt, and Estrada Palma hastily increased the Rural Guard by 2000 men. The opposition declared that the President had employed military forces to break the Liberal ranks, had pilfered funds to finance elections and now was spending the money to hire guerrilla assassins. The only choice, wrote one Liberal leader, was revolution.[20]

---

[19] Santovenia, *Estudios*, 199, 201, 203.

[20] Atherton Brownell, "The Cuban Republic on Trial," *Review of Reviews*, XXXIV (October, 1906), 427–428; Enrique Gay-Calbó, "Insurrection de 1906," in Guerra, *Historia nación cubana*, VIII, 17–29; Munro, *Intervention and Dollar Diplomacy*, 125–126; Faustino Guerra Puente, "Causes of the Cuban Insurrection," *North American Review*, vol. 183 (September, 1906), 538–539.

The stage was set for American intervention. Quickly Roosevelt sent William Howard Taft to conciliate the executive and the liberal combatants, but the result was unrewarding. Roosevelt blamed the failure of compromise on Estrada Palma, who threatened resignation each time the emissary broached a conciliatory agreement. Momentarily, there was a glimmer of hope for peace when the Cuban Congress entered the negotiations, but Estrada Palma killed all chances by resigning himself and compelling his cabinet members, who stood in the line of succession, to resign also. In the legislative branch, moderate supporters of the president refused to attend sessions and thus prevented a quorum. Cuba was left without a government. On September 28, 1906, Taft requested a squad of marines to guard the national treasury.[21]

Most Cubans expected a large-scale deployment of American troops, but Taft's proclamation called only for a small allotment of marines as protection for the provisional government. In the light of political frustration in 1906 and Cuba's seeming inability to abide by the noble dreams of Leonard Wood, some Americans considered once again the island's annexation. John W. Foster, former Secretary of State and grandfather of John Foster Dulles, pointed out the perils of annexation. In the first place, he wrote, annexation violated the Teller amendment and doubtless would mean a lengthy military occupation. Moreover, incorporation of Cuba would aggravate the racial and educational problems of the United States. Cuba was predominantly Catholic. Economically, annexation would prove harmful to the domestic beet sugar and tobacco industry.[22]

The military governor during the 1906–1909 intervention was Charles Magoon, whose colonial experience included service in the Canal Zone only a few years before. Magoon had been relatively successful in running the Canal Zone but proved a disap-

---

[21] Roosevelt to Joseph Foraker, 28 September 1906, quoted in Foraker, *Notes of a Busy Life*, II, 58–59; Munro, *Intervention and Dollar Diplomacy*, 132–3; Machado, *Enmienda Platt*, 102–103; Howard Hill, *Roosevelt and the Caribbean* (Chicago, 1927), 69–105.

[22] David Lockmiller, *Magoon in Cuba: A History of the Second Intervention, 1906–1909* (Chapel Hill, 1938), 58–59; Foster, "Annexation of Cuba," *Independent*, LXI (October 25, 1906), 966–967.

pointment in Cuba. The circumstances of his assumption of power were less auspicious than those surrounding the appointment of Wood, who served shortly after the war and before the erection of the Cuban republic. As administrator in Cuba, Magoon became less a ruler than a disseminator of patronage. Political factions, Cuban and American, hounded him for jobs; where positions did not exist, they were created for the faithful and deserving. Two public works concessions for sewage, paving, and aqueduct construction reeked of political jobbery; both were ordered from Washington; both were unwisely financed; and both companies rendered a shoddy product. In all fairness to Magoon, his administration did authorize a restudy of Cuban government. The Advisory Law Commission, which undertook this formidable task, recommended alterations in the methods of local taxation and accounting in an attempt to improve municipal and provincial government. Also, the Commission reevaluated the constitution and contributed to a strengthening of the legislative branch. Cuban statutes in 1905 were a conglomeration of Spanish codes, orders of Wood, and the national constitution. The Advisory Law Commission, headed by Enoch Crowder, examined the legal dilemma and came up with even more suggestions that led to a civil service law (patterned on that of the United States) and to the establishment of various executive branches, such as state, justice, and treasury. The labor of the Commission constituted the greatest success of the second intervention. Magoon, unfortunately, acquired only notoriety. Wood had been something of a hero to Cubans. Magoon was no military hero and, unlike Wood, he requested rather than ordered compliance with the rules. Successive Cuban generations looked with scorn at Magoon and with awe at Wood, but neither one accomplished the task of political instruction.[23]

On two other occasions, in the decade following the Magoon occupation, the United States employed the threat of intervention. The first came in 1912, as José Miguel Gomez's presidency

[23] Jenks, *Our Cuban Colony*, 97, 126–127; Advisory Law Commission to Provisional Governor, 15 January 1909, in *Senate Miscellaneous Documents*, 61st Cong., 1st Sess., No. 80, p. 23; Fitzgibbon, *U. S. and Cuba*, 135 *passim*; Lockmiller, *Magoon in Cuba*, 222.

was ending, and was precipitated by disenchanted Negroes and veterans. For several years, Negroes had protested legislation that allegedly deprived their electoral rights and had been organizing their own party, the *Partido Independiente de Color*. By presidential decree, officers of the Rural Guard and Army were forbidden to participate in politics. In May, 1912, these groups raised the standard of revolt in Santiago against the Gomez regime. At the outset, Secretary of State Philander Knox warned that Gomez was obligated to maintain republican government in Cuba and thus "prevent a threatened situation which would compel the Government of the United States, much against its desires, to consider what measures it must take in the pursuance of the obligation of its relations to Cuba." Unfortunately for the Cuban executive and the prestige of his administration, the revolt continued. Bands of Negroes fought with the Rural Guard in Oriente and Santa Clara provinces and even threatened Havana. As the fighting progressed, Gomez adopted harsh counterrevolutionary measures, hoping to convince Washington that his administration was capable of maintaining law and order. But when the rebels warned that foreign property would be destroyed, Knox responded with a call for 500 marines to land at Guantánamo. Gomez acquiesced and promised full cooperation with American troops. The intervention, wrote a Cuban historian, came at the behest of foreign property owners who foresaw destruction to their holdings and whose frantic appeals prompted Knox to act. The Secretary of State, however, explained that troops had indeed been dispatched to protect American lives and property but added the cryptic remark: "This is not intervention." [24]

The second intervention of the decade came just after American entrance into the World War. Considering the strategic ques-

---

[24] Rodolfo Z. Carballal, *Estudio sobre la administración del General José M. Gomez, 1909–1913* (Habana, 1915), 48–49, 58; *FR 1912*, 240–256. Knox disapproved a Senate proposal at the time that would have established conditions under which the President was empowered to intervene in Cuba to protect life, liberty, and property. See Knox to Elihu Root, 30 July 1912, 711.37/41, Department of State Correspondence, National Archives. The Department switched to the decimal system of recording in 1906.

tions confronting the United States in the Caribbean, Secretary of State Lansing carefully delineated the wartime role of Cuba. The island could not become a hiding place for German aliens, he believed, for there they might observe American naval movements. Cuban neutrality was equally unacceptable, since under that condition the United States would be prohibited from using the island's naval bases. There was only one answer, thought Mr. Lansing, and that was "to have the Cuban government follow our action." [25]

Cooperation by President Mario Menocal meant, of course, a reciprocal support for his regime by the United States. Already by 1917, Menocal possessed numerous political troubles that stemmed from his 1916 decision to succeed himself in the executive chair, after an earlier promise not to seek reelection. The Liberals, heretofore bitterly divided between the adherents of Alfredo Zayas and ex-President Gomez, consolidated their strength for the electoral battle. Menocal, frightened at the prospect of defeat, ordered transmission of election news to the presidential palace *before* public announcement. The Liberals charged fraud, brought their case before the election board and courts, and won another balloting in key provinces. When the returns from these areas, which were strongly pro-Liberal, proclaimed a Menocal victory, the Liberals resurrected their charges of fraud, asked for American intervention, and threatened revolution. It was mid-February, 1917, and the United States headed for war in Europe. Secretary Lansing sent a strong note to both sides, but the Liberals carried out their call to arms. Menocal, recognizing the security of his own position, refused to conciliate the Liberals, and obtained arms in the United States. When the President delivered his declaration of war against Germany in April, the Cuban revolt still flickered, but Menocal's power was stronger than ever. Ironically, the army that put down the uprising was the Liberal creation of several years before. Menocal, keenly attuned to the importance of the *threat* of intervention, paraded himself before the American government as a man who

[25] Lansing to Wilson, 26 March 1917, in Department of State, *Papers Relating to the Foreign Relations of the United States: The Lansing Papers, 1914–1920* (2 vols., Washington, 1939), I, 631.

protected foreign lives and property. Had the Liberals sustained the revolt for a longer time, doubtless they could have provoked full-scale American intervention. Maintenance of law and order now appeared as the only meaningful criterion for "good government" in Cuba, and a Cuban president learned how to employ the Platt amendment to his own advantage. A few years later, Secretary of the Navy Josephus Daniels wrote sarcastically in his diary that American power had put Menocal back in office when he had been rejected at the polls.[26]

Neither Menocal nor the American government forgot the mutual support during the 1917 Liberal uprising. After the declaration of war, Menocal opened up Cuba to agents of the Departments of Justice, Navy, and War, sent to the island to track down suspicious Germans. (The image of American officials in Cuba worsened considerably, for they apparently overreached delegated authority.) Enemy ships were dutifully interned in Cuban ports, Cuban naval and army officers were stationed in Washington, and Cuban ships came virtually under the command of American officers. The next year of war brought arms and munitions to the Menocal government in order that it might improve Cuban defenses. Two months before Armistice, Cuba offered to send troops to war, but the Department of State politely declined, arguing that insufficient ships existed to transport Cuban soldiers.[27]

III

"Americans generally are not liked in Cuba," wrote the American minister in 1910, "because most of those who come here (tourists excepted) wish to make money and to develop the coun-

[26] E. David Cronon, ed., *The Cabinet Diaries of Josephus Daniels, 1913–1921* (Lincoln, Nebraska, 1963), 106; Leo J. Meyer, "The United States and the Cuban Revolution of 1917," *Hispanic American Historical Review*, X (May, 1930), 138–166; León Primelles, *Crónica cubana, 1915–1921* (2 vols., Habana, 1955–58), I, 243–244, 245, 323–325; Cronon, *Diaries of Daniels*, 585.

[27] Guerra, *Cuba en la vida internacional*, 15; William Gonzales, American Minister, to Secretary of State, 30 July 1918, 711.37/56; Cuban Minister to Secretary of State, 15 June 1918, *FR 1918*, I, Supplement I, 704; Secretary of State to Cuban Minister, 23 September 1918, *ibid.*, 725–726.

try on American lines. . . ." Parallel to the rise of political interference in Cuba was an economic involvement that lingered as a decisive force until the advent of Fidel Castro.

The search for a Cuban market had constituted a persistent theme of American policy in the nineteenth century. Entrepreneurs cursed the bureaucratic walls that prevented selling their wares in Havana; Midwestern farmers looked to Cuba as an outlet for farm produce; and investors sought opportunities in the sugar industry after the Ten Years' War. American policy makers proclaimed the redeeming values of Cuban-American free trade for the political maturity of the island. On the eve of the 1898 war, writers condemned the economic backwardness of Cuba and blamed Spanish mercantilism. Cuba appeared as an unexploited prize whose rich potential could be realized only by American capital. Cuba's economic degenerance, another explained, was due to Spanish inability to consume the entire production of the island. Cuba's logical market was the United States. "No better field for the expenditure of capital," James Bryce observed of Cuba in 1902, "could be wished for. Under a wise and firm government, and in the hands of our energetic race, it might attain to a very high measure of prosperity." [28]

The negotiation of a commercial reciprocity treaty in 1902 symbolized the consummation of a special Cuban-American economic relationship. From 1895 the sugar production of the island had dwindled to such low production that the industry faced imminent bankruptcy in 1902. As the Wood occupation terminated its rule, the prospect of economic calamity in Cuba confronted the American government. Responsible for Cuba's political direction, the United States now appeared responsible for the island's economic future. The function of the military occupation was political tutelage leading towards stable govern-

[28] G. B. Jackson, American Minister, to Secretary of State, 30 April 1910, 711.37/19; "Cuba's Industrial Problems," *Gunton's Magazine*, XVI (February, 1899), 123; L. V. de Abad, "The Cuban Problem," *Gunton's Magazine*, XXI (December, 1901), 515; A. G. Robinson, "Cuba's Industrial Possibilities," *Review of Reviews*, XXIV (August, 1901), 200; James Bryce, "Some Reflections on the State of Cuba," *North American Review*, vol. 174 (April, 1902), 453.

ment, Elihu Root wrote, but orderly rule depended on Cuban prosperity. Specifically, this meant finding an outlet for sugar and tobacco. And the only prospective market for these products seemed to be the United States. Cuban planters, Root continued, trusted American guidance and deserved special consideration. The security of sugar held the key to Cuban prosperity and growth, Root believed, because

More than half of the people of the island are depending directly or indirectly upon the success of that industry. If it succeeds we may expect peace, plenty, domestic order, and the happiness of a free and contented people to reward the sacrifice of American lives and treasure through which Cuba was set free. If it fails we may expect that the fields will again become wasted, the mills will again be dismantled, the great body of laborers will be thrown out of employment; and that poverty and starvation, disorder and anarchy will ensue. . . .[29]

The chief opposition to reciprocity in 1902 came from the domestic beet sugar industry, which feared the economic competition of Cuban cane sugar. Ironically, the federal government that in 1902 pressed for reciprocity with Cuba had been responsible in the 1890's for the encouragement of the domestic sugar beet industry. In 1897 the Department of Agriculture imported huge stocks of beet sugar seeds and sent them free to Western farmers. By 1902 considerable investments were absorbed by the industry, and congressmen were under pressure to reject any arrangement whereby Cuban sugar would obtain commercial preference under tariff laws.[30]

For a year, the beet sugar interests delayed ratification of the commercial treaty, which was finally approved in December, 1902, after both the domestic planters and the Cubans reluctantly agreed on several amendments and after Roosevelt called

[29] Edwin F. Atkins, "Cuba's Imminent Bankruptcy," *North American Review*, vol. 173 (December, 1901), 773; Root, *Report, Secretary of War, 1901*, 57th Cong., 1st Sess., Serial Set 4269, p. 51; José M. Perez Cabrera, "Presidencia de Estrada Palma," in Guerra, *Historia nación cubana*, VIII, 5.

[30] Healy, *U. S. in Cuba*, 197; F. R. Rutter, "The Sugar Question in the United States," *Quarterly Journal of Economics*, XVII (November, 1902), 80.

a special session of Congress. Briefly, the treaty stipulated that Cuban products then entering on the free list would remain on the schedule and that other products would enter at a special discount of twenty percent less than similar items for other nations. American exports to Cuba received equal privileges, except for tobacco, and still other products were granted greater reductions in tariff. The United States concessions in the treaty were almost twice those granted by Cuba on a yearly, *ad valorem* scale. The important issue, Root explained to Andrew Carnegie, was not the tariff, but the recognition that Cuba occupied a special, intermediate place in the national economy.[31]

The impact of American investment in the Cuban sugar industry from 1902 was so influential that control passed to foreign hands. In the years after the Ten Years' War, American capital had been invested in bankrupt sugar plantations. The war and subsequent intervention merely facilitated the process. In 1910 the United States imported nearly all its sugar from Cuba, thus reflecting the benefits of the reciprocity treaty. But at the same time, Cuba tended to produce more sugar than could be sold in the United States, and thus the industry came more and more under the influence of the world price. During the World War, the demands for sugar were so heavy that Cuban producers built new mills and opened up new fields by borrowing heavily. When the war boom ended, the bubble collapsed, and Cuba faced financial ruin as the price of sugar dropped rapidly. The sugar collapse in the early 1920's brought more American capital into the Cuban industry and resulted in greater domination of Cuban sugar by American interests. Large companies, such as the American Refining Company, expanded their ownership of Cuban sugar *centrales*. Other corporations that purchased plantations in Cuba were the Hershey Chocolate Company, Hires Root Beer Company, and the Loft Candy Company.[32]

Parallel to the rise of American influence in Cuban sugar was

---

[31] Munro, *Intervention and Dollar Diplomacy*, 31; Root to Andrew Carnegie, 20 March 1902, in Jessup, *Root*, I, 327.

[32] Jenks, *Our Cuban Colony*, 139–140, 178–179; Robert Freeman Smith, *The United States and Cuba: Business and Diplomacy, 1917-1960* (New Haven, 1960), 29–30.

the increasing economic dependence of the Cuban sugar cane laborer and small planter. The application of technology to the industry—the creation of larger mills or *centrales* and railroads from the plantations to the *centrales*—accelerated the dependence of the cane grower. Competition between the *centrales* dictated harsh means in order to survive; the *colono,* or worker, became a vassal of the *central* through binding contracts that prevented independent sale of sugar or *colono* ownership of land. Once a class of free farmers, the *colono* in time became an economic serf. That, indeed, was the tragedy of Cuban sugar, wrote Ramiro Guerra, for the maturation of the Cuban sugar industry was accompanied by the rise of the *latifundia* (large plantation system), cheap labor, and foreign capital. Large trusts, such as the American Sugar Refining Company or the Hershey Company, both of which owned large properties in Cuba, emerged as dominant factors in the life of the *colonos.*[33] The economic despair of the Cuban sugar industry in the 1920's was blamed by nationalists on the inequities that arose from Cuban dependence on the United States. In 1925, the Department of State still recognized Elihu Root's judgment that Cuban-American commercial relations formed a "special category" distinct from United States trade intercourse with the rest of the world. Capital investment in Cuban sugar and other properties had increased from approximately $50 million in 1898 to 1.25 billion by the mid-1920's! In descending order of size, the most influential American investment came in sugar, railroads, public utilities, hotels and real estate, tobacco, mining properties, merchandise, banking, and warehouses. Still another $110 million American capital was invested in Cuban bonds. Cuba, complained the island's ambassador, failed to reap the benefits of this large-scale financial stake. Because Cuban trade depended on the United States market for survival, the amount of duties paid by Cuban exports to the American market was greater than that paid by all the other Latin American republics. The ambassador's answer was a temporary *Zollverein,* or customs union,

[33] Ramiro Guerra Sanchez, *Sugar and Society in the Caribbean: An Economic History of Cuban Agriculture* (New Haven, 1964), 67, 73–74, 159.

whereby Cuban and American articles would not be taxed and would pass freely between both countries.[34]

The reciprocity treaty, lauded as the economic salvation for Cuba by Elihu Root, failed to facilitate Cuban economic independence and, in fact, tied the republic closer to the American market. Other than the guarantee of a market, Cuban sugar producers benefited little financially by the twenty percent preferential duty, for the preference merely encouraged more capital investment in sugar production. Concentration on sugar meant that the Cuban economy was unable to diversify. Neither did Cuban sugar displace beet sugar or sugar from Hawaii. Similarly, the reciprocity convention greatly stimulated Cuban-American trade but discouraged Cuban trade with other nations. The appearance of the Fordney-McCumber tariff of 1922, which levied extra duties on imported Cuban sugar, stimulated the search for new markets. In 1928 the republic announced its readiness to sign a commercial convention with Nationalist China as a means of ending dependence on the American market.[35]

Cuba's economic crisis of the 1920's prompted a vigorous attempt to alter the commercial treaty. The Cuban case was summed up in the argument that the island's economy in 1925 was drastically different from that of 1903. Then Cuba required economic protection from the United States; now it demanded diversification and greater commercial links with the outside world. A survey of Cuba's trade balance in 1926 revealed that the island suffered a positive advantage only in trade with the

[34] Division of Latin American Affairs, Department of State, Memo, 19 February 1925, 711.37/9; Herbert Feis, "The Export of American Capital," *Foreign Affairs*, III, (July, 1925), 680; H. T. Collings, "Billions of Our Capital Invested in Latin America," *Current History*, XXVI (September, 1927), 849; Orestes Ferrara y Marino, "Cuba Again Asks Justice," *North American Review*, vol. 227 (June, 1929), 660; Ferrara, "Economic Loss from the High Tariff on Sugar," *Annals* of the American Academy of Political and Social Science, vol. 144 (July, 1929), 68.

[35] Lippert Ellis, *The Tariff on Sugar* (Freeport, Illinois, 1933), 68–69; Le Riverend Brusone, "Historia Económica," in Guerra, *Historia nación cubana*, IX, 327; *Diario de la Marina* (Habana), 8 March 1922, clippings in State Department files; *El Mundo* (Habana), 21 August 1928, clippings in State Department files.

United States and Great Britain. With all other countries, Cuba imported more than exported. But the rapid growth of American world trade and the large increase of Cuban sugar production during World War I witnessed a loss of benefits from the treaty for Cuba. It proved difficult, however, for the Cuban government to convince the Department of State. On paper, Cuba's preferential treatment seemed to be beneficial. The consumption of American sugar had risen from thirty-two percent in 1904 to sixty percent in 1928; during the same time, Cuban trade with the United Staes had increased five times. As for the lessened value of the price differential, observed the Secretary of State in 1928, treaty experts concluded that the declining advantage was due primarily to the rapid strides in Cuba's sugar production. While the Department of State was rejecting Cuban arguments for another commercial treaty, a special tariff commission, established to study the island's economic ills, was concluding its survey. The report of the commission, issued in 1929, was mildly sympathetic and pointed out that Cuba's economic crisis emanated from sugar overproduction during the World War.[36]

The Cuban government was unsuccessful in obtaining a new commercial treaty in the 1920's, but private interests did attempt to control the sugar market. When the price of sugar dropped drastically, a New York lawyer, Thomas Chadbourne, submitted a proposal to Havana that aimed at raising prices. The plan called for the segregation of 1,500,000 tons of sugar, payment in government bonds, limitations on sugar exports to the United States, and agreements with European producers to control the sugar market. Chadbourne's idea was acceptable to Cuban president Gerado Machado, and in 1931 the lawyer represented Cuba at the Brussels convention. The meeting, composed of Cuba, Java, Czechoslovakia, Germany, Poland, Belgium, and Hungary

[36] Crowder to Hughes, 8 April 1926, *FR 1926*, II, 11–12; Cuban Secretary of State to Crowder, 5 May 1926, *ibid.*, 15–16; Gustavo Gutierrez y Sanchez, "Necesidad de adoptar una política exterior definida," 49–50, pamphlet in State Department files; Cuban Ambassador to Secretary of State, 11 April 1927, *FR 1927*, II, 504; Kellogg Memo, 2 December 1927, *ibid.*, 507–508, Kellogg to Ambassador in Cuba, 23 June 1928, *FR 1928*, II, 642, Cuban Ambassador to Secretary of State, 10 January 1929, *FR 1929*, II, 891–892.

(countries that produced approximately seventy percent of the world's sugar supply), resulted in a pact by which the signatories agreed to segregate surpluses of sugar over a five-year period, to limit production, and to increase sugar exports if prices rose.[37]

Chadbourne's plan illustrated a denial of traditional American beliefs about the Cuban economy. One legacy of the nineteenth century told that the exploitation of the island's resources by American capital paved the route towards stability and prosperity. The generation of '98 that "freed Cuba from a tyrannical Spain" accepted the idea that the key to Cuba's economic future lay in *production*. The twentieth century proved the fallacy of this theory, for Cuba was encouraged to produce the one product that maintained the island's economic servitude. Economically, Cuba remained as much a colony in the twentieth century as it had been under four centuries of Spanish rule.

IV

The 1917 American intervention in Cuban politics guaranteed the reelection of Menocal but simultaneously laid a foundation for revision of the island's electoral procedure. Broadly interpreted, the Platt amendment provided a vehicle for interference in politics on the judgment that internal turmoil endangered Cuban independence. The shape of American policy following the 1917 affair was the erection of legal and electoral arrangements whose successful operation made for honest elections and thus precluded outright intervention. "Preventive policy" was the term applied to these measures.

The man who established the rules for honest elections under the "preventive policy" was Enoch Crowder. A native Missourian, Crowder had served with distinction on the Advisory Law Committee during the Magoon intervention. After the war, he was sent to Cuba by Woodrow Wilson to erect a legal basis for Cuban elections. Crowder shared the attitudes of his generation: he believed the Cubans a pleasant people who were politically immature and therefore required American guardian-

---

[37] Ellis, *Tariff on Sugar*, 176–177.

ship. Like Wilson and Lansing, he accepted the logic of the "preventive policy" as a necessary device to prevent intervention and to satisfy the prerequisites for stable rule. Crowder's 1919 assignment to Cuba was welcomed by the disenchanted Liberals, who wanted the emissary to supervise election results. His mission, however, was not one of supervision but of legislating a new electoral code, which was proclaimed in August. The code established rules and procedures that were designed to mold the Cuban party system along lines similar to the two-party balance in the United States. Candidates were forbidden to run on two or more tickets; separate ballots for national and local elections were drawn up to avoid confusion on issues; judges and electoral officials would be selected by a means designed to prevent fraud; and the returns were subjected to a public canvass. The code went into great detail regarding still other methods to assure honesty, but Crowder placed emphasis on the role of the judiciary in determining electoral victories. In reporting from Havana, Crowder argued that the United States was morally obligated to provide stable government in Cuba. This goal, however, must not be brought about by intervention but by diplomacy.[38]

The first test of the Crowder code in the 1920 elections proved to be an embarrassment. President Menocal, in a desperate move to keep the Conservatives in power, united his party with the Popular Alliance, appointed military supervisors at polling places, and stripped electoral powers from duly elected municipal and provincial officials—all in violation of the code. Menocal's strategy aimed at the defeat of José Miguel Gomez, leader of the Liberal defeat of 1917, who allegedly was preparing the eventual purge of his former enemies. When Menocal's earlier tactics failed to dim Gomez's chances for victory, the president next approached Alfredo Zayas, who was encouraged to lead a Liberal faction away from the Gomez camp. The Conservatives saw in Zayas the lesser of two evils, for he was presumed to be

[38] Primelles, *Crónica cubana,* II, 13; David Lockmiller, *Enoch Crowder: Soldier, Lawyer, Statesman* (Columbia, Missouri, 1955), 217, 222; Crowder Report, 30 August 1919, 711.37/68.

an indecisive leader. Once in the executive chair, Menocal hoped, Zayas would fail to provide strong guidance, and the Cuban populace would cry for the return of Mario Menocal.[39]

Once again, a Cuban president gambled that American political attitudes would support his party's cause. Repeating their ploy of 1917, the Gomez Liberals announced withdrawal from the elections and charged Menocal with a repetition of fraudulent practices. In 1917, the Department of State had defended its support for Menocal as a wartime emergency. In 1920, it condemned the Liberal move as "undemocratic" and "as tending to undermine the foundations of popular government." To withdraw from an election was to withdraw from the political environment of the nation. In the view of the State Department, the Liberal refusal to participate in an election was tantamount to a declaration of incapacity to govern and unwillingness to uphold constructive political institutions. When the Liberals appealed for American supervision, the Department rejected the plea on Menocal's pledge of honest elections. Other complaints that were channeled to the American legation by the Liberals were redirected to officials provided for in the Crowder code. In August, 1920, however, the earlier refusal to supervise the national elections was followed by a reluctant admission that the United States was obliged to act as an observer. The fact that the electoral code was untested and that Cuban-United States relations were of a special nature now prompted the American government to observe the electoral contest.[40]

The decision to send an observer to Cuba reflected a growing disgust with the maneuvers of both political parties. When disturbances broke out in Camagüey province in September, 1920, and threatened American property owners, Menocal promised adequate protection but quietly informed the American minister, Boaz Long, that his administration would not protest the sending of marines into the province. Menocal's concern centered on the

[39] Lockmiller, *Crowder*, 228; Primelles, *Crónica cubana*, II, 155–156.

[40] Secretary of State to Minister in Cuba, 31 March 1920, 13 April 1920, *FR 1920*, II, 10, 12; Secretary of State to *chargé d'affaires* in Cuba, 4 June 1920, *ibid.*, 13–14, 18.

possible political repercussions for his party if American troops were dispatched to the Cuban interior. President Wilson, however, was disinclined to augment forces in Cuba with additional soldiers and warships unless the Cuban government declared its inability to protect life, liberty, and property. The Liberals, who had sanctioned the Camagüey protest, passed resolutions in November that demanded annulment of the elections and a new balloting under American supervision.[41] As in 1906, Cuban politics approached a crisis in which both political parties refused to negotiate their differences and hoped that American interference would support their respective positions.

The upshot of the 1920 debacle was the second Crowder mission, which began early in 1921. Crowder now went to Cuba as the personal representative of the President. Instructed to interview Menocal, Crowder was to convince the Cuban executive that the island faced political and financial calamity unless the major political parties abided by electoral outcomes and the Cuban government adopted financial retrenchment. (In the previous year, the Menocal administration had attempted to borrow money to bolster the treasury's resources. At that time a special investigator had been sent to Cuba as economic adviser. His report to the Secretary of State in December had been optimistic, concluding that Cuba was potentially prosperous but financially maladministered. What Cuba required was a strict deflationary policy for Havana. For present emergencies and future needs, the economic adviser had recommended a $100 million loan, half of it from American banks, which would be loaned to solvent Cuban banks. Any money borrowed in the United States was to have the approval of the American government.) Crowder was not authorized to threaten Menocal with disapproval of any loan but merely to reiterate to the Cuban executive the obvious reluctance of American bankers to lend money to a nation plagued by internal political disruption.[42]

---

[41] Acting Secretary of State to Boaz Long, 27 September 1920, *ibid.*, 23–24; Minister in Cuba to Secretary of State, 1 October 1920, *ibid.*, 24–25; Secretary of State to Minister in Cuba, 20 October 1920, *ibid.*, 29; Minister in Cuba to Secretary of State, 11 November 1920, *ibid.*, 39.

[42] Economic Adviser to Menocal, 17 December 1920, *ibid.*, 52–57; Acting Secretary of State to Crowder, 31 December 1920, *ibid.*, 41–43.

Asserting that his mission was not "intervention," Crowder met not only with Menocal but Zayas and Gomez. On board the *Minnesota*, Crowder was given assurances from the two Liberals that *neither* would run for the Cuban presidency. The announced withdrawal of both Liberals, Crowder reported, was no improvement and probably unconstitutional (he did not explain why), for the result would be distrust and instability. Far better if only Gomez withdrew, then Zayas automatically would be named! The State Department judgment on Crowder's suggestions was a reluctance to approve of any candidate's withdrawal and a reassertion that the United States' only interest in the presidential contest was an honest election. A short time later, the electoral courts announced their restudy of the 1920 balloting and declared Alfredo Zayas the next president of Cuba. In form, the Crowder code of 1919 appeared to have solved the dilemma of presidential succession; in fact, the United States, particularly Crowder himself, chose Menocal's successor.[43]

Crowder did not terminate his sojourn in Cuba but remained as American minister and as informal political and economic solon for the new Cuban executive. Zayas inaugurated his presidency with a bankrupt treasury, a depressed sugar market, and amidst numerous bank failures. He reduced the miltary budget, which saved the government a sizable expenditure. It was not enough, and like Menocal before him, Zayas began negotiations for a loan. The loan request provided Crowder with an excellent opportunity to lecture Zayas on the virtues of responsible government, and he prepared a 126-page memorandum. Crowder stressed that Cuban prosperity depended on a reduced budget, adoption of new auditing procedures, termination of sinecures and graft in the national bureaucracy, and a general improvement in the morality of government. The proposed loan, which would be negotiated with J. P. Morgan and Co., was made conditional on a budget reduction to $55 million annually and ap-

[43] Acting Secretary of State to Boaz Long, 4 January 1921, *FR 1921*, I, 671–672; Crowder to Secretary of State, 16 February 1921, *ibid.*, 675–676; Secretary of State to Crowder, 21 February 1921, *ibid.*, 676–677; *ibid.*, 686–687; *Diario de la Marina*, 7 March 1922, clippings in State Department files; *New York Times*, 16 July 1922, Sec. 6, 4:1.

proval of the Cuban assembly and U. S. Department of State. When Zayas proposed a $64 million budget in November, 1921, Secretary of State Charles Evans Hughes warned that overexpenditures prevented any loan approbation. His reasoning, later conveyed by Crowder to Zayas, was prefaced on article II of the Platt amendment, which had intended to provide for a solvent Cuba. Finally, in October, 1922, Zayas explained that his administration had revised internal revenues and tariffs sufficiently to service a loan of $50 million. Under these conditions the State Department approved the Morgan loan.[44]

One gesture that indicated a possible retrenchment in American power in Cuba was the ratification of the Isle of Pines treaty in March, 1925, which returned jurisdiction over the island to the Cuban government. Signed in 1904, the treaty's ratification was delayed for two decades because of legal and political complications. In the Treaty of Paris with Spain, the United States had agreed to study the legal position of the island to determine if it was a part of Cuba (and thus excluded from annexation). By 1904 American settlers had ventured to the Isle of Pines; investment increased rapidly, so that by 1923, 10,000 Americans owned property in the Isle. Seven hundred of these investors were residents. Crowder estimated the American investment in the Isle was about $15 million. The investors, of course, opposed the 1904 treaty and fought its ratification successfully for twenty years on the argument that, if Cuba resumed domination over the island, they would be taxed heavily. Secretary Hughes, however, considered the unratified treaty as unfinished Departmental business and successfully persuaded a number of influential Senators to extend approval early in 1925. Proclaimed as law in March, the treaty ended colonial claims to the Isle of Pines. The explanation for relinquishment was that Cuba had provided adequate naval and coaling stations to the United

[44] Emeterio S. Santovenia, "Experiencias del gobierno propio," in Guerra, *Historia nación cubana*, VIII, 59; Lockmiller, *Crowder*, 233–241; Hughes to *chargé*, 20 October 1921, 19 November 1921, *FR 1921*, I, 754–755; 759–761; Crowder to Zayas, 24 February 1922, *FR 1922*; I, 1014; Acting Secretary of State to Cuban *chargé*, 1 November 1922, *ibid.*, 1047–1048.

States. As for the American property owners, their investments were safeguarded by the treaty.[45]

V

The succession of Zayas by Gerado Machado in 1925 seemed to represent a new maturity in Cuban politics. Unlike 1916 and 1920, the 1924 election witnessed minimal disturbances. The opposition appeared willing to abide by its electoral defeat. Machado's inauguration was to herald a stable era in Cuban politics. These predictions would prove premature, for in the next few years Machado would consolidate his power and impose one of the most brutal tyrannies Cuba has ever known.

Machado paraded as a democratic president who intended to reestablish the prestige of the Cuban government by respecting individual liberties and by inaugurating firm, but benevolent, rule. Noting the rapid increase of population, he stressed the imperative need to renovate Cuba's educational system. Cuba had arrived at political maturity, Machado proclaimed; the republic could not expand geographically but it could broaden its moral and intellectual purpose. His pledge of *moralización*, an honest, business administration of government, was welcomed by Cubans who had observed four years of graft during the Zayas years. Here and there, public works projects moved ahead as a tangible fulfillment of the president's plan for Cuban material improvement. Machado even managed to retard the precipitous fall of sugar prices.[46]

Machado's foreign policy was anti-American and nationalistic in tone but pro-American in intent. Cuban intellectuals spoke openly of a new epoch in Cuban internationalism and the imminent removal of restrictions under the Permanent

---

[45] M. E. Clapp, "Have We Mislaid a Valuable Possession?" *North American Review*, vol. 190 (September, 1909), 330–337; Janet D. Frost, "Cuban-American Relations Concerning the Isle of Pines," *Hispanic American Historical Review*, XI (August, 1931), 336–337, 341, 343, 345–346; Merlo Pusey, *Charles Evans Hughes* (2 vols., New York, 1951), 535; *Treaty Series 709*, 11–13.

[46] Manuel Marquez Sterling, *La política exterior y la política nacional del Presidente Machado* (Habana, 1926), 12–13, 23, 26; Ernest Gruening, "Cuba Under the Machado Regime," *Current History*, XXXIV (May, 1931), 214.

Treaty and the Platt amendment. Dr. Emilio Roig de Leuchsenring, a famous Cuban historian and critic of American power, condemned the Platt amendment as a tool for the creation of a Cuban protectorate and praised Machado as a nationalistic leader. While Machado was executive, the movement to terminate the Platt amendment grew in strength; Cubans organized a League Against the Platt Amendment, which planned to initiate debate at the upcoming 1928 Pan American conference in Havana. Machado himself grumbled that the Amendment was a limitation of Cuban sovereignty and expressed resentment of the Guantánamo naval base. But in 1927, when the Cuban ambassador was queried about Machado's proposed topics for the 1928 conference, the Cuban president was willing to abide by the selections of Calvin Coolidge.[47]

Because Machado provided protection to American investments and property in Cuba, his anti-American public utterances produced no hint of intervention. The Department of State expressed its goal of stability in Cuban government as a necessary corollary to the safeguarding of private investments in the island. Machado's reputation among American bankers was more favorable than that of any predecessor, for they recognized that his nationalistic diatribes were intended for public consumption. Machado possessed interests in Cuban public utilities and various American-owned properties; when he was victorious in the 1924 campaign, he received an invitation to visit the United States in order to meet President Coolidge and American business leaders. In a telephone address to the Cuban Exposition at the Pennsylvania Hotel, New York City, in 1925, Machado referred to the Cuban-American commercial marriage and predicted an intensification of Cuban-American trade, since Cuba constituted the "natural and logical market of the United States . . . ." When he did visit Coolidge, Machado did not demand but requested, as a personal favor, the abroga-

[47] Gutierrez y Sanchez, "Necesidad de adoptar una política exterior definida," 37; Roig de Leuchsenring, Address to Cuban Society of International Law, in *Diario de la Marina*, 27 August 1926, clippings in State Department files; Roig, *Historia de la Enmienda Platt*, I, 261; Crowder to Secretary of State, 2 September 1926, 15 September 1926, 711.37/85 and 86; *Diario de la Marina*, 2 December 1926; Morgan Memo, 21 February 1927, 711.37/101.

tion of the Platt Amendment. Coolidge replied that it was just as much a Cuban as an American amendment. Later, an American *chargé d' affaires* in Havana described Machado as a "businessman of considerable force, unusual personality, and political acumen." [48]

Machado's consolidation of power, interpreted by many Americans as a necessary means for providing Cuba with stable rule, transformed his presidency into a brutal dictatorship. Previous Cuban presidents had been unsuccessful in crushing completely their political opposition; Machado was the first to succeed. He began by forcing a coalition of various political factions and then by placing his chosen officials in key party slots. The Nationalist Union, organized by Machado's enemies, found itself completely circumscribed by law. Machado forbade the establishment of new parties, public assemblies, and press criticism. The famous Crowder election code became a dead letter, and in 1927 a subject congress extended Machado's term by two years and provided for a six-year presidential office. When opponents could not be bought with bribes, they were beaten, jailed, or assassinated. Armed Machado thugs disrupted professional meetings of lawyers, doctors, engineers, and scientists and compelled the selection of pro-Machado officers. From 1925, politicians, newspaper editors, and labor leaders who defied the regime disappeared under mysterious circumstances. Cuban exiles in the United States wrote of police visitations in the night, prison torturing, and official terrorizing.[49]

Initial official criticism of Machado's regime came not from the State Department but from the Senate. In April, 1928, Senator Henrik Shipstead of the Foreign Relations Committee pro-

---

[48] Department of State Solicitor, Memo, 15 July 1925, 711.37/4; Marquez, *Política exterior . . . Machado*, 15–16; Smith, *U. S. and Cuba*, 113–114; Machado telephone address, 27 November 1925, 711.37/80; Chief, Division of Latin American Affairs, Memo, 23 April 1927, *FR 1927*, II, 526–528; C. B. Curtis, *chargé*, Memo, November 1927, 711.37/111.

[49] Carleton Beals, *The Crime of Cuba* (Philadelphia, 1933), 244–245; R. L. Buell in the *New York Times*, 12 May 1929, Sec. 10, 13:1; R. B. Porter, "Cuba Under President Machado," *Current History*, XXXVIII (April, 1933), 29–30; Roig, *Historia de Enmienda Platt*, I, 285; "Where is the Dynamite?" *The Nation*, vol. 136 (June 14, 1933), 664–665.

posed a resolution calling for an investigation of the Cuban government. The Shipstead resolution condemned a "virtual dictatorship" that denied basic political privileges, destroyed the opposition, closed the national university, carried out assassinations, and suborned public officials. But Machado carefully countered with assertions that his administration respected American lives and property and that the Senate was not empowered to interfere in Cuba's internal problems. Machado had earned the respect of American business and the Department of State. A resurrection of the old cry "Cuba Libre!" wrote a French observer in 1929, would need to change American opinion about Gerado Machado.[50]

And, in 1929, official disavowal of the Machado government seemed remote. The new ambassador in Havana was Harry Frank Guggenheim, whose family had risen to economic prominence in Anaconda Copper, American Smelting and Refining Company and in Chilean nitrates. Guggenheim lauded the accomplishments of capital in Cuba, which was ravaged in 1898 but in 1929 boasted highways, public works, railroads, and the material benefits of advanced civilization. If Cuba was dominated by foreigners, Guggenheim believed, it was explained by the logical working of a free enterprise economy. The average Cuban did not possess the personal drive to climb the ladder of success. Younger Cubans who cried out for economic reform pursued an unrealizable goal, for Cuba boasted no middle class that prepared the populace for independent small land ownership. The republic's abuses were not social or economic, but political: the national lottery, frequent amnesty laws that pardoned criminals and undermined justice, and congressional license of immunity privileges. Guggenheim singled out the lottery as a symbol of inherent corruption in national politics.[51] Years later, after the fall of Machado, Guggenheim qualified his earlier espousal of the Cuban dictator, but only after it was

[50] Senate Resolution 201, 70th Cong., 1st Sess., copy in State Department files; *El Mundo*, 4 May 1928, clippings in State Department files; Léon Rollin, "Cuba en 1929," *L'Europe Nouvelle* (27 April 1929), 555.

[51] Beals, *Crime of Cuba*, 326–327; Guggenheim, *U. S. and Cuba*, 113, 118–119, 151, 162–166.

obvious that the American government intended to disassociate itself completely from the Machado regime.

Machado's ouster in 1933 came only after a prolonged agitation and his rejection by the United States. American involvement in the Machado regime was inevitable, wrote Raymond L. Buell, because the Platt Amendment made the United States a judge of Cuban government. The sporadic outbursts of the late twenties, led mostly by university students, mushroomed into the widespread disorders in 1930. Angered over the closing of the national university, students rioted, staged anti-Machado demonstrations, and clashed with police. Such affrays became frequent occurrences in late 1930 and 1931. The students, armed, would open fire; the police would respond with random bursts that caused more injury to bystanders than to the rioting youth. Machado insisted that the student revolt had been whipped up by communist agitators and that the police used their weapons only in self-defense. It soon became obvious that Machado counted on American intervention (or at least diplomatic interference) to save his regime, but the State Department's press release of October 2, 1930, claimed that the United States intervened in Cuba whenever there was no government to maintain order. The opposition, too, according to Guggenheim, was asking for intervention.[52]

With student agitation an everyday occurrence, Guggenheim saw himself as the logical mediator between Machado and the leaders of the opposition. His decision to act as conciliator was refused at first by Secretary of State Henry Stimson, who suggested that Machado was obligated to ask for assistance. Otherwise, wrote Stimson, the American ambassador might be accused of political interference. For the final months of 1930, then, Guggenheim seemed content to perform the role of an impartial observer of the Cuban calamity. In successive memoranda, he blamed Cuba's misfortune on the diverse problems of sugar surpluses, denial of political liberties, administrative overspending, dissemination of revolutionary propaganda, and

[52] R. L. Buell, *New York Times*, 12 May 1929, Sec. 10, 13:4; *Chargé* to Secretary of State, 30 September 1930, *FR 1930*, II, 660; Secretary of State, Memo of Press Conference, 2 October 1930, *ibid.*, 662–664.

a perpetual conspiracy to overthrow the government. The probable eventualities were: (1) Machado would resign and chaos would follow; (2) Machado would be ousted by a coup and chaos would follow; (3) a coup would be unsuccessful; (4) Machado could maintain himself possibly another two months; or (5) Machado might resign, followed by a provisional presidency.[53]

However pessimistic these choices were for the United States, they numbered more than the alternatives for Machado himself. In 1931 the disorder erupted into open rebellion that counted among its adherents not only students but also ex-president Menocal, Carlos Mendieta, and thousands of townspeople, sailors, and soldiers. Many of the citizenry had organized anti-Machado cells, known as A. B. C., etc., thus the title "ABC" movement. Composed of students, professors, and professional groups, the ABC advocated a program of social and economic renovation and pledged itself to Machado's overthrow. The organization employed propaganda and terror to alarm Machado's followers and frighten the unfaithful. Its diverse triumphs included bombings of public buildings and assassinations of government, military, and police officers. In the most daring spree, the ABC terrorists eliminated two of Machado's top lieutenants in a burst of machine gun and shotgun fire. In September, 1931, Guggenheim warned the Cuban executive to extend reforms, but the appeal brought only half-hearted support. In December, Machado announced a perpetuation of his presidency until 1935. The next year Cuba fell into total discord: Machado organized the remaining loyal military and police into terrorist squads. The opposition met death with death, assassination with assassination.[54]

But, far away, other men were debating Cuba's fate. In the early days of 1933, as Machado exhausted his repressive re-

[53] Secretary of State to Guggenheim, 15 November 1930, *ibid.*, 671; Guggenheim to Secretary of State, 24 November 1930, 12 December 1930, *ibid.*, 673–676, 679.

[54] Santovenia, "Experiencias del gobierno propio," Guerra, *Historia nación cubana*, VIII, 74–75, 76; Beals, *Crime of Cuba*, 260–261, 314–315; Porter, "Cuba Under Machado," *Current History* XXXVII, 31; Guggenheim to Secretary of State, 2 September 1931, 24 December 1931, *FR 1931*, II, 71–75, 80–82.

sources, a new President of the United States prepared to inaugurate his administration. A thousand miles from Havana, a new Cuban policy was emerging. The era of paternalism, begun in the fervor of war in 1898, was coming to an end.

VI

Why, during these years after the Spanish-American War, did the United States choose Cuba for an unprecedented interference in the internal affairs of a foreign state? One persistent argument has been that the American government, particularly the Department of State, sought to assure easier access for private American capital into the island. Still another explanation, employed by contemporary Secretaries of State, was the paramount necessity to protect the vital isthmian waterway in Panama and to prevent European encroachment in the weaker republics of the Caribbean area. Thoughtful scholars, particularly Dana Gardner Munro, have subjected the official contentions to exhaustive inquiry and concluded that, with some qualification, they are indeed honest and sincere. Although Munro (himself a State Department official during this period) admits that many of the decisions were unfortunate and unwise, he believes that the ultimate goal of the United States in the Caribbean, especially Cuba, was the achievement of political and economic conditions that prevented the discord and anarchy which might impair American security interests. With the important exception of Cuba, little private capital followed the flag of intervention in the "banana republics." [55]

As the era of paternalism recedes into the past, however, it appears that the roots of the Cuban protectorate lay in the nineteenth century. Certainly, the rise of America to the status of a world power with the defeat of Spain and the construction of the Panama Canal provided contemporaries with some justification for pursuing a policy of intervention. Yet, the men who fought in Cuba against Spain and who later erected the protectorate in the aftermath of war were influenced more in their thinking by the nineteenth than by the twentieth century. They

---

[55] Munro, *Intervention and Dollar Diplomacy*, 530–546.

applied old ways to new conditions. The strategic value of Cuba was not a creation of any post-1898 power struggle for control of the Caribbean but a legacy of the 1820's. The enormous American investment (an estimated $1.5 billion in 1925) in Cuba after 1898 was the logical culmination of the nineteenth century search for an ever greater share of the Cuban market. Finally, the intensive effort to reform Cuba politically with the Wood trusteeship, the guarantees of the Platt Amendment, or the Crowder mission, derived its justification from the hallowed conviction that democracy and material progress created stability and well-being. Before the struggle with Spain, Americans had contended that Cuba ("Voluptuous Cuba," many called it) was naturally rich but brutally exploited by Spanish maladministration. Once liberated, the island was subjected to a third of a century of paternalism in a futile attempt to tutor the people in the traditional American political and economic values.

CHAPTER VI

Batista and Castro

I

BETWEEN THE SPANISH-AMERICAN WAR and the beginning of Castro's government, the most crucial year in Cuban history was 1933. Within six months, from August 1933 to January 1934, the republic changed leadership three times, experimented with socialism, confronted a severe economic crisis, and witnessed the meteoric rise of Sergeant Fulgencio Batista. The generation that wrought these profound changes sought a democratic order, social-economic justice, and the destruction of the American protectorate. Cuba in 1933 was a society in revolt against the earlier revolutionaries who had prostituted their idealism of 1895 by accepting American paternalism and the consolidation of economic colonialism. Those who led the protest against Machado comprised the youth of Cuba—students, young professionals, and the lower echelons of the Cuban army.[1]

When Franklin Delano Roosevelt assumed the Presidency in March, he confronted the likely prospect of political and economic disruption in Cuba. Even Harry Frank Guggenheim, the retiring ambassador in Havana, lost faith in Machado's ability to maintain order. In the final months of his office, Guggenheim abruptly altered his view of Cuba and recommended a scuttling of the Platt amendment. The 1903 policy, he wrote later, was

[1] Aurelio Concheso, *Cuba en la vida internacional* (Jena and Leipzig, 1935), 16; Carleton Beals, "Young Cuba Rises," *Scribner's Magazine*, XCIV (November, 1933), 269. The most detailed analysis of these confusing months of Cuban-American relations is Bryce Wood, *The Making of the Good Neighbor Policy* (New York, 1961), 48–117.

unprogressive, for Cuban governments responded to reform appeals only if faced with a loan disapproval or an imminent *coup d'etat*. Guggenheim suggested a new political and commercial treaty.[2] Roosevelt's Cuban policy, however faced a greater test than that of treaty alteration. During the Hoover years, Roosevelt had criticized the intervention policy, and his first Inaugural promised an end to the protectorate system and the initiation of a "good neighbor" policy. But only a few months in office, the new President saw possible calamity in one of the most strategically important Caribbean sites.

That the adminstration considered Cuba's strategic value of more immediate worth than a credo of absolute nonintervention soon became evident. Early in April, Roosevelt and Secretary of State Hull decided to send Sumner Welles, a career diplomat who had just been named Assistant Secretary of State, to act as intermediary between Machado and his enemies. Welles' attitudes reflected the imprint of past policy. In a press release delivered before his departure to Havana, the Assistant Secretary referred to the island's historical relationship to the United States: the intervention of 1898, the geographic proximity of Cuba, and, finally, the important Cuban market for American products. His instructions from Hull, which were dated May 1, looked as much to the past as the future. The basis of American action in Cuba remained the policy of 1902–1903. The Secretary recognized that Machado's arbitrary extension of the presidential term and the severe economic crisis had schooled an entire generation of Cubans in the belief that political change came only through force. As a special emissary, Welles was to safeguard American lives and property, work for a settlement between Machado and the opposition, and convince Machado that the American people were shocked by the wave of terrorism. A promise of United States' mediation and a new reciprocity treaty were included as measures to facilitate an end to the discord.[3]

Welles viewed Machado as a vigorous, formerly popular executive who expressed deep hostility towards a people who

---

[2] Guggenheim, *U. S. and Cuba*, 236–237.

[3] Cordell Hull, *The Memoirs of Cordell Hull* (2 vols., New York, 1948), I, 313; Welles, Press Release, 15 April 1933, in *FR 1933*, V, 278; Hull to Welles, 1 May 1933, *ibid.*, 279–286.

turned against him. Assassins lurked everywhere, Machado related to Welles, and the Cuban executive moved from his Havana offices to his country villa by secret routes. On one occasion, Welles wrote in *The Time for Decision,* the police guard encountered a band of orderly demonstrators and opened fire. The ambassador's first reports from Havana were guarded approvals of Machado's ability to maintain law and order, suggestions for economic agreements, and pressure for electoral reform. Later, in early June, he advised Machado to announce an alteration of the constitution that would allow the representations of all major political organizations. Welles recommended also an immediate restoration of the vice-presidency, an office that Machado had abolished several years before.[4]

The appeal was futile. Throughout the summer, Machado lingered on, barely able to assert any power over a nation that approached economic and political collapse. In August, the government confronted a general strike that disrupted completely the transportation system. By this time, Welles had decided that Machado must resign by naming a Secretary of State who would assume temporary power and reorganize the cabinet, by allowing the resurrection of the vice-presidency, and by acquiescing to constitutional reforms limiting congressional terms. These changes completed, the new vice-president would advance to the executive chair. Apparently, Machado was furious when these suggestions were broached, but Welles predicted acceptance by the major political factions and warned that only this route would prevent widespread disorder. A few days later, having found no support from the Army, Machado agreed to step down. When Welles entered Cuba in April, Machado had been cooperative because he believed that delay and time would strengthen his position. The revolutionary element, he thought, was diverse and disorganized. Three months of strikes, assassinations, and demonstrations proved him wrong, and on August 13, one of Cuba's most terrible dictatorships terminated.[5]

[4] Welles, *The Time for Decision* (New York, 1944), 195; Welles to Hull and Acting Secretary of State, 13 May 1933, 6 June 1933, 7 July 1933, *FR 1933,* V, 289–296, 302–303, 318.

[5] Welles to Hull, 7 August 1933, 12 August 1933, *ibid.,* 336–337, 359; Roig, *Historia Enmienda Platt,* II, 5.

The abrupt departure of Machado was followed by the rapid formation of a coalition government under Dr. Carlos de Céspedes and accompanied by public disorder. Roosevelt immediately ordered two destroyers to Cuban waters but maintained that the action had no connection with intervention or interference in Cuban politics. In the next few weeks, the coalition de Céspedes government barely survived. Welles wrote condemnatory reports that blamed various factions for attempting to launch still another revolutionary movement and warned that de Céspedes was doomed to failure. The coalition proved unable to obtain support of the military or to quell the continuing public disruption and wave of strikes. Welles' solution to prevent inevitable revolt was a general election.[6]

If Cuban politics were unpredictable and uncertain in these days, perhaps it was because American policy was unpredictable and uncertain. For thirty years, the United States had followed a pattern of intervention and interference in Cuba. Now, in 1933, the Roosevelt administration announced the demise of the intervention policy. What Welles overlooked in his analyses was that United States' policy had proved *decisive* heretofore in Cuban politics; political parties had recognized the influence of American favoritism and recognition. Factions in 1933 groped for power in a political maelstrom. Each searched for the key that would satisfy Welles' criteria for good government because only his approval would bring diplomatic recognition and permanent power.

The impatience for power among de Céspedes opponents soon manifested itself in a barracks revolt led by Sergeant Fulgencio Batista on the nights of September 3 and 4. In a sense, the Batista coup was a revolt within a revolt: the noncommissioned officers, resentful over a proposed pay reduction, vied with their officers for the loyalty of the men, and won. The decision to upturn the government came after Batista and his associates were approached by another anti-de Céspedes element from the Student Directory. Alarmed over this unexpected happening, Welles

[6] Hull, *Memoirs*, I, 314; Welles to Hull, 22 August 1933, 25 August 1933, *FR 1933*, V, 369–370, 371–373.

cabled for two warships in Havana and one in Santiago. On the same day, September 5, he telephoned Washington and asked for the landing of 1000 troops to maintain order and protect the American Embassy. Welles justified the intervention as necessary to safeguard the de Céspedes government from a mutinous army and argued that the troops would withdraw as soon as new elections were held.[7]

Roosevelt and Hull, having extended American authority in the form of the Welles' mission, now stepped back. In his *Memoirs*, the Secretary of State related how he carried the news to the White House, argued that Welles exaggerated the danger of the Cuban situation, strongly opposed intervention, and found the President in agreement. In a terse paragraph, Hull relayed Roosevelt's decision: intervention was rejected on the grounds that it constituted an undue expression of partiality and violated neutrality. Any Cuban administration receiving American support would be regarded as a creation of Washington. The President did approve the idea of sending warships to Cuban waters, but these were solely a measure of precaution and did not signify any involvement in the island's internal affairs.[8]

In the next four months, the government of Cuba was led by Dr. Ramón Grau San Martín, a physician and National University professor. The new executive confronted almost insurmountable obstacles: pressure from the left for social-economic reforms and increasing militancy in Camp Colombia, scene of Batista's sergeants' coup. Leaning towards the reformist element, Grau promised punishment for the hated *machadista* henchmen and legislative enactment of progressive legislation. Orderly government seemed out of the question. Across the island, labor troubles continued as workers seized sugar mills and alarmed property interests. The president appeared to rule by decree. He

---

[7] C. A. Thomson, "The Cuban Revolution: Fall of Machado," *Foreign Policy Report*, XI (18 December 1935), 262; Welles to Hull, 5 September 1933, 7 September 1933, *FR 1933*, 379, 397–398; Memo, Telephone conversation between Welles and Jefferson Caffery, 5 September 1933, *ibid.*, 386.
[8] Hull, *Memoirs*, I, 314–315; Hull to Welles, 7 September 1933, *FR 1933*, V, 402; Hull to Certain Diplomatic and Consular Missions, 11 September 1933, *ibid.*, 422.

announced the establishment of the eight-hour day, minimum wage system, compulsory arbitration of labor-management arguments, temporary nationalization of certain large sugar and public utilities holdings, and the beginnings of agrarian reforms.[9]

Whatever the merits of its social reform laws, the Grau administration found disfavor in the mind of Sumner Welles. The Secretary of State's instructions to the special emissary listed one criterion for diplomatic recognition: a government supported by the public and able to maintain order. To Welles, Grau was a well-meaning but naive executive whose administration failed to provide stability. The labor legislation that Grau had passed, wrote Welles, doubtless was beneficial, but throughout Cuba laborers were still seizing plants and industries and thus preventing a return of economic prosperity. Bands of students were able to invade cabinet offices and compel public officials to do their bidding. In several encounters with Grau, Welles emerged with the belief that there was little hope of stable rule from such an impractical, visionary intellectual. In late September, fearing another revolt, Welles appealed to Roosevelt for a strong statement calling for conciliation between the warring factions. A few days later FDR declined. Welles' refusal to recommend recognition for Grau followed on October 5.[10]

In *The Time for Decision,* Welles answered the critics who condemned nonrecognition of Grau San Martín as rejection of social reform in Cuba. The former ambassador based his judgment on the obligations of the Platt Amendment, especially the right of intervention, pledging the United States to the support of a Cuban government capable of safeguarding life, liberty, and property. The Grau regime had been unable to perform this task, Welles wrote, and diplomatic recognition in 1933 would have constituted a breach of faith. Grau's overthrow by Batista

[9] Thomson, "Cuban Revolution," *Foreign Policy Reports,* XI, 263–269; Smith, *U. S. and Cuba,* 149–150; Raymond L. Buell *et al., Problems of the New Cuba: Report of the Commission on Cuban Affairs* (New York, 1935), 14–15.

[10] Hull to Welles, 11 September 1933, *FR 1933,* V, 424; Welles, *Time for Decision,* 198; Welles to Hull, 16 September 1933, 17 September 1933, 25 September 1933, 5 October 1933, *FR 1933,* V, 441, 443–445, 457–458, 473–474.

and Mendieta in January, 1934, proved that the professor's administration was unpopular with Cubans. Despite this explanation, there is evidence to suggest the plausibility of the anti-Welles' charge. The Department of State, particularly Welles and Hull, interpreted the labor unrest as the work of communists. Hull, moreover, leaned towards the conspiratoral thesis that the 1933 Cuban discord was directed from Moscow. But it proved virtually impossible to obtain conclusive evidence of Russian subversion in a western hemispheric republic.[11] Welles held firmly to his original explanation, but many Cubans in later years would adhere to the notion that American interference prevented a "new deal" for Cuba in 1933 and paved the way for the Batista era.

Since the "barracks revolt," Batista had carefully segregated himself from the Grau regime and emerged gradually as the man who could provide Cuba with law and order. On September 21, Welles reported a lengthy conversation with Batista in which the ambassador expressed his respect for Batista's reasonableness. He had none of the "stubbornness" of Grau or the student directorate. Reiterating the criterion for recognition of a Cuban government, Welles informed Batista that the United States had no partiality in the contest for power. ". . . We would welcome any government in Cuba," he related to Batista, "no matter by what individuals it was composed which fulfilled the requirements made clear in the official declaration of the Secretary of State. . . ." Following this encounter, the sergeant met with student leaders and thrashed out a compromise whereby Grau would be substituted by a president mutually acceptable to the army and to the students. The Batista faction continued to operate completely outside the Grau government. In late October, the army announced its selection of Carlos Mendieta and warned the students that their rejection of Mendieta would result in a forced return to the university. A week later, Welles wrote Hull to inform the Secretary that Batista had decided to compel Grau's resignation. Another month passed, and Grau was still in office,

[11] Welles, *Time for Decision*, 198–199; Robert Bowers, "Hull, Russian Subversion in Cuba, and Recognition of the U. S. S. R.," *Journal of American History*, LIII (December, 1966), 547–554.

but by this time Welles had completely lost faith in the Cuban executive.[12]

Welles departed Cuba shortly afterwards and was replaced by Jefferson Caffery, also a career diplomat, who shared his predecessor's lack of faith in Grau's ability to govern Cuba. Grau now received support, wrote Caffery, only from the "ignorant masses who have been misled by utopian promises." He believed, however, that Grau's government would end only through voluntary resignation or an army coup. On January 13, Caffery conferred with Batista, restated the conditions for diplomatic recognition, and learned that the sergeant was preparing to place Mendieta in the executive palace. Mendieta, however, agreed to the plan only if promised recognition in advance, a suggestion that Caffery accepted. To do otherwise, Caffery wrote, would drive Batista over to the leftists or cause him to establish a military dictatorship. The reply from Roosevelt was refusal and a reiteration of Hull's criterion. Within ten days, Grau resigned under pressure, Mendieta assumed the presidency, and the United States extended diplomatic recognition.[13]

The extension of full recognition only five days after Mendieta took power was interpreted by many Cubans as unfair. Grau had remained in office for four months and was unsuccessful in obtaining the approbation that Mendieta received in less than a week. Certainly, the provisional government of Grau proved unable to quiet the labor troubles and public discord, but Mendieta encountered similar frustrations. In 1933 the anti-Machado movement had resurrected a lofty nationalism and patriotism which found expression in a social and economic reform program. Within a year Grau was out, Mendieta (and Batista) were in, and the vaunted ideals of the previous months gave way to frustration and defeat. The question still remained, as Hubert Herring asked, "Can Cuba Save Herself?"[14]

---

[12] Welles to Hull, 21 September 1933, 23 September 1933, 29 October 1933, 1 November 1933, 7 December 1933, *FR 1933*, V, 451, 457, 503, 506, 535–536.

[13] Caffery to Acting Secretary of State, 10 January 1934, 13 January 1934, 14 January 1934, *FR 1934*, V, 95–96, 97–98; Acting Secretary of State to Caffery, 14 January 1934, *ibid.*, 100.

[14] Buell, *Problems of the New Cuba*, 498; Herring, "Can Cuba Save Herself?" *Current History*, XXXIX (November, 1933), 157.

II

The emergence of Batista in the post-Machado era of Cuban politics represented the transformation of the military into a powerful political instrument. Prior to 1933, the Cuban army was a weapon of presidents who wished to coerce the opposition. Menocal, for instance, had employed the military to supervise electoral balloting. Under Batista, however, the armed forces constituted the most decisive element in national politics, and Camp Colombia overshadowed the National Palace. When it was advantageous to the army's interests, Batista intervened directly in politics by removing presidents or indirectly by exerting pressure in order to obtain votes favorable to his program. In January, 1936, Mendieta lost favor and resigned under fire. He was succeeded by José Barnet, who survived five months in the National Palace, and Mariano Miguel Gomez, who committed the error of opposing Batista's program of military control of rural education. Gomez lasted six months. Batista had become, as Carleton Beals noted, a "new Machado." He was still the head of the "revolution" and *jefe máximo* of the armed forces of Cuba. He had become the maker of Cuban executives.[15]

While Batista exploited national politics for his own benefit, the Roosevelt administration systematically relinquished the old interventionist policy. In May, 1934, came a new treaty that abrogated the convention of 1903 and, more importantly, abolished the Platt Amendment. The only military legacy from Root's structure was an agreement to continue the Guantánamo naval lease. Later, when the opposition in Cuba made discreet inquiries to American involvement in the island's politics in 1935, Sumner Welles informed Ambassador Caffrey that the United States did not intend to intervene directly or indirectly in internal affairs.[16]

---

[15] H. B. Murkland, "Cuba's National Unity Move," *ibid.*, n. s., III (September, 1942), 51–52; "Le Nouveau Président de la République Cubaine," *L'Illustration* (11 Janvier 1936), 53; *New York Times*, 11 March 1952, 13:1; *Newsweek* (26 December 1936), 10; Carleton Beals, "New Machado in Cuba," *Nation*, vol. 141 (7 August 1935), 152.

[16] Department of State, *Treaty Series 866*; Welles to Caffery, 4 March 1935, *FR 1935*, V, 476–477.

What satisfied traditional economic interests in Cuba was the acceptance of Batista as a force for political stability and the negotiation of a new trade treaty to promote American products. The alteration of the 1902 reciprocity convention did not eradicate American business domination in Cuba. Under the New Deal approach, the Roosevelt administration produced a new trade agreement with Cuba that substituted a sugar quota for the former twenty percent tariff reduction.

The aim of this "new" economic program was to sustain the search for markets in Cuba but within a different structure. Secretary Hull believed that prior high tariffs of the 1920's had severely reduced the dollar amount of American exports to Cuba. In 1933, the value of those exports was only one-tenth of what it amounted to in 1924. The new reciprocity treaty, however, would regain a potentially wealthy market for the products of American farmers and industrialists.[17] It was a reiteration of a familiar nineteenth century theme.

Batista's public role in the 1930's was that of a *neo-caudillo* who labored to provide his country with political order and social-economic reform. Under his aegis, the Cuban government sponsored labor legislation that benefited the sugar *colonos,* child labor, and the industrial worker by guaranteeing a minimum wage, an eight-hour day, paid vacations, and the right to strike. The army, which was augmented to 14,000 soldiers, 3,000 marines, 3,000 Havana police, and 3,000 rural police, was given the task of rural education. In the Constitution of 1940, the nation guaranteed employment and a minimum wage to manual and professional workers, extended social security, and accepted the principle of equal pay for equal work. There were also references citing the need to control foreign land ownership and vague promises of land reform. In 1937 the *colonos* of the

---

[17] Smith, *U. S. and Cuba,* 160–162; A. A. Berle, "America Embarks on a New Trade Policy," *New York Times,* 26 August 1934, Sec. VIII, 1:5, 8; Press Release, Department of State, 24 August 1934, *FR 1934,* V, 177; Hull to Caffery, 26 July 1934, *ibid.,* 143; Thomson, "Cuban Revolution," *Foreign Policy Reports,* XI, 272; G. Patterson y de Jaureguí (Cuban ambassador to the United States), "Commercial Relations between Cuba and the United States," *Annals* of the American Academy of Political and Social Science, vol. 186 (July, 1936), 192.

sugar plantations were favored with the Law of Sugar Coordination, which proclaimed sugar as a national industry and provided for a division of sugar income between the worker and landowner.[18]

If the Cuban *caudillo* espoused nationalistic and reformist ideals that frightened Cuban and American property holders, why was Batista acceptable to the United States? The fact was that Batista's progressivism was more a yearning for power than an expression of conviction. Following the ousting of Gomez in 1937, Batista feared that his political maneuvers were alienating the Roosevelt administration. He spoke of plots in the United States against his life. The old landowning elite was becoming disenchanted with the succession of presidents. Abruptly Batista proclaimed reformist intentions. He blamed the failure of social and economic advances on the big sugar planters. Turning towards the left, he contracted a political arrangement with the communists, agreeing to legalize the party, appoint a member to a future cabinet, and grant the party political spoils. Publicly, he spoke of the danger of foreign control yet, at the same time, emphasized the role of Cuba as a traditional market for American machines, automobiles, gasoline, and agricultural produce. American investors who became uneasy over such statements and the language of the 1940 constitution in reality had little to fear. In 1939 they still controlled more than fifty percent of the sugar production of Cuba, based on a $600 million investment in that industry alone. The end of Machado and the Platt Amendment had not destroyed American economic influence, which in 1940 rested on a $1400 million investment in Cuba. Those who predicted that radical land reform would end this business venture soon discovered that enforcement of the new constitution would be gradual. Cuba, wrote *Business Week*, would not be able to expropriate foreign holdings, for the island was politically and

[18] Beals, "New Machado," *Nation*, vol. 143, 153; Edmund C. Chester, *A Sergeant Named Batista* (New York, 1954), 170; *Literary Digest* (17 October 1936), 16; "Labour Provisions of the New Cuban Constitution," *International Labour Review*, XLII (December, 1940), 282–283; Ramiro Guerra, "Sugar: Index of Cuban-American Co-operation," *Foreign Affairs*, XX (July, 1942), 749–750.

economically an adjunct of the United States.[19] Similarly, the Roosevelt administration protected investments by withholding economic assistance. As the Havana conference of July 1940 proceeded, Secretary Hull explained to President Laredo Bru and President-Elect Batista that Cuba must honor its obligations to investors before receiving aid. A number of American firms that had contracted public works programs in the islands in the 1920's were still in the process of settling with the Cuban government. Simultaneously, the Department of State refused to approve loans to Cuba in 1940 until a thorough study of tax reform, monetary and banking changes, and proposed public works projects. The recommendations of the study were similar to those of Crowder almost two decades before: Cuba required a fiscal and taxing reorganization and a reduction in budget expenditures.[20]

During World War II, Batista, who became president in 1940, cooperated willingly with the United States in a program of hemispheric defense. Recognizing the strategic importance of the island, the Cuban government accepted the need for American domination of Guantánamo and approved Roosevelt's "safety belt" measure, adopted at the 1939 Panama conference, which prohibited belligerent activity in hemispheric waters. Two weeks following State Department approbation of a $25 million Export-Import Bank loan, Batista sanctioned the idea of a military mission to Cuba. During the summer of 1941, the Cuban president proclaimed that Cuba would follow the United States into war, asked for military equipment to strengthen the army, and suggested that American forces might use Cuban soil for training and for building airfields. To offset the economic losses resulting from the closing of trade to Europe, the American government

---

[19] A. Pincus, "Cuba's Puppet Democracy," *Nation*, vol. 147 (17 December 1938), 659–660; Fulgencio Batista, *Cuba, su política interna y sus relaciones exteriores* (Habana, 1939), 26; Le Riverend Brusone, "Historia Económica," in Guerra, *Historia nacíon cubana*, IX, 315; *Business Week* (12 October 1940), 63–64.

[20] Messersmith Memo, 30 July 1940, *FR 1940*, V, 757; Welles to Secretary of the Treasury Henry Morgenthau, 14 September 1940, *ibid.*, 778–779; Ambassador in Cuba to Hull, 29 October 1940, *ibid.*, 783; "A Program of Economic Cooperation between the United States and Cuba," *ibid.*, 785–788.

guaranteed a scheme to purchase the entire 1942 sugar crop through the Federal Loan Agency. A lend-lease agreement came a month before Pearl Harbor. It provided the granting of $7,200,000 in armaments and munitions to Batista's defense program.[21]

Batista promoted himself as the "first chief of the revolution of 1933" but proved unable to overcome rival politicians and programs. Throughout the 1930's, Grau San Martín maintained a solid hold over a portion of the anti-Machado movement. Half a decade after his ouster from the National Palace, Grau and his associates formed the *Auténtico* party, claiming that it inherited the revolutionary spirit of the 1933 era. The *Auténticos* stressed economic nationalism and called for limitations of foreign property, castigated financial imperialism, and sounded a rally for immediate national action to regain economic control of the country. Grau condemned the American government for its support of post-Machado regimes and, more importantly, for the Welles mission, which allegedly destroyed the revolutionary goal of Cuba for Cubans. As president from 1940-1944, Batista allowed the *Auténticos* to survive and maintained that he would not seek reelection in 1944. In the campaign, Batista seemed assured that his progressivism of the war years and the government party coalition could not possibly suffer defeat. But Grau roamed the island, calling for an end to administrative corruption and fulfillment of agrarian reform promise. When Batista lost, he was stupefied, but stepped down from the executive chair.[22]

Had Grau San Martín and his successor, Carlos Prío Socarrás, satisfied the revolutionary promises of 1933 and the reformist

[21] Miguel Ángel Campa, *Un año de política exterior cubana* (Habana, 1941), ii, 67; C. de la Torriente, "Cuba, America, and the War," *Foreign Affairs*, XIX (October, 1940), 151; Cuban Ambassador to Welles, 5 May 1941, *FR 1941*, VII, 157; Messersmith to Welles, 20 May 1940, *ibid.*, 97–101; Messersmith to Secretary of State, 19 June 1941, *ibid.*, 104–107; Secretary of State to Ambassador in Cuba, 21 October 1941, *ibid.*, 237; Lend Lease Agreement, 7 November 1941, *ibid.*, 122–125.

[22] W. A. Roberts, "Cuba goes Democratic," *American Mercury*, LIX (October, 1944), 450–456; Grau San Martín, *La revolución cubana ante América; conferencias* (Mexico City, 1936), 25–26, 91–92.

plan of the 1940 constitution, Cuba might have avoided the strife of the Castroite rebellion of the 1950's. Grau promised continued support for the Allied cause and the American military effort, a departure from his earlier pronouncements against the influence of the Yankee in Cuba. His administration committed itself also to industrialization, debt reduction, and agricultural diversification. Every scheme seemed to fail: Cuban economic domination by American investment continued apace; the goal for agricultural diversification vanished, and Grau's ministers misappropriated public funds. When he turned over the presidency to Prío Socarrás in 1948, the Cuban revolutionary movement was a structure without substance. It was soon evident that the authentic party of the revolution had little intention of remolding the nation socially and economically. Prío did sponsor a national bank, promote crop diversification, encourage low-cost housing, but these hardly touched the deeper issues of land redistribution and foreign investment power.[23]

In 1950 Cuba was still an economic colony. Only Bolivia and Haiti had more prolonged economic stagnation from the 1920's to the 1950's. Most of the sugar land remained in the hands of a few large companies, which sent the unrefined sugar to industrial countries. The income from sugar refining went outside Cuba. The Reciprocal Trade Agreement Act of 1934 discouraged industrialization by favoring importation of American products, which were paid for by sugar exports. From the 1920's, Cuba's volume sales to the United States stayed at a net level, for the island suffered an actual decline in the burgeoning American market. In 1950 the International Bank for Reconstruction and Development surveyed the Cuban economy and concluded that sugar dominated the island more than ever. The recommendations of the IBRD pointed to diversification as the answer and based the

[23] Enrique Lumen, *La revolución cubana: crónica de nuestro tiempo, 1902–1934* (Mexico City, 1934), 104–105; "Ramon Grau San Martin. . ." *Bulletin* of the Pan American Union, LXXVII (November, 1944), 601–603; William Stokes, "Cuban Revolution and the Presidential Elections of 1948," *Hispanic American Historical Review*, XXXI (February, 1951), 40–41, 75; *New York Times*, 11 March 1952, 13:2.

claim on Cuba's favorable geography, fertile soil, mineral resources, and *proximity to the American market.*[24]

In lightning fashion, Batista returned to the National Palace via a barracks coup on March 10, 1952. The only losses were two lives and the interruption of business for one day. Everything was so well timed—seizure of police headquarters, a military convergence on the presidential residence, and a carefully-prepared radio broadcast—that the returning *caudillo* did not even bother to have a DC-3 warming up at the airport for a quick getaway. In the radio address, Batista professed no ambition for power but a deep affection for his *patria* that moved him to restore public tranquillity. In franker language, Batista told reporters that President Prío was plotting to overturn the upcoming June elections and inaugurate a new revolutionary era. The Batista coup, then, forestalled an inevitable period of strife. His enemies maintained that the dictator saw defeat at the polls in June and decided to act promptly with forceful means. Or perhaps, as a political scientist later reported, the 1952 seizure was merely an example of violence inherent in Cuban politics. The real tragedy, wrote Herbert Matthews, was the loss of faith in Cuban political leadership.[25]

In the aftermath of the 1952 coup, Batista struggled to legitimize his usurpation of a constitutional government by encouraging business support and by declaring his undying hostility to the Soviet bloc. For those who favored a middle course to Cuban material progress, Batista appeared as the answer. He spared the island from the turbulence of 1933 and promised a quick surge

---

[24] Dudley Seers, "Economic and Social Background," in Seers, ed., *Cuba: The Economic and Social Revolution* (Chapel Hill, 1964), 10–11, 13–14; Julián Alienes y Mosa, *Características fundamentales de la economía cubana* (Habana, 1950), xv; International Bank for Reconstruction and Development, *Report on Cuba* (Washington, 1951), 4–5, 7; Henry Wallich, *Monetary Problems of an Export Economy* (Cambridge, Mass., 1950), 6.

[25] *Illustrated London News*, 11 March 1952, vol. 220, 508; Batista, Speech to Cubans, in *Diario de la Marina*, 11 March 1952, 1:4–5; Chester, *Sergeant Named Batista*, 224; *New York Times*, 11 March 1952, 12:6; Stokes, "National and Local Violence in Cuban Politics," *Southwestern Social Science Quarterly*, XXXIV (September, 1953), 61–62; Herbert Matthews, *New York Times Magazine* (18 May 1952), 45.

of economic prosperity. The economic sectors of the republic seemed more interested in a speedy return of "business as usual" rather than a sincere questioning of the legality of Batista's government. Later, Batista would claim that his coup was made legitimate by international recognition from non-Communist states and by his inauguration in 1955 as president.[26]

To foreign observers, especially investors, Batista-ruled Cuba possessed all the desiderata of export capitalism: political stability, encouragement of tourism, protection of foreign investment, and an expanding market for industrial products. The newspapers of Havana advertised a vast array of items imported from the United States: autos, tractors, sewing machines, tires—the list was endless. Movie marquees showed the impact of Hollywood; Havana was a glittering playground of swank clubs that catered to the incoming American tourist. (In "Guys and Dolls," a hit musical, the hero Sky Masterson won the heart of a Salvation Army worker after a night on the town in Havana.) Batista attracted commercial interest by his support of government agencies, such as an Agricultural and Industrial Development Bank, a Cuban Foreign Trade Bank, and a Technological Research Institute, which served as foundations for industrial advancement. Although the sugar industry still overshadowed other economic areas, wrote a Department of Commerce bulletin, Cuba was not underdeveloped, boasted ports, highways, and railways, and its people had "one of the highest standards of living in Latin America . . . ." Batista's Cuba was a magnificent facade, a culmination of the nineteenth century ideal of a prosperous and happy land.[27]

Behind the facade of prosperity, however, was an island economy in colonial status. The reformist pleas of the 1940 constitution, especially those referring to land reform, remained largely unsatisfied. American investment in the sugar industry had de-

[26] Armando Giménez, *Sierra Maestra; la revolución de Fidel Castro* (Buenos Aires, 1959), 19–20; *Diario de la Marina*, 12 March 1952, 1:3; *ibid.*, 14 March 1952, 1:1; "El momento económico y financiero," *Cuba Económica y Financiera* (March, 1952), 7; Batista, *The Growth and Decline of the Cuban Republic* (New York, 1964), 261.

[27] United States Department of Commerce, *Investment in Cuba: Basic Information for United States Businessmen* (Washington, 1956), 5–6, 17.

clined by the 1950's to about one-third of the productive facilities, but these interests continued to wield effective power in controlling the annual Cuban sugar quota in the United States. In other areas of the Cuban economy, particularly in public utilities, railroads, banking, nickel mining, and various retail concerns, American capital was prevalent. From Batista, American investment received beneficial treatment. His periodical xenophobic statements and proclamations of widescale reform were passed over as political electioneering by an American people and government which equated *Batistismo* with stability, prosperity, and protection. Beneath the gilded shell of a wealthy and democratic Cuba loomed a revolutionary force that would proclaim social and economic reformation, political regeneration, and the termination of American influence in Cuba. That revolutionary force would be commanded by Fidel Castro.[28]

III

Castro's career from the 1948 *bogotazo* to the 1953 "History Will Absolve Me" speech was a representation of the landowner's son crusading as the young revolutionary. His student days at Havana University convinced Castro of his capabilities as a leader of men and a promoter of causes. During the Bogotá Conference, he was a member of a Cuban student delegation, and when the riots erupted in the famous *bogotazo* Castro joined in the affray. Years later, after his Marxist-Leninist professions were made, Castro's venture to Bogotá would be interpreted by his detractors as evidence of his communist leanings in those early days. Still a student, Castro and his comrades launched an abortive raid against the Dominican Republic in a desperate bid to overthrow Rafael Trujillo. When he graduated in 1950, Castro found little opportunity professionally in a society that boasted too many lawyers and too few technicians. He undertook a few

---

[28] Philip W. Bonsal, "Cuba, Castro, and the United States," *Foreign Affairs*, XLV (January, 1967), 265; Giménez, *Sierra Maestra*, 24; Smith, *U. S. and Cuba*, 170–171; "U. S.-Cuban Discussions on Economic Relations," Department of State *Bulletin*, XXXI (29 November 1954), 815–816; J. Cloyd, "Cuba, Our Gayest Neighbor," *American Magazine*, vol. 160 (September, 1955), 99.

charity cases, but most of his time he spent in the political circles of the Orthodox party, which declared itself the inheritor of revolution. The Batista coup of March, 1952, upset all of Fidel's bright hopes, and from this date he became an unremitting foe of the dictator.[29]

The famous speech of 1953 occurred after Castro led a fantastic raid on the Moncada barracks in Santiago de Cuba. An ill-planned scheme called for the taking of the post, a daring proclamation, and the winning of the people to the cause. Fidel was captured in the countryside nearby and probably would have been shot on the spot had it not been for the intervention of the archbishop, who pleaded for clemency. His trial before imprisonment brought Castro first into prominence as a Cuban revolutionary. In what must have been an agonizing ordeal for the court, Castro summed up the tragedy of Cuban history, a record of revolutionary promises and broken pledges. The oration was a condemnation of Batista for violation of the 1940 constitution and for social and economic neglect. The purpose of his rebellion, Castro said, was political; it aimed at the restoration of constitutional government. But a large part of the speech was interspersed with statistics dealing with the unemployed—*colonos*, tenants, and thousands of young professional doctors, lawyers, and educators who saw little hope of success. If successful, the revolutionary movement would reestablish the 1940 constitution, inaugurate land reform, provide profit sharing for sugar workers, and confiscate illegal land holdings.[30]

With Castro sentenced to prison for fifteen years, Batista felt secure once more. In 1954 he granted an interview with American correspondents and noted that Cuba had achieved political stability, was becoming more diversified economically, and had learned how to deal with communists. His political grip as firm as ever, Batista decided to prove that democracy existed in Cuba by releasing political prisoners. Castro and the survivors of the Moncada attack thus found freedom under a government am-

---

[29] Teresa Casuso, *Cuba and Castro* (New York, 1961), 96–97; Ward Morton, *Castro as Charismatic Hero* (Lawrence, Kansas, 1965), 14.

[30] Casuso, *Cuba and Castro*, 98–99; Morton, *Castro*, 20; Castro, *History Will Absolve Me* (Havana, 1960), 21, 34, 35–36.

nesty. Batista underestimated the determination of his enemy. In December, 1956, Castro led another escapade on Cuban shores, this time in Oriente province. The boat, *Granma,* which carried them to Cuba from their Mexican base, was left in open view; Batista's air force struck at the revolutionaries as they made their way into the hills. Few of them knew the terrain; most were captured by Batista's scouts before reaching the Sierra Maestra.[31]

From late 1956 until he assumed control of Cuba in early 1959, Castro's image was transformed from that of the revolutionary guerrilla to the people's warrior. While Batista promoted tourism, announced social reforms, and erected a statue of Christ in Havana harbor, Castro carried out an effective guerrilla campaign. Incendiaries burned cane fields and vehicles; others disrupted communications by cutting telephone and telegraph lines, and daring saboteurs planted bombs. For a long time, Batista denied that Castro was a threat and published accounts that his enemy had been killed. But others believed differently, and one of them, Herbert Matthews of the *New York Times,* journeyed to the Sierra Maestra, and interviewed and photographed Castro, thus disproving Batista's boast. (Castro fooled Matthews, too, into believing that the guerrillas numbered a larger force.) Castro's appeal to reformist elements now went outside Cuba. Batista's tactics from the rediscovery of Castro became brutal and alienated the professional classes of Cuba. Government censors carefully scrutinized incoming American newspapers and cut out stories relating to the guerrillas. The national police dealt harshly with captured plotters, and Batista ordered the publication of photographs showing dead revolutionaries, castrated, with their testicles stuffed in the mouth. News coverage of guerrilla terrorism was overshadowed by reports of Batista's counterrevolutionary brutalities. Fidel Castro became the hero of Cuba.[32]

Once these revelations of Batista's police methods were made known, his association with the United States left the American

[31] *Newsweek* (15 November 1954), 67; Casuso, *Cuba and Castro,* 125–126.
[32] *Time* (7 January 1957), 33; Batista, *Growth and Decline,* 254–255; Casuso, *Cuba and Castro,* 126–127; Earl E. T. Smith, *The Fourth Floor: An Account of the Castro Communist Revolution* (New York, 1962), 39; Victor Franco, *The Morning After: A French Journalist's Impressions of Cuba under Castro* (New York, 1963), 103.

government in an uncomfortable position. It was obvious to critics that the million dollars in military aid granted to the Cuban dictator in 1958 played only a minor role in hemispheric defense and was interpreted as aid to Batista in his struggle with Castro. The American ambassador, Earl Smith, who had condemned the Castroite movement *and* Batista's anti-Castroite measures, was now instructed to express impartial neutrality. An arms embargo was imposed. Fearful of what Castro would do in power and repelled by Batista's dictatorship, the Department of State, according to Smith, approved a secret mission to Batista. The emissary, William Pawley, went to Cuba in December, 1958, in an effort to secure Batista's resignation. In return, the Cuban president would be guaranteed protection in Daytona Beach, Florida (a favorite vacation spot of Batista) and would be succeeded by an anti-Castro regime. The mission failed, as Pawley later testified, because he could not promise the full support of the American government.[33]

As a private citizen, Smith wrote later that Castro came to power partially by the failure of the Department of State to act decisively. The Matthews interview gave Castro prestige in the United States; guerrilla terrorism was given little press coverage. Most damaging of all, in Smith's view, was the fact that Cuban policy was shaped by the lesser bureaucrats of the fourth floor of the Department of State. There labored men who longed for the triumph of Castro's rebellion. Smith's portrayal of the Cuban middle classes as anti-Castroite as well as anti-Batista reinforced the beliefs of those who contended that Castro was always a Marxist-Leninist. Actually, his most ardent support came from doctors, teachers, and lawyers, members of the middle class who were repelled by the graft and intolerance of the Batista dictatorship. When Castro entered Havana triumphantly in January, 1959, he was able to do so because the middle classes had lost faith in Batista.[34]

[33] John Hickey, "The Role of the Congress in Foreign Policy: Case, The Cuban Disaster," *Inter-American Economic Affairs*, 14:4 (Spring, 1961), 79; Smith, *Fourth Floor*, 20 166–167.

[34] *Ibid.*, 6–7, 29–30, 41, 228; "Cuba's Rightist Rebel," *Economist*, vol. 187 (26 April 1958), 328; the interpretation of Castro's triumph is based on Theodore Draper, *Castro's Revolution: Myths and Realities* (New York, 1962), *passim*.

IV

The early admirers of Castro who subsequently were alienated by his Marxist professions still maintain that the Castro revolution was initially justified as an anti-Batista struggle for political democracy. Castro himself had spoken often of the need to restore the constitution of 1940. His pre-1959 political associations were with the Orthodox party, whose declared program was a restoration of the promises of 1933 revolutionary Cuba. Once in power, however, Castro rejected previous pledges of political democracy in favor of a totalitarian regime that spouted anti-Americanism and espoused rapid social and economic reformation. The first open signs of Castro's alienation from American influence came only a few months after he seized power. In April, 1959, when he was still popular with the American public, Castro made an official visit to the United States. Perhaps he came with the intention of negotiating a loan; probably he wanted the Eisenhower administration to offer economic aid. In this manner Castro could have had his foreign aid (which his new government needed desperately) yet not appear as an American puppet.[35] The truth about his encounter with American officials will not be known for a long time. It seems reasonable to assume, however, that the April visit was the last real hope for friendly relations between Washington and Havana, and that hope was doomed because neither Castro nor the Eisenhower administration was willing to trust each other.

The following months of the Eisenhower presidency witnessed a steady breakdown in communication between Washington and Havana. In its initial stages, the Castro government systematically hunted down and tried Batista henchmen under the aegis of special tribunals and in the spirit of revolutionary justice. The American public was simply unprepared to accept the manner by which the guilty were punished: public trials, thousands of jeer-

[35] José M. Illán, *Cuba: Facts and Figures of an Economy in Ruins* (Miami, 1964), 7; Loree Wilkerson, *Fidel Castro's Political Programs from Reformism to 'Marxism-Leninism'* (Gainesville, Florida, 1965), 7–8; International Commission of Jurists, *Cuba and the Rule of Law* (Geneva, 1962), 78; Casuso, Cuba and Castro, 207–208; Eisenhower, *The White House Years: Waging Peace, 1956–61* (Garden City, 1965), 523; W. A. Williams, *The United States, Cuba and Castro: An Essay on the Dynamics of Revolution and the Dissolution of Empire* (New York, 1962), 100.

ing spectators, and an atmosphere of tribal justice. The ritual was portrayed in condemnatory rhetoric in hundreds of American newspapers. What damage revolutionary justice did to Castro's image in the United States was compounded by new Cuban laws nationalizing foreign-owned businesses. Castro's hostility to private investment—his contention that it subverted Cuba to foreign control—found expression in the appointment of "intervenors" who supervised the operation of American companies, particularly the Cuban Telephone and Electric Companies. Under Law 851, the Cuban government began the seizure of foreign-controlled landholdings that produced rice, tobacco, and coffee. New mining and pertoleum legislation wiped away old contracts, and more taxes were levied on foreign companies. In May, the Cuban Court of Social and Constitutional Guarantees approved nationalization of lands owned by Nicaro Nickel, Moa Bay Mining, and Freeport Sulphur Companies. When the companies protested and threatened to close down, the Cuban regime took over operations in these industries. On behalf of the investors, the American government filed legal protests, arguing that the nationalization laws were in violation of international law.[36]

In early 1960, the Eisenhower administration issued a statement on Cuban-American relations that implied a prolongation of the firm stand against the Castro government. The announcement, drafted with the aid of Philip Bonsal, the ambassador to Havana, pledged American support of the noninterventionist principle, declared that American soil would not be employed by anti-Castro guerrillas, expressed dismay at the unwillingness of Cuba to accept the overtures of Washington, asserted that Cuba must abide by the obligations of international law, and maintained that the American government would use legal remedies to protect the interests of its citizens in Cuba. These utterances were scoffed at, however, by other Latin American nations and intellectuals who contended that the United States was still try-

[36] Nicholas Rivero, *Castro's Cuba: An American Dilemma* (Washington, 1962), 10–11; Casuso, *Cuba and Castro*, 159; L. H. Johnson, *U. S. Business Interests in Cuba and the Rise of Castro* (Santa Monica, Calif., 1964), 20, 33; *Cuba, the U. S. and Russia, 1960–63* (New York, 1964), 9–10; Williams, *U. S., Cuba, and Castro*, 143–144.

ing to dominate the Cuban economy. When Castro initiated discussions with the Soviet Union over the possibility of commercial intercourse, he appeared to many as a national leader attempting to foster Cuban trade with the rest of the world. After all, asked the Mexican writer Isidro Fabela, the United States trades with Russia, why not Cuba? The deal with Moscow to purchase Cuban sugar, contracted partly out of necessity, partly out of spite for the United States, appeared as a windfall to Castro's economy. In 1960 the Russians, obviously delighted over the Cuban-American rift, contracted to purchase 1,700,000 tons of Cuban sugar. The price of trade with the USSR was high, for the Russians demanded that most of the payment be made in trade, rather than money, and at a price lower than that paid previously by American purchasers.[37] But for Fidel Castro in 1960 there was no turning back.

For the Eisenhower administration, too, there seemed to be no reversal in the course leading to a diplomatic rupture. In May, 1960, the Cuban government announced that American and British refineries would be required to process Soviet crude oil instead of Venezuelan oil. Apparently, the company managers were at first willing to agree with the demand but refused after consultation with the Secretary of the Treasury. Castro, of course, merely ordered the seizure of the oil companies. Doubtless, he would have done so in any event, but the circumstances of the seizure gave Castro a diplomatic victory. When the President retaliated with a suspension of the Cuban sugar quota for the remainder of the year, Castro replied with nationalization of remaining American sugar mills.[38]

Meanwhile, the Eisenhower team began planning to equip and train anti-Castro exiles for a future invasion of the island. The exiles, who ranged the entire spectrum in political ideology, could agree on little else except their deep detestation of the

---

[37] Bonsal, "Cuba, Castro, and U. S.," *Foreign Affairs*, XLV, 270–271; Fernando Benítez, *La batalla de Cuba* (Mexico City, 1966), 17; José Gatria, "Política de aritmética plutocrática," *Cuba Económica y Financiera* (October, 1959), 21; Maurice Zeitlin and Robert Scheer, *Cuba: Tragedy in our Hemisphere* (New York, 1963), 184; Casuso, *Cuba and Castro*, 165, 199–200.
[38] Bonsal, "Cuba, Castro, and U. S.," *Foreign Affairs*, XLV, 272–273.

Castro regime and their willingness to participate in its overthrow. Under the supervision of the Central Intelligence Agency, the arming and instruction of the future invaders began in isolated camps in Central America. Throughout the Presidential campaign of 1960, the preparations continued. (Richard Nixon, in *Six Crises,* wrote that he had long championed the idea of aiding an invasion but could not relate his views in the 1960 debates with Senator Kennedy. Thus, for reasons of national security, Nixon maintained, he had to remain silent and endure the Kennedy accusation that Eisenhower and Nixon were "soft" on Castro.) The diplomatic breakdown came in early January, 1961, when Castro ordered the American embassy staff in Havana reduced to eleven persons within two days' time. Shortly after, Eisenhower announced the termination of diplomatic relations. He was already committed to the invasion idea; in fact, back in December, he had suggested the erection of a Cuban government in exile and its recognition by the United States.[39] But, before this idea could be carried through, John Fitzgerald Kennedy became President of the United States.

For all the rhetoric of the New Frontier, there was actually little difference between the Eisenhower and Kennedy approaches to Castro. The new executive inherited the invasion plans, which now called for a conventional military force rather than a guerrilla attack. Kennedy's advisers, notably Theodore Sorenson, noted afterwards that the new President was deeply disturbed about the CIA maneuvers and probably would have rescinded the orders. For several reasons, however, he allowed the preparations to continue. Cuba was moving ever closer towards the Soviet orbit; Castro was sending his pilots to Czechoslovakia for training; and he was ordering sporadic raids against Caribbean republics. Kennedy was surrounded by advisers who warned that the landings must come quickly, for the exiles were trained and becoming restless. If the invasion was called off, the brigades would have to be brought to the United States, where revelations of their disenchantment would reap unfavorable opinion, or left in Guatemala, where they would be able to over-

[39] Nixon, *Six Crises* (Garden City, 1962), 352, 354–355; Eisenhower, *Waging Peace*, 613–614.

throw any one of the Central American governments. Once again, Sorenson has defended the late President on the grounds that (a) he was unaware of the publicity the invasion would receive; (b) he believed that the invaders would infiltrate Cuba and continue guerrilla operations if initially unsuccessful; (c) he thought the American support was covert, whereas the Cuban exiles expected open and direct assistance; and (d) he misunderstood the strength of Castro's hold in Cuba and the unwillingness of the population to rise up in arms with the coming of their liberators. The exiles' leaders in the United States were granted no effective control over the planning and, as later inquiries revealed, the invasion was pretty much a CIA operation.[40]

The tragedy of the Bay of Pigs marked a low point in Kennedy's career at home and the prestige of the United States throughout the world. Once the invaders hit the beaches, everything went wrong. Castro's miniature air force, which was supposed to have been destroyed days before, controlled the skies. One of the planes sank a major supply ship. The exiles remained stranded on shore without food, water, or reinforcements. It was only a matter of time before Castro's land forces were able to round up the ragged band of survivors. The Cuban dictator's image, tarnished somewhat by revolutionary laws and justice, was strengthened immensely. In December, he would make the famous speech proclaiming his conversion to Marxism-Leninism. That announcement, coupled with the Bay of Pigs fiasco, underscored the shock of American defeat in dealing with Castro.

The Cuban Revolution and Castro had been misinterpreted. In the thirty months since he had come to power, congressmen and responsible public officials received insufficient information about the impact of the revolution and the strength of Castro in Cuba. The press gave widespread coverage to Cuban-Russian relations but inadequate analyses of social and economic reforms that Castro's regime undertook. Castro himself appeared in newspaper editorials as a maniacal fiend who was goading the

[40] Stuart Novins, "The Invasion that Could Not Succeed," *The Reporter*, XXIV (11 May 1961), 19–20; Theodore Sorenson, *Kennedy* (New York, 1965), 295, 296, 302–303; Zeitlin and Scheer, *Cuba*, 206.

United States into a fight.[41] The Bay of Pigs was an irrational outburst, a striking back at a petty Latin dictator who irritated Uncle Sam and got away with it. It was a lashing out at Castro himself, who did not fit into the traditional pattern of the Cuban revolutionary fighting valiantly against Spanish oppression. Instead, the bearded warrior of the Sierra Maestra turned out to be just another Marxist-Leninist ideologue.

Castro, inflated by his triumph in the Bay of Pigs, proceeded to negotiate the infamous pact leading to the erection of Soviet missiles in Cuba. Those who tried to discern Khrushchev's motives in sending missiles to a western hemispheric republic could only speculate. But, essentially, the Soviet logic probably was (a) to alter rapidly the nuclear balance of power by placing missiles ninety miles from American shores, and (b) to illustrate to the Latin American world that a small republic such as Cuba was able, with the aid of the Soviet Union, to counteract traditional United States domination of the hemisphere. In the summer of 1962, the Kennedy administration withstood press and public criticism that it was allowing the buildup of offensive missiles in Cuba. A persistent critic was Senator Kenneth Keating (Rep., N.Y.), who stated publicly that his private sources of information confirmed the shipment and installation of nuclear missiles on the island. On September 4, the President tried to counter the charges of Russian influence in Cuba by admitting that the Soviets had supplied antiaircraft defensive missiles. He noted also that the additional weaponry did not constitute an *offensive* threat, nor was Cuba violating her Guantánamo treaty commitments. In the same remarks, however, Kennedy was careful to point out that the Cuban issue had to be viewed as part of the global communist challenge and that the United States would not permit Castro to export his revolution by violence or threats of war. A week later, *Tass*, the Soviet News Agency,

[41] Haynes Johnson, *et al.*, *The Bay of Pigs: The Leaders' Story of Brigade 2506* (New York, 1964), 349; Rivero, *Castro's Cuba*, 2–3; Wilkerson, *Fidel Castro's Political Programs*, 81; Michael J. Francis, "The United States Press and the Cuban Revolution: A Study in Declining Relations," (Unpublished paper, Southwestern Social Science Convention, 1966), 28–29; Hickey, "Role of the Congress . . . Cuban Disaster," *Inter-American Economic Affairs*, XIV, No. 4, 77.

announced that the Soviet Union had not sent offensive missiles to Cuba.[42]

Kennedy, according to Theodore Sorenson, believed neither the Cuban refugee statements about offensive missiles nor Soviet assurance to the contrary. Under increasing political pressure from a bellicose Congress and press, he stood firm against both and waited for incontrovertible proof. He could not afford another Bay of Pigs fiasco on the assumption that offensive missiles *might* exist in Cuba; neither could he allow the Soviet Union to transform the island into a nuclear threat. Publicly, the President warned that if the Soviet military aid to Cuba endangered the security of the United States, specifically if Cuba became an offensive military base, then the United States would undertake whatever retaliatory action was necessary. Air flights over Cuba in September and the first week of October revealed a large-scale military increase but not offensive in nature. Soviet aid seemed still to constitute more a political than military weapon in the communist determination to win over Latin American minds.[43]

When later overflights and accumulated photographic evidence proved the existence of offensive weapons in mid-October, there began two of the most dangerous weeks in the history of the Cold War. Unlike the Bay of Pigs invasion more than a year before, the Cuban missile crisis of late October, 1962, would be handled with cold logic and precise maneuvering. The first task was the calling of an extraordinary meeting, made up of Vice-President Johnson, Secretary of State Rusk, Attorney-General Kennedy, Secretary of Defense McNamara, Generals Taylor and Carter, McGeorge Bundy, Sorenson, Kenneth O'Donnell, Douglas Dillon, and Charles Bohlen. For the next few days, these men would have to decide the reason for the Soviet missiles in Cuba, the response of the United States, and the risks of world nuclear

---

[42] Robert Crane, "The Cuban Crisis: A Strategic Analysis of American and Soviet Policy," *Orbis*, VI, No. 4 (Winter, 1963), 529; Kennedy, Press Statement, 4 September 1962, quoted in David L. Larson, ed., *The 'Cuban Crisis' of 1962: Selected Documents and Chronology* (Boston, 1963), 3; Soviet Statement, 11 September 1962, in *ibid.*, 11–12.

[43] Sorenson, *Kennedy*, 671; Arthur M. Schlesinger, Jr., *A Thousand Days: John F. Kennedy in the White House* (Boston, 1965), 799–800.

annihilation. Of the theories projected on Soviet behavior, the discussants noted the following: (a) Khrushchev believed that the United States would do nothing to risk nuclear war and thus took the chance of installing offensive weapons in Cuba; (b) if the American government did respond militarily, the Allies would be divided, and the Soviet Union could seize Berlin during the crisis; (c) Khrushchev could not permit Cuba to be attacked in another exile invasion; (d) Khrushchev intended to employ the missile threat as a bargaining weapon in Cold War politics; or (e) the Soviet Union needed the Cuban missiles to catch up with the United States in the missile race.[44]

The answer? From the published accounts of the missile crisis, the solutions advanced by the discussants included half a dozen possibilities. The first, which was "do nothing and hope for the best" apparently was considered briefly and then promptly rejected. The remainder ranged all the way from diplomatic overtures to the Soviets or to Castro, trying to woo him from the communist orbit, to various forms of military action, a blockade, an air strike, or to an invasion of the island. For obvious reasons, the choice of "doing nothing" was unacceptable. As for a full scale invasion of Cuba, this solution appealed to several in the President's special advisory committee, but its political implications in Latin America, particularly after the abortive Bay of Pigs affair, limited its effectiveness as a *first* step. Actually, the group, especially Attorney-General Kennedy and Secretary of Defense McNamara, kept insisting that Kennedy had a scale of options. He might begin with a blockade of Cuba, preventing the unloading of certain materials, missiles, petroleum, or similar items. If this failed, he could call for a selective air strike at the missile sites; then, if necessary, an invasion. The important thing was to start with the less dangerous end of the scale and work from there.[45]

The ships were in place around Cuba by Monday, October 22, and Kennedy appeared on nationwide television in the early evening and confirmed publicly the missile buildup, the counter-

---

[44] Elie Abel, *The Missile Crisis* (Philadelphia, 1966), 44; Sorenson, *Kennedy*, 676–677.

[45] *Ibid.*, 682, 687–688; Abel, *Missile Crisis*, 81.

action by the United States, and the risk of nuclear war. The missiles, he said, were capable of hitting any hemispheric city within 1000 nautical miles: Washington, D.C., Mexico City, Caracas, or Panama City. He warned of continuing efforts in Cuba to strengthen the air bases and missile sites. The first step was a quarantine of offensive military supplies headed for Cuba; the second, constant surveillance of the island and directions to the armed forces to prepare for "any eventualities"; and the third, an explicit statement that a missile launched from Cuba against any hemispheric country would be interpreted as an attack against the United States and would require a retaliatory nuclear response. The President warned the Soviet Union not to interfere with its access to West Berlin. He called for military reinforcements at Guantánamo, a meeting of the Organ of Consultation of the Organization of American States, and a convening of the Security Council of the United States. Finally, the President appealed to Khrushchev to withdraw the missiles.[46]

What followed was hours on end of agonized waiting. The Russian ships already *en route* to Cuba remained on course. An American U-2 was shot down over the island. Khrushchev was talking about a *quid pro quo:* the Soviet Union would dismantle its missiles in Cuba if the United States would remove similar offensive weapons from Turkey. On October 26, the Soviet premier sent a lengthy letter to Kennedy. It was the first sign of a thaw in the confrontation. The Soviet Union had transported missiles to Cuba, Khrushchev wrote, because the United States had attempted to overthrow a Communist state in the Bay of Pigs invasion. He then applauded Kennedy's frankness in accepting responsibility for that occurrence, rambled on about the holocaust of nuclear war, and asked for specific assurances not to invade Cuba. The Soviet leader could not speak for Castro but suggested that if the blockade was lifted, then the Cuban premier would demobilize his armed forces. What was missing from the letter was a commitment by Khrushchev to remove the missiles. That, however, was one commitment Khrushchev probably could not afford to put in writing. One aide suggested that Khruschev's

[46] Kennedy, Address to the Nation, 22 October 1962, in Larson, *Documents*, 41, 43–44.

letter be interpreted in view of another incident, the informal meeting between a Soviet Embassy official, Alexander S. Fomin, and a network correspondent, John Scali. As Scali later recounted the encounter to the State Department, Fomin's proposal *had* included a promise to remove the missiles in return for a no-invasion pledge. If this meant a promise to dismantle the missiles, then it was certainly a weak one, for it had not come from Khrushchev but from a Soviet embassy official. On Saturday, October 27, there came another letter from Moscow that spoke once again of the Turkey-Cuba analogy. Its tone was much more harsh than the Friday message, and, for a while, the special group of advisers sensed that the crisis was worsening. Then, apparently following the suggestion of Robert Kennedy, the group decided to *ignore* the Saturday letter and answer the one received from Khrushchev on Friday. Indeed, the so-called "second letter" of Saturday was probably written in the Soviet Foreign Office and thus was delayed in its transmission by the usual bureaucratic processes. The Friday letter, however, was sent directly from the Soviet Premier and reached Washington ahead of the other message. In any event, the decision to respond as the Attorney-General proposed was not without its risks. Saturday night was suspenseful: nobody knew what was going on inside the Kremlin. Khrushchev might have been deposed. The Soviets perhaps were preparing to move on Berlin. October 28 came with the Department of Defense preparing for the worst, possibly an air strike, when another Khrushchev letter arrived. The third paragraph told the whole story: the missiles would be removed.[47]

Thus concluded the most dangerous hours in Cuban-American

[47] Schlesinger, *Thousand Days*, 827–829; Abel, *Missile Crisis, passim*, especially 180–185. For an analysis of the missile crisis see also Henry Pachter, *Collision Course* (New York, 1963), 17–18.

Conflicting legal views of the "quarantine" are given by Charles G. Fenwick, "Quarantine Against Cuba: Legal or Illegal," *American Journal of International Law*, LVII (July, 1963), 588–599, and Quincy Wright, "The Cuban Quarantine," *ibid.*, 546–565.

The Department of State position on the legality of the "quarantine" was written by Abraham Chayes, Legal Advisor, 3 November 1962, and is quoted in Larson, *Documents*, 246–247.

relations. October, 1962, was more terrifying than March, 1898, because in that earlier confrontation with Spain many knew what kind of war was coming and greeted the prospect; in the showdown with the Soviet Union, men saw what kind of war *might* come and recoiled in horror. The President was able to regain much of the prestige he had lost in the Bay of Pigs affair. The crisis demonstrated to the world, and most importantly, to Latin America, that Castro was responsive to Soviet command. And the danger of nuclear annihilation—the collision of Soviet-American power on the world stage—cast the confrontation as the climactic moment of the Cold War. But Kennedy's speech to the nation concerned the strategic implications of missiles in Cuba and resurrected the logic of past crises and former leaders. The legacy of John Quincy Adams and Hamilton Fish and William McKinley was very real in October, 1962.

CHAPTER VII

Epilogue: The Cuban Policy of the United States

THE SOVIET-AMERICAN CONFRONTATION OVER CUBA in October, 1962, dramatically illustrated the permanency of the island's strategic value in American foreign policy. In 1823, when John Quincy Adams wrote his famous instruction on Cuba, the United States stood as a young revolutionary nation opposed to British and French manipulation in the Caribbean. The reasoning of Adams called for the maintenance of Spanish colonialism, no matter how repugnant to New World ideologies, because Spain's presence in Cuba satisfied America's interests. Similarly, the Cuban missile crisis of 1962 reflected strategic rather than ideological forces. To be sure, the obsessive hatred of Castro by the American public doubtless influenced the belligerent tone of Congress, but the President's decisions during that crucial month were based on a determination to prevent the Soviet Union from upsetting the nuclear balance of power by planting offensive missiles in Cuba.

The ideological theme in Cuban-American relations has served often as an impulsive force calling for the invasion of Cuba and the overthrow of its government. In the nineteenth century, the revolutionary heritage of hostility to Old World rule found expression in movements to attack Spanish authority on the island. Narciso Lopez' expeditions of 1849-1851, for instance, received enthusiastic support from both the Northern and Southern public simply because Lopez symbolized the valiant Cuban warrior struggling against tyranny and oppression. And the Southern slavocracy interpreted the Cuban annexationist movement as a crusade for the protection of Southern society. Once slavery was eradicated from American soil, a dominant motif of the Cuban policy in the late nineteenth century was the repeated demand that Spain must reform Cuba by abolishing slavery and incorporating the principles of representative government. Spanish administration failing to fulfill pledges of Cuban reform, the proponents of change accepted the belief that Spain could not "save" Cuba from internal destruction. The solution was the application of force, or war to terminate war, in 1898. The generation that fought the Spanish-American War devoutly believed that it was saving Cuba from inevitable destruction and that only the transplanting of Anglo-Saxon governmental institutions would guarantee Cuba's political and economic salvation.

The economic theme in the Cuban policy has been intertwined with the ideological. From the age of Jackson, the United States pressured Spain to open the ports of Cuba to the produce of the American agricultural heartland. The *Black Warrior* incident of 1854, for example, was as much a protest against Spanish mercantilism and a demand for free trade as it was a ruse to annex Cuba for the slave South. After the Ten Years' War, American investment emerged as an important factor in the Cuban sugar industry. The crusade of 1898 and the subsequent domination of Cuba facilitated and greatly amplified the economic power of American capital. Historians of late nineteenth century expansion have traced the parallelism between expansionism and industrialism—the territorial urge accompanied by a search for markets. This economic impetus was not solely exploitative in nature. Rather, it was imbedded in the broader ideological commitment to the Jacksonian equation of democracy and capitalism. The removal of Spanish power in Cuba, then, was lauded as necessary for the reformation of Cuba politically *and* economically. Free trade and unrestricted investment appeared as key elements in the political rehabilitation of Cuba. Spanish political oppression received no less scorn than Spanish *economic* oppression. Throughout the nineteenth century, policy makers, newspaper editors, and journalists praised the political effect of entrepreneurial capitalism and applied it to Cuba. In this view, it is possible to see how capitalism and humanitarianism joined hands in the 1898 intervention. Humanitarianism promised relief to a ravaged land, and capitalism pledged to restore the productive capacity of a rich island plagued by political and economic discord.

Cuba's experience in the twentieth century was a denial of nineteenth century judgments. Opened to American investment, Cuba remained an economic colony through continued dependence on sugar. The paternalistic tutelage of the first and second interventions failed to implant permanently Anglo-Saxon political principles. Instead, Cuban politics was geared to the prospect of American intervention. The abrogation of the Platt amendment in 1934 in the aftermath of a violent year in Cuba's history was a sign that Cuba no longer needed direct parental guidance. But, in a sense, Batista and the matured Cuban army filled the political void vacated by the United States. The economic pattern of pre-1934 days was continued, and American capital was granted a favored role under Batista. If Batista did not live up to the prototype of a democratic ruler that Leonard Wood and his generation dreamed of, he nevertheless satisfied post-1934 Washington administrations by assuring political stability. And Batista successfully cultivated American favoritism because his regime presented the facade of Cuban prosperity: a gay tourist land, abundant markets for American industrial products, and the tacit acceptance of Anglo-Saxon culture. The emphasis was on *productivity* and *stability* even though Cuba was still a sugar economy and was ruled by a dictator.

Had Castro never allowed the erection of Soviet missiles nor tried to export violent revolution, his government still would not be compatible with the traditional Cuban policy of the United States. By proclaiming communism, Castro has not only irritated the American government but denied a fundamental American assumption about Cuba. He has declared Cuba's problem to be one of distribution of wealth rather than the lack of democracy or unrestricted investment. He has not only taken Cuba into the Soviet orbit politically but he has transformed the Cuban economy along Marxist lines. It is not Castro's political dictatorship that is so reprehensible as his open denial of the Jacksonian credos of democracy, capitalism, and progress. For that reason alone, there will be probably be no reconciliation with Cuba as long as Castro is in power. His successors, like the inheritors of the Mexican Revolution, may moderate their anti-Americanism; a future American President may call for a fresh appraisal of the Cuban policy. But the resumption of Cuban-United States harmony will mean necessarily the rejection of much of the nineteenth century view about Cuba.

Bibliographical Essay

This bibliographical essay, selective rather than exhaustive, is intended to be a guide to the published literature on Cuban-American relations.

General histories of Cuba are Charles Chapman, *History of the Cuban Republic* (New York, 1927), which remains useful for student and scholar; Willis F. Johnson, *The History of Cuba* (5 vols., New York, 1920); and the journalistic but informative account in Hudson Strode, *The Pageant of Cuba* (New York, 1936). None of these goes beyond the 1930's, and each should be supplemented by the detailed labors of Cuban scholars in *Historia de la nación cubana* (10 vols., Habana, 1952). The *Historia* is less condemnatory of the American protectorate than Castroite studies, of course, but it does provide excellent chapters on the republic's early political leaders and Cuba's blessing and nemesis—sugar.

There is no up-to-date history of Cuban-American relations from 1789 to 1967. An older reliable study of the story to 1899 is James M. Callahan, *Cuba and International Relations: A Historical Study in American Diplomacy* (Baltimore, 1899), which stresses Cuba's international importance in the nineteenth century. Philip Foner is writing a multivolume *History of Cuba and its Relations with the United States* (2 vols. thus far, New York, 1962-), which is detailed, pro-Cuban and Marxist-oriented, and therefore should be used with care. Two recent works are Robert Smith's *The United States and Cuba: Business and Diplomacy, 1917-1960* (New York, 1961), which is strongest on the influence of American business in Cuba during the 1920's, and his edited work, *What Happened in Cuba* (New York, 1963), a collection of documents. On the Cuban side, the above should be balanced with Ramiro Guerra Sanchez, *Cuba en la vida inter-*

nacional (Habana, 1923), and Aurelio Concheso, *Cuba en la vida internacional* (Jena and Leipzig, 1935). Two authors who interpret the nineteenth century independence movement as a Cuban rather than American triumph are Herminio Portell Vilá, *Historia de Cuba en sus relaciones con los Estados Unidos* (4 vols., Habana, 1938), and Emilio Roig de Leuchsenring, *Cuba y los Estados Unidos, 1805-1898* (Habana, 1949). Both are foremost Cuban historians. The most detailed diplomatic history from the Spanish point of view is Jerónimo Becker, *Historia de las relaciones exteriores de España durante el siglo xix* (3 vols., Madrid, 1924-1926). On the American side, French E. Chadwick, *The Relations of the United States with Spain: Diplomacy* (New York, 1909), remains a standard diplomatic history.

Unfortunately, no one has written a satisfactory account of Cuba's international role from colonial times to the era of the Monroe Doctrine. A classic work is Germán Arcienagas, *The Caribbean: Sea of the New World* (New York, 1946), which makes the history of the Spanish Main and the exploits of English buccaneers all the more exciting. Irene Wright has written *The Early History of Cuba, 1492-1586* (New York, 1916), and has rendered yeoman service in her editing of *Spanish Documents Concerning English Voyages to the Caribbean, 1527-1568* (London, 1929). Two important articles dealing with Cuba's international status during this period are Roland D. Hussey, "Spanish Reaction to Foreign Aggression in the Caribbean to about 1680," *Hispanic American Historical Review,* IX (August, 1929), 286-302; and N. V. Russell, "The Reaction in England and America to the Capture of Havana, 1762," *ibid.,* 303-316. British interest and activity is delineated in the excellent *War and Trade in the West Indies, 1739-63* (London, 1963, orig. pub., 1936), by the late Sir Richard Pares. From 1789, the evolving American statement on Cuba may be traced in the various published papers of Adams, Jefferson, Gallatin, and the *Diary* of John Quincy Adams. All distinguished carefully between revolution in mainland Latin America and the Antilles. Rayford W. Logan, *The Diplomatic Relations of the United States with Haiti, 1776-1891* (Chapel Hill, 1941), demonstrates the impact of the Haitian revolution on the United States. For those unable to plow through the voluminous diplomatic correspondence, there is the monumental *Diplomatic History of the United States Concerning the Independence of the Latin American Nations* (3 vols., New York, 1925), edited by William Ray Manning. Dexter Perkins, *The Monroe Doctrine, 1823-26* (Cambridge, 1927) is the definitive study of the origin of this policy. Perkins relates also the ancillary development of the Cuban policy in the Monroe and Adams administrations. British policy is conveniently summarized in A. P. Newton, "United States and Colonial Development, 1815-1846," in the *Cambridge History of British Foreign Policy*, II, 220-286; and C. J. Bartlett, *Great Britain and Sea Power*, 1815-1853 (Oxford, 1963). W. C. Ford, "John Quincy Adams and the Monroe Doctrine," *American Historical Review*, VII (July, 1902), 676-696, and VIII (October, 1902), 28-52, expounds on the Secretary of State's primary role in the formulation of Monroe's message of December. A key monograph is John Logan, *No Transfer: An American Security Principle* (New Haven, 1961).

The annexationist movement of the late forties and early fifties is illuminated in Allan Nevins, ed., *Polk: The Diary of a President, 1845-49* (New York, 1929); Robert Caldwell, *The Lopez Expeditions to Cuba, 1848-51* (Princeton, 1915); and Basil Rauch, *American Interest in Cuba, 1848-55* (New York, 1948). Herminio Portell Vilá, *Narciso Lopez y su época* (3 vols., Habana, 1930-1958), portrays the subject as a crusader for Cuban independence. Revealing insights into the spirit of the Southern Democracy are various contemporary periodicals, especially *DeBow's Review* and the *Democratic Review*. Standard biographies of key individuals are Roy Nichols, *Franklin Pierce: Young Hickory of the Granite Hills* (Philadelphia, 1958); A. A. Ettinger, *The Mission to Spain of Pierre Soulé, 1853-55* (New Haven, 1937), which lays bare the philosophy of a European revolutionist and Southern slavocrat; and Ivor Spencer, *The Victor and the Spoils; A Life of William L. Marcy* (Providence, 1959), which is good political history.

No adequate English language history of the Ten Years' War has appeared. Ramiro Guerra Sanchez, *Guerra de los diez años, 1868-78* (2 vols., Habana, 1950-1952), provides detailed analysis from the Cuban point of view. Spanish honor in the preservation of colonial Cuba is expressed in dogmatic fashion in José de Ahumanda y Centurión, *Memoria histórica-política de la isla de Cuba, redactada del orden del señor ministro de ultramar* (Habana, 1874), and Justo Zaragoza, *Las insurreciones en Cuba. Apuntes para la historia política de esta isla en presente siglo* (Madrid, 1872-73), written by an official of the Volunteers. By far the most extensive study from the American position is provided in Nevins' two-volume biography of *Hamilton Fish: An Inner History of the Grant Administration* (New York, rev. ed., 1957). The Caleb Cushing papers, Manuscripts Division, Library of Congress, and Claude Fuess, *The Life of Caleb Cushing* (2 vols., New York, 1923), point to Cushing's conservative outlook towards Cuban revolution. Edgcumb Pinchon, *Dan Sickles, Hero of Gettysburg and "Yankee King" of Spain* (Garden City, 1945), is adequate for a minister who often confused diplomacy and personal political philosophy. Contemporary articles on Cuba in such polite magazines as *Appleton's Journal* should be compared with the stinging antiimperialist messages of the *Nation*.

The Spanish-American War has attracted more scholarly attention than any other era of Cuban-American relations. The older works of Julius Pratt, *Expansionists of 1898: The Acquisition of Hawaii and the Spanish Islands* (Baltimore, 1936); and Walter Millis, *The Martial Spirit* (Boston, 1931), have been supplemented by newer interpretations, particularly E. R. May, *Imperial Democracy: The Emergence of America as a Great Power* (New York, 1961), and Walter LaFeber, *The New Empire: An Interpretation of American Expansion, 1860-1898* (Ithaca, N. Y., 1963). May interprets the war within the structure of European power politics, and LaFeber shows the relationship between expansion and the late nineteenth century search for markets. The standard biography of Cleveland is still Nevins, *Grover Cleveland: A Study in Courage* (New York, 1932). Fortunately, H. Wayne Morgan has resurrected McKinley's reputation from textbook innuendo in *William McKinley and his America* (Syracuse, 1963), and *America's Road to Empire: The War with Spain and Overseas Expansion* (New York, 1965). Julio Romano, *Weyler: hombre de hierro* (Madrid, 1934), fails to exonerate a Spanish general condemned by Americans in 1897. The thinking of Lodge, Mahan, Roosevelt, Hannis Taylor, Fitzhugh Lee, and others may be found in articles contributed to the *North American Review* and similar periodicals of the 1890's. A work that emphasizes Anglo-Saxon ethnic influences on diplomacy is A. E. Campbell, *Great Britain and the United States, 1895-1903* (London, 1960). Charles C. Campbell, Jr., *Anglo-American Understanding, 1898-1903* (Baltimore, 1957), provides the view from Washington. A famous revolutionary is lauded in Félix Lizaso, *Martí: Martyr of Cuban Independence* (Albuquerque, 1953). Emilio Roig de Leuchsenring, *Por su propio esfuerzo conquistó el pueblo cubano su independencia* (Habana, 1957), stresses the Cuban contribution to independence. The student interested in Castroite influences on Cuban historiography should begin with Duvon Corbitt's article, "Cuban Revisionist Interpretations of Cuba's Struggle for Independence," *Hispanic American Historical Review*, XLIII (August, 1963), 395-404.

With the exception of the Spanish-American War, no era in Cuban-American relations has received so much attention as the period 1898-1934, the "Years of Paternalism." Chapman's *History of the Cuban Republic* appeared in 1927, and Smith's *The United States and Cuba*, now available in paperback, concentrates on the 1920's. Students of this important epoch owe the greatest debt to Russell H. Fitzgibbon's *Cuba and the United States, 1900-1935* (New York, 1964, orig. pub., 1935). Fitzgibbon, a well-known Latin Americanist, analyzes the interplay of politics and economics in the shaping of Cuban history during the first years of the republic. David Healy, *The United States in Cuba, 1898-1902* (Madison, 1963), takes the position that politicians, not businessmen, formulated policy during these crucial years. The various *Reports* of John Brooke and Leonard Wood, especially the latter, are revealing for their paternalistic temper as well as for coverage of postwar Cuba. Root's colonial theory is explored by Philip C. Jessup, *Elihu Root* (2 vols., New York, 1938). Hermann Hagedorn, the first writer to gain access to the papers of Wood, is adulatory but captures Wood's messianic zeal in *Leonard Wood: A Biography* (2 vols., New York, 1931). David Lockmiller, *Magoon in Cuba: A History of the Second Interven-*

tion, 1906-1910 (Chapel Hill, 1938), and his *Enoch Crowder: Soldier, Lawyer, and Statesman* (Columbia, Mo., 1955), attempt to salvage the diplomatic careers of two criticized emissaries to Cuba. Theodore Roosevelt's correspondence has been ably edited by Elting E. Morison, *et al.*, in *The Letters of Theodore Roosevelt* (8 vols., Cambridge, 1951-1954). A basic source of these years is the *Foreign Relations* series of the Department of State. Dana G. Munro's *Intervention and Dollar Diplomacy in the Caribbean, 1900-1921* (Princeton, 1964), untangles many threads in United States policy in Cuba during the political debacle of 1905-1906 and the Wilsonian years of 1913-1921. Chapter V of this study relies heavily on the pioneering works by Fitzgibbon, Smith, Healy, and Munro. From the Cuban outlook, León Primelles, *Crónica cubana, 1915-21* (2 vols., Habana, 1955-58), supplies detailed information on Cuba's critical war and postwar years. Caustic criticism of the Machado era may be found in several articles by Hubert Herring in the contemporary volumes of *Current History* and by Carleton Beals, *The Crime of Cuba* (Philadelphia, 1933), which is also a condemnation of American policy. Ramiro Guerra Sanchez' *Sugar and Society in the Caribbean: An Economic History of Cuban Agriculture*, now translated and reissued by Yale University Press (1964), is a classic portrayal of the plight of a monoculture economy.

The *Foreign Relations* volumes for the year 1933 give detailed coverage to the Cuban unrest of that year, but the reader must begin with Bryce Wood's *The Making of the Good Neighbor Policy* (New York, 1961), which demonstrates that the American experience in Cuba before 1934 helped to shape the contours of Roosevelt's Good Neighbor Policy. Wood makes intensive use of State Department material but balances his account with Spanish sources. Cordell Hull's *Memoirs* (2 vols., New York, 1948), show the Secretary's moral judgments as well as his jealousy of Sumner Welles. There will be no biography of Welles until his papers are opened to scholars. The special emissary gave his opinion of Cuban events in *The Time for Decision* (New York, 1944). An objective biography of Batista does not exist, and therefore scholars must rely on the woefully inadequate Edmund Chester, *A Sergeant Named Batista* (New York, 1954), and Batista's

Growth and Decline of the Cuban Republic (New York, 1964), obviously designed for the uninformed audience. No one has produced a sequel to Fitzgibbon's *Cuba and the United States*, but detailed works on Cuba's continuing political and economic woes after 1934 are Raymond L. Buell, *et al.*, *Problems of the New Cuba* (New York, 1935); International Bank for Reconstruction and Development, *Report on Cuba* (Washington, 1951); Henry Wallich, *Monetary Problems of an Export Economy* (Cambridge, 1950); and Wyatt McGaffey and Clifford Barnett, *Twentieth Century Cuba: The Background of the Castro Revolution* (paperback edition, Garden City, N.Y., 1965). A general introduction to American policy is Donald Dozer, *Are We Good Neighbors? Three Decades of Inter-American Relations, 1930-1960* (Gainesville, Fla., 1959).

Books dealing with Castro, the Bay of Pigs, and the "Missile Crisis" are numerous but uneven in scholarship. Castro's *History Will Absolve Me* (Havana, 1960), has gone through several English-language editions. Informative insights are Teresa Casuso, *Cuba and Castro* (New York, 1961), and the little-known but brilliant study, Ward Morton, *Castro as a Charismatic Hero* (Lawrence, Kansas, 1965). Earl Smith's *The Fourth Floor: An Account of the Castro Communist Revolution* (New York, 1962) reveals more about Smith's distrust for the policymakers in "Foggy Bottom" than it does about Batista or Castro. Philip Bonsal, Smith's successor, writes honestly in "Cuba, Castro, and the United States," *Foreign Affairs*, XLV (January, 1967), 260-276. For the Bay of Pigs, the author has used the accounts of Kennedy men Theodore Sorenson, *Kennedy* (New York, 1965); A. M. Schlesinger, Jr., *A Thousand Days: John F. Kennedy in the White House* (Boston, 1965), now praised as the best book on the Kennedy years; and Haynes Johnson, *et al.*, *The Bay of Pigs: The Leaders' Story of Brigade 2506* (New York, 1964). Both Sorenson and Schlesinger are invaluable for the "Missile Crisis." David Larson, ed., *The "Cuban Crisis" of 1962: Selected Documents and Chronology* (Boston, 1963), is a handy reference tool, and Elie Abel, *The Missile Crisis* (Philadelphia, 1966), writes an exciting story about the dramatic days of October, 1962. Castro's revolution has been interpreted and misinterpreted. This volume has relied on the judgments contained in Dudley Seers, ed., *Cuba: The Economic and Social Revolution* (Chapel Hill, 1964), and Theodore Draper, *Castro's Revolution: Myths and Realities* (New York, 1962). Finally, a little book with a stinging message, with which this author disagrees but from which he has learned, is W. A. Williams, *The U. S., Cuba, and Castro* (New York, 1962).

Index